HUBLOT
GENEVE

GRAND COMPLICATIONS®

THE ORIGINAL ANNUAL OF THE WORLD'S WATCH COMPLICATIONS AND MANUFACTURERS®

SPECIAL MOONPHASES EDITION

First published in the United States in 2010 by

TOURBILLON INTERNATIONAL
A MODERN LUXURY MEDIA COMPANY
11 West 25th Street, 8th floor
New York, NY 10010
Tel: +1 (212) 627-7732 Fax +1 (312) 274-8418
www.modernluxury.com/watches

In association with RIZZOLI INTERNATIONAL PUBLICATIONS INC.

300 Park Avenue South, New York, NY 10010

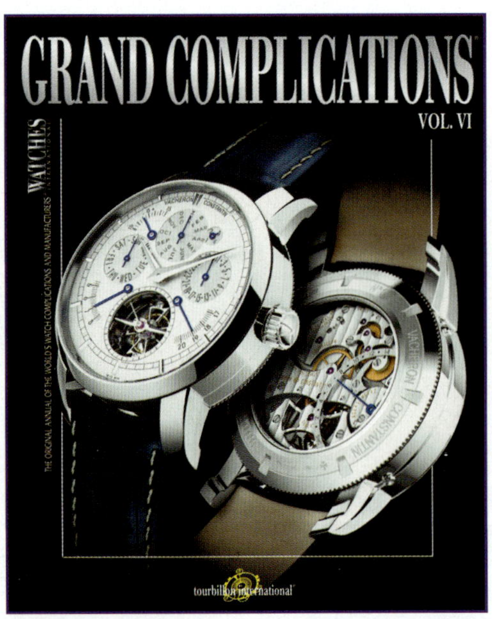

ISBN: 978-0-8478-3421-1

DISCLAIMER: THE INFORMATION CONTAINED IN GRAND COMPLICATIONS VOLUME VI HAS BEEN PROVIDED BY THIRD PARTIES. WHILE WE BELIEVE THESE SOURCES TO BE RELIABLE, WE ASSUME NO RESPONSIBILITY OR LIABILITY FOR THE ACCURACY OF TECHNICAL DETAILS CONTAINED IN THIS BOOK.

EVERY EFFORT HAS BEEN MADE TO LOCATE THE COPYRIGHT HOLDERS OF MATERIALS PRINTED IN THIS BOOK. SHOULD THERE BE ANY ERRORS OR OMISSIONS, WE APOLOGIZE AND SHALL BE PLEASED TO MAKE ACKNOWLEDGMENTS IN FUTURE EDITIONS.

PRINTED IN ITALY

AP
AUDEMARS PIGUET
Le maître de l'horlogerie depuis 1875
LE BRASSUS 12h35
JULES AUDEMARS
EQUATION OF TIME
AUDEMARS PIGUET, LE BRASSUS (VALLÉE DE JOUX), SWITZERLAND, TEL. +41 21 845 14 00 – www.audemarspiguet.com

CALIBER RM 020
TOURBILLON POCKET WATCH

Carbon nanofiber baseplate
Variable inertia, free sprung balance
Power reserve : circa 10 days
Barrel pawl with progressive recoil
Function selector
Modular time setting mecanism fitted against the case back
Winding barrel teeth and third-wheel pinion with central involute profile
Titanium watch chain with fast release / attach mecanism
Can be used as a "pendulette de bureau"
Frequency : 21 600 vph
Moment of inertia : 10 mg.cm2
Anglage, locking sections and contact points hand finished

Available in titanium, 18 carat white or red gold
Titanium caseband

CALIBER RM 025

CHRONOGRAPH DIVER'S WATCH

Manual winding tourbillon movement
Carbon nanofiber baseplate
Chronograph (Column wheel in titanium)
Power reserve : circa 50 hours
Torque indicator
Power reserve indicator
Function indicator
Variable inertia, free sprung balance with overcoil
New in-line escapement design
Fast rotating barrel
(6 hours per revolution instead of 7.5 hours)
Winding barrel teeth and third-wheel pinion
with central involute profile
Barrel pawl with progressive recoil
Modular time setting mechanism fitted against the case back
Torque limiting crown
Wheel based time setting system (back of the movement)
Closure of the barrel cover using excentric screws
Spline screws in grade 5 titanium for the bridges and case
Bezel turning unidirectionally following ISO 6425 norm
300 meter water resistant case in titanium and red gold

cellini

NEW YORK, NY

When Cellini Jewelers opened in the lobby of the Waldorf-Astoria in 1977, it arrived at a time when Americans were rediscovering the art of watchmaking. More than a fashion statement, for some the survival of mechanical watches signified a gentle pushback against the rapid proliferation of quartz clocks and a longing for handmade authenticity amid a mass-production society.

Many of those early collectors found a kindred spirit in Cellini's president Leon Adams, whose appreciation for rare timepieces and demanding standards echoed their own. Early on, his showcases were home to rare editions from venerable firms and inventions from exclusive ateliers.

Guests who frequented Cellini in those early years witnessed the mechanical watch industry undergo a rapid renaissance. Advances in computer-aided design and production redefined what was possible in the realms of mechanics and aesthetics, from fine-tuning performance to expanding imaginations.

The next generation of timepieces resonated among collectors, whose ranks grew steadily in the '80s. To keep apace of the growing thirst for fine watchmaking, Cellini added a boutique on New York's Madison Avenue in 1987. Today, the two locations combine to form one of the world's largest and most prestigious collections of timepieces from Europe's historic manufactures and independent watchmakers.

Chapter Two (Maîtres du Temps)

Blue Blazes: Sapphires and diamonds artfully set in platinum.

cellini

RAISING THE BAR

That well-edited selection has elevated Cellini's reputation among the industry's cognoscenti, making it an influential arbiter of style and an important proving ground for rising watch brands. In fact, a number of successful brands first found a home in the U.S. at Cellini, where collectors were introduced to A. Lange & Söhne, Guy Ellia, H. Moser & Cie., Maîtres du Temps, and of course Audemars Piguet, which was part of Cellini's collection from the start.

Through the years, watchmakers have recognized Cellini's influence and created limited editions exclusively for the independent jeweler. Companies like Panerai, Jaeger-LeCoultre and IWC are among the most recent brands to honor Cellini with special timepieces.

Today, these watchmakers are cornerstones of a collection dominated by watch brands with strong and varied personalities. "One of our biggest strengths is that our collection never stops changing and growing," Adams says. "We'll always make room for a brand that has a fresh look or is technically advanced. I'm not afraid to take a chance on a new brand if it's one I believe in."

Adams's attention to the smallest detail extends to the service provided by the watch experts at Cellini. Welcoming and fluent in the eccentricities of high horology, they are available to answer questions about both the art and value of mechanical timepieces.

"Most people ask: 'Am I going to love this watch two years from now?' and 'Will this watch be an asset in the future?' It's our responsibility to help them find the right answers," says Abe Azaria, a Cellini watch specialist. "To do that, we ask questions to get a sense of the person and offer them guidance based on their answers and our own experiences. That honest approach is why clients trust our opinions and keep coming back."

Perpetual Calendar Chronograph (Vacheron Constantin)

GOTHAM GLAMOUR

For those who prefer haute couture to haute horlogerie, sparkling scintillation beckons from Cellini's windows, tempting passers-by with a breathtaking array of jewelry that ranks among New York City's best.

Adams maintains the jewelry collection's reputation for excellence by personally choosing each gemstone featured in Cellini's one-of-a-kind pieces. "We've earned people's trust and I take that responsibility very seriously. Clients expect an impeccably high standard and I make sure we exceed their expectations."

From elegant understatement to over-the-top glitz, imagination is the only limit when it comes to creating custom jewelry, says Lauren Goldsmith, the company's certified gemologist. "Starting with a simple drawing or an idea, we can design something tailored to the individual's unique style. Another advantage of custom jewelry is that it's properly proportioned to fit the client's features. That personalized sizing is what makes a piece truly look and feel one-of-a-kind."

Skilled at restoring everything from family heirlooms to sentimental favorites, Cellini's workshop can also redesign an existing piece. "People still enjoy handing down jewelry to their children, but that tradition has changed," Goldsmith explains. "One woman wanted to give her mother's ring to her daughter, but she knew her daughter wouldn't like the antique setting. We suggested she use the ring's three diamonds to make a necklace for herself and earrings for her daughter. What's old is new again."

After just one visit, it's easy to see why any conversation about the world's finest jewelry and best watches would be incomplete without Cellini.

Symphony of Color: These one-of-a-kind pieces highlight Cellini's vast assortment of natural color diamonds with an extraordinary array of pink, blue, green, orange, and yellow stones.

STORE LOCATIONS

Hotel Waldorf-Astoria • 301 Park Avenue at 50th Street • New York, NY 10022
tel: 212-751-9824

509 Madison Avenue at 53rd Street • New York, NY 10022
tel: 212-888-0505

800-CELLINI • www.CelliniJewelers.com

BRANDS CARRIED

A. Lange & Söhne
Audemars Piguet
Bell & Ross
Cartier
Chopard
Daniel Roth
De Bethune
DeWitt
F.P. Journe
Franck Muller
Gérald Genta
Girard-Perregaux
Guy Ellia
H. Moser & Cie.
Hublot
IWC
Jaeger-LeCoultre
Jean Dunand
Maîtres du Temps
Panerai
Parmigiani Fleurier
Piaget
Richard Mille
Ulysse Nardin
Vacheron Constantin

Watch in black high-tech ceramic and 18K yellow gold. Self-winding mechanical movement custom-made by AUDEMARS PIGUET exclusively for CHANEL: CHANEL - AP3125 (40 jewels, 21'600 vibrations/hour).
Rotor in black high-tech ceramic with a segment in rhodium-plated 22K yellow gold mounted on high-tech ceramic ball bearings.
Balance with 8 giromax regulating weights. 60-hour power reserve.

CHANEL
CHANEL
J12
AUTOMATIC
J 12
CALIBRE
3125
www.chanel.com

LETTER FROM THE PUBLISHER

Scanning the Horizons

Haute horology is a strange mix of tradition and innovation – watchmakers love to use this apparent paradox to mark their territory and let everyone know that they are authentic players in this ever more competitive universe. It is tradition that sustains the savoir-faire that distinguishes all timepieces crafted with its conventions, and tradition that fosters skills passed from generation to generation. On the other side of the coin, innovation is the sign of dynamism, of a will to change, to progress and to improve.

Between these two poles, haute horology presents a diverse range of brands and products. Among the conservative watchmakers and the more progressive ones, a horde of players are staking their claims by joining, to varying degrees of success, the comfort of tradition and the thrill of innovation. Those who most skillfully combine the reassuring side of history and the intriguing aspect of evolution are also those who most attract and keep the attention of observers and collectors. This is no accident: the subtle alchemy between tradition and innovation is never the result of chance, but the hallmark of the biggest names of horology, today as in years past.

Though the inventions of Abraham-Louis Breguet are now considered to be the foundations of horology, many of them were seen as the equivalent of today's UFOs – mysterious mechanisms that seemed to come from an alien intelligence. The watches' reputations stemmed from their questioning of long-established principles. Two centuries later, haute horology is still exploring unknown paths. Every day brings a new high-tech watch material or another triumph in the quest, now nearly realized, for a watch that needs no lubricant, the fields of new research are numerous, and the years to come will certainly bring new evolutions and dazzling innovations.

More than just technology, the evolution of horology is also that of the genius minds who regularly present watch lovers with exceptional pieces. Still often compared with UFOs for the breaks they make with more conventional products, these timepieces mark their eras. Whether they are proposed by historic brands or by gutsy new watchmakers, these UFOs – or the most significant among them – will become the new touchstones in the history of haute horology. Little wonder all the passionate watch lovers constantly scan the horizon, hoping to discover the next out-of-this world invention. Which will illuminate the year 2010?

Caroline Childers

PIAGET
SWISS
MADE

PIAGET POLO
FortyFive
Piaget Manufacture movement 880P
Mechanical self-winding chronograph
Flyback, dual time
100 meter water resistant
Titanium, sapphire case-back
Rubber strap
PIAGET
www.piagetpolo.com
NEW YORK - LAS VEGAS - COSTA MESA - BAL HARBOUR
1-877-8PIAGET

LETTER FROM THE EDITOR IN CHIEF

Cracking the Whip

Was 2009 an annus horribilis? Not necessarily! In terms of sales, and especially the sales of Swiss watches abroad, a strong argument certainly presents itself. Over the year, the total value of Swiss watch exports plunged by more than 20%. Certain brands – among them the most prestigious houses – are now sitting on a mountain of unsold inventory. Paradoxically, 2009 was actually one of the most dynamic years the watch industry had seen in a long time. However, this was on another front: production capacity.

Vaucher Manufacture ($20 million), Minerva (an estimated $2 million), Chopard ($15 million), Armin Strom ($2 million), Greubel Forsey ($11 million), Jaquet Droz (an estimated $10 million), Audemars Piguet ($35 million), Vincent Bérard (an estimated $5 million), Patek Philippe (an estimated $25 million), Ulysse Nardin ($15 million), TAG Heuer ($20 million), Rolex ($200 million), Jaeger-LeCoultre (an estimated $15 million), Hublot ($35 million): all of these companies have been constructing, enlarging, renovating, transforming – in short, equipping themselves for the days ahead. Indeed, rarely has horology invested in itself as much as it did in 2009!

How to explain this turn of events? In 2002, Nicolas G. Hayek, president of Swatch Group, triggered a veritable tsunami in the industry when he announced his intention to stop selling movements, a decision that will take effect in 2011. In December of 2009, the patriarch of the largest watch group in the world upped the ante by announcing that Swatch would no longer provide any watch part whatsoever to outside brands.

This shock to the system has resulted in more and more brands developing and releasing their own exclusive in-house mechanical movements, usually for their own use. In the past few years, more than twenty brands have chosen to take this step and work towards internally producing all or some of the movements that they had formerly acquired from Swatch Group. And so the beat goes on...

History is ironic, and the history of horology is even more so. Just as the sales of watches are slowing down, watchmaking houses have never invested so much! It is a wager in three parts: part one is Nicolas G. Hayek, who will no longer allow his strategic companies – ETA (movements), Nivarox (spirals), or Universo (hands) – to be used as supermarkets for the horological world. The second part is the industry's sudden doubt about Hayek: after having officially saved the watch industry, will he destroy it? The third part is a crack of the whip, urging everyone on, which resounds like a terrific wakeup call and a test of strength. This whip crack may be just what we need for the crisis to dissipate.

Michel Jeannot

Westime

LOS ANGELES & BEVERLY HILLS, CA

For two decades, Westime has distinguished itself as the ultimate retail destination for finding extraordinary watches. Throughout those 20 years, Westime has earned the return business of discriminating clients from around the globe who value Westime's extraordinary service as well as its watch selection.

Westime's two elegant boutiques create the perfect settings for watch shopping. At its original location, a 6,000-square-foot showroom at Los Angeles's Westside Pavilion, Westime features a wide range of brands at every price point. Within the boutique are expansive showcases, comfortable seating arrangements and two specialty boutiques. Two full-time master watchmakers are on site at all times and utilize state-of-the-art equipment for service and repairs. In Beverly Hills, Westime's intimate, multilevel boutique resides at the heart of the city's most glamorous shopping district. Here, connoisseurs and fashionistas alike will find the most sought-after timepieces in the world.

Westime prides itself on offering highly regarded and rare watches. Limited editions, unique pieces, and even custom models created exclusively for Westime take pride of place in the boutiques' showcases. Westime is frequently selected by brands to carry their most complicated timepieces on an exclusive basis.

From day one, Westime has also dedicated itself to seeking the new guard in haute horology by presenting the finest creations of contemporary watchmakers. Three brands stand powerfully for the new watchmaking vanguard. Richard Mille is regarded as the master of materials that are redefining the vocabulary of luxury; Greubel Forsey hails as a tourbillon revolutionary; and URWERK has emerged as the master of kinetic sculpture.

THIS PAGE
UR-202 (URWERK)

FACING PAGE
Westime boutique on Rodeo Drive in Beverly Hills.

254
RICHARD MILLE
A RACING MACHINE ON THE WRIST
Audemars Piguet . Breguet . Glashutte . Jaquet Droz
DeGrisogono . Harry Winston . Franck Muller . IWC
FP Journe . Breitling . Zenith . ST Dupont
Parmigiani . Michel Jordi . Richard Mille

Westime boutique on West Pico Boulevard, Los Angeles

Westime hosts unique customer events to introduce preferred clients to the newest watches, or to meet the owners, presidents and even master watchmakers of some of the key brands.

Founded 20 years ago, Westime is owned by a third-generation watch connoisseur with a passion for mechanical timepieces and a true love of the business; now, the fourth generation is taking an instrumental role in Westime's future. Every member of Westime's affable, multi-lingual staff is dedicated to providing exceptional service—from explaining the specifics of complications, to hand-delivering a watch across the country.

The purchase of a watch from Westime marks only the beginning of a relationship. "We believe fine timepieces should be a source of pleasure, not frustration, to our clients. Should a watch require service, we strive to ensure that it is done as expeditiously as possible and with the highest level of skill," says Barbara Simonian, co-founder of Westime. "Of course, our close relationship with the unique and sophisticated brands, whom it is our privilege to represent, helps ensure the quality communication and impeccable service our clients have come to expect."

BRANDS CARRIED

A. Lange & Söhne
Alain Silberstein
Audemars Piguet
Baume & Mercier
Bell & Ross
Blancpain
Bovet
Breguet
Breitling
Chanel
Chopard
Concord
Corum
DeWitt
Dimier
Dior Phones
Ebel
F.P. Journe
Franck Muller
Gérald Genta
Girard-Perregaux
Glashütte Original
Greubel Forsey
Guy Ellia
Hamilton
Harry Winston
Hautlence
HD3
Hermès
Hublot
Ikepod
IWC
Longines
MB&F
MCT
Milus
Nubeo
Omega
Richard Mille
Roland Iten Mechanical Luxury
Romain Jerome
TAG Heuer
TAG Heuer Meridiist
Tissot
URWERK
Vacheron Constantin
Vertu
Vincent Bérard
Wyler Genève
Zenith

STORE LOCATIONS

10800 West Pico Blvd., #197 • Los Angeles, CA 90064
tel: 310-470-1388 • fax: 310-475-0628

254 North Rodeo Drive • Beverly Hills, CA 90210
tel: 310-271-0000 • fax: 310-271-3091

www.westime.com

RM 028
(Richard Mille)

World First Mechanical Digital Watch

Limited edition of 177 pieces

Having devised a new timepiece language, de GRISOGONO presents its new digital-display mechanical timepiece.

Conceived by de GRISOGONO founder Fawaz Gruosi, the meccanico dg gives high watchmakimg a **powerful new dimension,** propelling it into the third millenium.

Incorporating pioneering technology, the Meccanico dG provides the time in both the **analog style** (with rotating hands) and the **digital mode** (with figures or digits).

Patented by, and exclusive to de GRISOGONO, the timepiece's groundbreaking movement comprises **651 parts and components**.

A triumph of nanomechanics, the Meccanico dG's exceptional design incorporates a variety of microsystems featuring preprogrammed cams driven by complex geartrains, making the watch's revolutionary **double mechanical time display** possible.

Supremely complex in design, the Meccanico dG features two timezone indications along with two distinct time displays.

meccanico dG
by de GRISOGONO

de GRISOGONO
GENEVE
de GRISOGONO
GENEVE
SWISS MADE
www.degrisogono.com

GRAND COMPLICATIONS®

THE ORIGINAL ANNUAL OF THE WORLD'S WATCH COMPLICATIONS AND MANUFACTURERS®

TOURBILLON INTERNATIONAL

A MODERN LUXURY MEDIA COMPANY

ADMINISTRATION, ADVERTISING SALES,
EDITORIAL, BOOK SALES

11 West 25th Street, 8th Floor, New York, NY 10010
Tel: +1 (212) 627-7732 Fax: +1 (312) 274-8418

HUBLOT
GENEVE
BIG BANG
Aero Bang, Skeleton Chronograph in 18K Red Gold, Tantalum and Rubber.
HUBLOT SA • Switzerland • +41 (0)22 990 90 00 • Hublot TV on: www.hublot.com

1969
2010
TAG Heuer
SWISS AVANT-GARDE SINCE 1860

SUMMARY

WEB SITE DIRECTORY

A. Lange & Söhne	www.alange-soehne.com
Artya	artya.luxuryartpieces.com
Audemars Piguet	www.audemarspiguet.com
Bell & Ross	www.bellross.com
Blancpain	www.blancpain.com
Bovet	www.bovet.com
Breguet	www.breguet.com
Breitling	www.breitling.com
Chanel	www.chanel.com
Chopard	www.chopard.com
Concord	www.concord.ch
De Bethune	www.debethune.ch
de GRISOGONO	www.degrisogono.com
F.P. Journe	www.fpjourne.com
Frédérique Constant	www.frederique-constant.com
Greubel Forsey	www.greubelforsey.com
Guy Ellia	www.guyellia.com
Hublot	www.hublot.com
IWC	www.iwc.com
Jacob & Co.	www.jacobandco.com
Jaeger-Lecoultre	www.jaeger-lecoultre.com
Leviev	www.leviev.com
Montblanc	www.montblanc.com
Panerai	www.panerai.com
Parmigiani Fleurier	www.parmigiani.ch
Patek Philippe	www.patek.com
Piaget	www.piaget.com
Richard Mille	www.richardmille.com
Rolex	www.rolex.com
Stührling Original	www.stuhrling.com
TAG Heuer	www.tagheuer.com
Ulysse Nardin	www.ulysse-nardin.com
Vacheron Constantin	www.vacheron-constantin.com
Zannetti	www.zannettiwatches.it
Zenith	www.zenith-watches.ch

Bell & Ross
12
3
SWISS
MADE

INDEX

LONGINES
self-winding mechanical movement with four retrograde functions
second timezone
date
day of the week
seconds
The Longines Master Collection Retrograde
www.longines.com

INDEX

GUY ELLIA

REPETITION MINUTE
« ZEPHYR »

Arije Paris
Doux Joaillier Courchevel   Zegg & Cerlati Monaco   Doux Joaillier Saint Tropez
Carat & Time Saint Barthelemy   Piantelli London   Avakian Geneva
Hubner Vienna   Diamond Time Athens   Steltman Den Haag   Lydion Mucevher Antalya
Azal Dubaï   Harvey Nichols Dubaï   Louvre Moscow   Crystal Kiev   Sincere Kuala Lumpur
Sincere Singapore   Cellini New York   Westime Los Angeles

www.guyellia.com

INDEX

WATCHES
INTERNATIONAL

Kiss, Kiss, dar-leeng,
where do you want to go?

CLOSE-UP ON MOONPHASES

July 21, 1969, 2:56 am, Greenwich Mean Time: The first time a man walked on the moon. This event, widely celebrated on its 40th anniversary in 2009, represented not only, as Neil Armstrong famously said, "one small step for man, one giant leap for mankind." It also marked a milestone for Swiss watchmaking (and for all watchmaking), as Omega Speedmaster, the famous Moonwatch, was on board. Forty years after this historic day, the first moon landing remains one of the most powerful moments of human history, and we have even seen Romain Jerome create a dial that includes moon dust and a bezel in steel that incorporates parts of Apollo 11 for its "Moon Dust-DNA" (second in its "DNA of Famous Legends" series).

But the moon has always enjoyed a much more intimate, ancient relationship with horology. Along with the sun, the moon has inspired numerous calendar systems, and shows its face on timepieces as early as the first large mechanical clocks of the Middle Ages. The moonphase display later became a prominent element of pocket watches with astronomical, astrological or calendar indications, most notably the famous perpetual calendars. Once miniaturized to the dimensions of a wristwatch, the moonphase display would remain in its subordinate, essentially decorative role throughout the 20th century.

Today, the moonphase is experiencing a resurgence in popularity. Better still, it seems to be asserting itself, finally, as a complication in and of itself. More and more watches give pride of place to the moonphase, and each year brings a crop of technical and aesthetic innovations.

The moonphase owes this success to its visual appearance, but also to the dreamy touch it brings to the dial. A window on the night sky, it reminds us that our time is indissolubly linked to the stars and the great cycles of nature.

The year 2009 was proclaimed by UNESCO to be the International Year of Astronomy, to commemorate Galileo's first observations of the night sky in 1609. Armed with his telescope, the famous scientist discovered, among other things, that Venus orbits around the sun, that Jupiter has satellites and that the moon is covered with mountains similar to those on Earth. Four hundred years later, now that we have actually explored, photographed and analyzed the lunar surface, the heavenly body has lost none of its magic. All aboard for a trip through the universe of moonphase watches!

New moon, first quarter, full moon, last quarter: moonphase displays reproduce the changing faces of the celestial body throughout its cycle, which lasts about 29 and a half days. The small portion of the night sky portrayed on the dial adds a touch of poetry and vitality to the timepiece. Long a mere element of perpetual calendars, the moonphase has come into its own and is experiencing unprecedented success. Among watchmakers, it has inspired several variations of traditional displays and shows its face in sometimes quite spectacular stagings.

***L. Leroy**, Grande Osmior Platine*
***De Bethune**, DBW1*
***Blancpain**, Equation Marchante*
***Blancpain**, Blancpain Woman*
Quantième complet Phases de lune

***Perrelet**, Grande Phase de lune centrale*
***Blancpain**, L-evolution 8 Jours*
Complete Calendar Moon Phases
***Bovet**, Fleurier Triple Date*

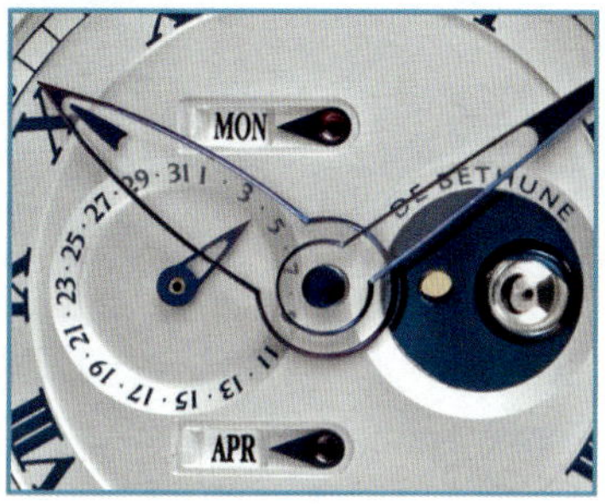

MOONPHASES

CELESTIAL MATHEMATICS

The observation of the moon's path—along with the sun, the cycle of the seasons and the alternation of day and night—has always constituted one of the fundamentals of calendar systems. It was the moon that inspired the ancient Egyptians to divide the year into twelve months, a system that we have inherited via the Greeks and Romans, and that most likely also led to the division of the day into two sets of twelve hours each. Despite the nearly universal adoption of the Gregorian calendar, which is essentially sun-based, ancient lunar or lunisolar calendars (which are based on both the sun and the moon) still maintain their importance in certain cultures, especially in determining the dates of traditional holidays or religious events, or for astrological calculations. For example, this is the case with the Jewish and Chinese lunisolar calendars. This is also the case for the Muslim lunar calendar, in which the year consists of twelve lunar months of 29.53059 solar days—or about eleven days fewer than the Gregorian calendar—which explains why Ramadan begins about ten days earlier each year. In many countries, the exact start date of Ramadan is still determined by local observation of the first sliver of a new moon. The moon also plays a role in Christianity, in which the date of Easter has traditionally been cele-

FACING PAGE
***Breguet**, Classique 7337*

THIS PAGE
***IWC**, Portuguese Perpetual Calendar*

brated on the first Sunday after the first full moon following the vernal equinox.

WINDOW ON THE NIGHT SKY

In the West, the moonphase display was an essential element of the large early clocks of the Middle Ages. For instance, the French cathedral at Saint-Etienne de Bourges (1424) and the clock at Prague's City Hall (also 15th century) both feature moonphases. It also shows up on the dials of the first pocket watches, starting in the 16th century, next to other astronomical and astrological indications—long before anyone was able to display the minute, let alone the second. At the end of the 18th century, the great Abraham-Louis Breguet would use it in his numerous watches with multiple complications, creating purified, refined dials whose echoes are heard in the recent Breguet Classique 7337, a wristwatch with an off-center hour hand, asymmetrical small seconds, moonphase and indications of the date and the day of the week in windows at 2:00 and 10:00 respectively.

In the 20th century, though the moon had lost some of its power of attraction on the human spirit, watchmakers sought to miniaturize the mechanism so as to place it within the format of the smaller wristwatch while keeping it as precise as possible—not an easy thing to do (see sidebar, "How does it work?"). But the moonphase display has long been restricted to just one indication among others on the dials of perpetual or annual calendars, complementing the displays of day, date and month (see "Perpetual Calendar" chapter). Generally placed at 6:00, its window on the night sky lends a note of visual poetry as well as a sense of balance to the dial. In 2009, Blancpain

HOW DOES IT WORK?

The moonphase display is generally driven by a system of mobile discs that depict two perfectly round moons that rotate around the disc's axis. A specially shaped window, with two rounded cutouts reproducing the "shadow" of the Earth, reveals a part of the disc and shows the changing face of the moon throughout its cycle (waxing moon, full moon, waning moon, new moon). The indicator is activated once a day, usually around 7:00 PM, via a system of gears.

A VARIABLE LEVEL OF PRECISION

Though they are based on the same principle, not all moonphases with windows operate with the same level of precision. Their accuracy especially depends on the number of teeth on the disc. The length of a lunar season (also called a month or a synodic revolution) is actually 29 days, 12 hours, 44 minutes and 2.8 seconds, or 29.53 days—which means that the watchmaker cannot use simple multiples of units from mean solar time. The more teeth on the disc, the more precise the moonphase.

ORDINARY MOONPHASES

On ordinary moonphases, the disc with two moons is linked to a gear with 59 teeth corresponding to two lunar cycles (2 x 29.5 days). This system entails a lag of 44 minutes and 2.8 seconds per month, or almost nine hours per year. Over 2 years, 7 months and around 20 days, this adds up to a lag of one full day, requiring manual correction.

ASTRONOMICAL MOONPHASES

High-end watches are equipped with a much more precise and complex mechanism called "astronomical moonphase," with 135 teeth on the gear. The lag between the mechanism and the true lunar cycle is thus just one day in 122 years and 44 days.

RECORDS IN PRECISION

On its Portuguese Perpetual Calendar, IWC has further improved that precision. Thanks to an innovative system with three toothed gears, the lag is reduced to just one day in 577 years! As for Arnold & Son's True Moon, it is claimed to reproduce with perfect accuracy the waxing and waning faces of the moon according to the length of the "synodic periods.

THIS PAGE
TOP LEFT
***Louis Erard**, 1931 Jubilé Moonphase*

TOP CENTER
***Ebel**, 1911 BTR Perpetual Calendar Chronograph*

CENTER
***Hermès**, Moonphase Cape Cod*

FACING PAGE
TOP LEFT
***Maurice Lacroix**, Masterpiece Lune Rétrograde*

TOP CENTER
***Pierre Kunz**, A014 HMRL*

TOP RIGHT
***Girard-Perregaux**, Vintage 1945 King Size*

BOTTOM
***Frédérique Constant**, Heart Beat Manufacture Automatique Moonphase-Date*

masterfully reinterpreted the classical calendar tradition of the moonphase in its new L-evolution collection named 8 Jours Complete Calendar Moon Phases. Equipped with a new in-house movement with three barrels, a power reserve of eight days, a titanium balance with adjustment via micrometric screws. This timepiece shows the moonphase on a large subdial at 6:00, the day and the month in two small windows at 12:00, and the date via a central hand tipped with a red crescent. The two large Roman numerals III and IX, as well as the openings that show the calendar discs, lend the dial a decidedly geometrical, avant-garde look. Thanks to a security system, the date, day, month, and moonphase can be corrected at any hour of the day or night, even midnight, which is generally impossible on perpetual calendars, as it can damage the movement. The moonphase is even placed in a majestic, openworked dial on the Ebel 1911 BTR Perpetual Calendar Chronograph in rose gold, with an exclusive chronometer-certified movement. The Louis Erard 1931 Jubilé Moonphase shows visible discs, as well as an annual calendar and moonphase at 6:00.

A GROWING ROLE

Over the last few years, the moonphase display seems to have been liberated from the straitjacket of the perpetual or annual calendar and its unavoidable auxiliary role, taking its place as a complication in its own right. Keeping the traditional moonphase position at 6:00, certain watchmakers have decided to give it a more visible role, for example by associating it with a simple date display. On its Cape Cod Moonphase, equipped with an exclusive automatic Vaucher

Manufacture Fleurier movement, Hermès elegantly combines an "astronomical" moonphase (see "How does it work?" sidebar) with a retrograde date display along a 225° arc. The new Maurice Lacroix Masterpiece Lune Rétrograde, equipped with an in-house movement, displays the moonphase in a large counter at 6:00 that also boasts a hand for the day of the week; while the other two-thirds of the dial showcase the retrograde date display and the power-reserve display—all on a modern-looking skeletonized dial. Pierre Kunz, on its A014 HMRL, has created an entirely new dial configuration. The retrograde hours and -minutes are shown on two "fans" on the top half; the moonphase is displayed in a window with a stunning depth effect in the center of an oval cartridge sprinkled with stars. Reinterpreting one of its signature Art Deco models, Girard-Perregaux offers in its rectangular Vintage 1945 King Size collection a model of sobriety and refinement, with moonphase and date at 6:00.

Departing from its obligatory station at the bottom of the dial, the moonphase sometimes rises to the much more prominent position at 12:00. The Genevan brand Frédérique Constant has enriched its range of exclusive movements with its Heart Beat Manufacture Automatique Moonphase-Date, also available in a version with a silicon escapement wheel; the moonphase window, placed at 12:00, in the middle of a calendar with a hand, hangs over the "beating

THIS PAGE
TOP LEFT
***Hermès**, Arceau Pocket Retrograde Calendar Moonphase*

TOP RIGHT
***F.P. Journe**, Octa Automatique Lune*

CENTER
***Perrelet**, Large Central Moonphase, men's version with titanium case and black dial*

FACING PAGE
TOP LEFT
***Jaeger-LeCoultre**, Reverso Grande Sun Moon*

TOP RIGHT
***Patek Philippe**, Nautilus Ref. 5712/1*

BOTTOM
***Vacheron Constantin**, Malte Moon Phase and Power Reserve*

heart" opening that reveals the balance spring. Perrelet grants the moon a place of honor on its Large Central Moonphase, with a window spanning the entire top half of the dial. This watch, with its titanium case, black dial and calendar hand, also includes an indicator of the moon's "age" (the number of days since the last new moon). The French company L. Leroy gives the moonphase the same privileged position on its Grand Osmior Platine, whose white-gold moon disc is set against a sky of polished, flame-blued steel.

MOON STRIKES

Another striking trend: the moonphase window is venturing more and more often from its symmetrical position along the vertical axis of the dial, to occupy a more off-center location—allowing the designers to create timepieces that present original and dynamic faces. F.P. Journe provides a refined example of this trend with its Octa Automatique Lune; the moonphase display at 7:00 is joined by small seconds at 5:00, a power-reserve indicator (120 hours) in a segment between 8:00 and 10:00, and a large double date-window at 11:30—a real study in geometry! On the Arceau Pocket Retrograde Calendar Moonphase pocket watch, which Hermès launched in 2009, the moonphase plays among the stars at 5:30, next to a retrograde calendar hand that moves through 225 degrees. Patek Philippe's Nautilus Ref. 5712/1, released in 2006 on the occasion of the 30th anniversary of the sporty chic collection, also sets its sights on asymmetry and originality. Its moonphase occupies the center of a pointer-type date display at 7:00, a power reserve indicator at 10:30 and

small seconds at 4:30. The same madness occurs on Vacheron Constantin's new tonneau watch Malte Moon Phase and Power Reserve, bearing the prestigious Poinçon de Genève quality hallmark; the moonphase is obliquely displayed at 8:30, combining several finishings, and the power reserve is at 10:30. A slanted window also appears in Daniel Roth's Athys Moon 2134, launched in 2009 to celebrate the International Year of Astronomy and designed to require no manual adjustment for 125 years—hence its name. On Jaeger-LeCoultre's Reverso Grande Sun Moon, the moonphase occupies the whole lower right quadrant of the dial, in the middle of the small seconds; it is complemented by a day/night indication at 1:30. The transparent back of the reversible case reveals the hand-decorated movement, with its jewels and blued screws joined by lines evoking the constellations of the night sky.

THIS PAGE
TOP LEFT
de GRISOGONO, *OtturatOre*

CENTER
Harry Winston, *Opus 4*

LEFT
Patek Philippe, *Celestial Ref. 5106*

FACING PAGE
TOP LEFT
Chopard, *L.U.C Lunar One*

TOP RIGHT
deLaCour, *Bitourbillon*

LEFT
Louis Moinet, *Variograph*

CENTER
Zenith, *Class Tourbillon Moon & Sunphase*

The traditional window display also appears on watches with unusual constructions, as on Harry Winston's Opus 4 (2004), created by watchmaker-artist and complications master Christophe Claret. This completely reversible timepiece (via a device in the lugs) is distinguished by its twin face: a "technical" face which presents a tourbillon paired with a cathedral-chime minute repeater; and a "romantic" face with a slightly off-center large moon at 11:00 and a pointer-type date display around the dial rim. Though invisible at first glance, the moonphase also counts among the functions on the highly original OtturatOre, released by de GRISOGONO in 2008. So as to maintain a pure, understated dial aesthetic—and appeal to fans of technical curiosities—the brand developed a patented "sequential display" system. Thanks to its bi-directional mobile dial, OtturatOre reveals the indication of the wearer's choice of seconds, date, power reserve or moonphase (at 6:00), while masking the other three displays. Simply pressing on one of the two pushers performs this magic trick in a few dozen milliseconds.

VARIATIONS ON A THEME

The disc/window system can give rise to several technical or aesthetic variations, often with poetic results. Zenith has opted to represent the alternation of day and night in the background of its moonphase display via a device with two superposed discs (the one with the two moons is transparent; the background disc is opaque). Every morning, the night sky gives way to a radiant sun. This mechanism has featured in several

models in the collection, including the Class Tourbillon Moon & Sunphase, with the El Primero chronograph caliber. On the Bitourbillon from deLaCour, equipped with a large moon holding court at 12:00 just above the tourbillon's double cage, a small shooting star (painted on a sapphire crystal disc) zips across the moonphase window every six minutes at lightning speed—just enough time to make a wish. On its Variograph model, Louis Moinet decided instead to indicate not the different phases of the moon, but, more precisely, the date of the full moon in the middle of the window. The perpetual calendar L.U.C Lunar One from Chopard offers a so-called "orbital" moonphase: the small round window in which the moon waxes and wanes spins around the same axis as the small seconds, on a disc that simulates the star-spangled sky. Boasting a mobile sky chart, the highly complex Celestial Ref. 5106 by Patek Philippe reveals at any moment the exact configuration of the night sky, with the visible movement of the stars, moonphases and the position of the moon in the sky. A golden ellipse placed on the sapphire crystal of the watch outlines an opening for the sky visible from Geneva and all cities on the same latitude. The entire heavenly vision thus unfolds on the wrist.

FROM ONE HEMISPHERE TO THE OTHER

Several recent timepieces have stood out by simultaneously displaying the moonphases in both hemispheres—this particularity is not in and of itself a remarkable technical achievement

THIS PAGE
TOP LEFT
***Chopard**, L.U.C Lunar Big Date*

TOP RIGHT
***Jaeger-LeCoultre**, Master Grand Réveil*

FACING PAGE
TOP
***A. Lange & Söhne**,*
Grande Lange 1 "Luna Mundi"

RIGHT
***MB&F**, Horological Machine N° 2*

CENTER
***Piaget**, Emperador Coussin Grande Lune*

(all one needs to do is reveal the two moons that are already present on most mobile discs), but it does add an original note to the dial. Such is the case with the Portugaise Perpetual Calendar from IWC. This watch, equipped with an ultra-precise moonphase display (see "How does it work?" sidebar) also possesses a countdown indicating the number of days until the next full moon. A double moon also figures prominently in Chopard's L.U.C Lunar Big Date, which is equipped with the latest addition to the brand's collection of in-house movements, the L.U.C. 96 LD, a chronometer-certified automatic movement with two barrels and a 65-hour power reserve. The orbital double moonphase is displayed in an oversized window, with Ursa Major in the northern part of the disc and the Southern Cross opposite. The window rotates on the same axis as that of the small seconds, cut into a disc that simulates the star-spangled night sky. Yet another double moon pops up on Jaeger-LeCoultre's Master Grand Réveil, which joins a perpetual calendar with an alarm mechanism that chimes or vibrates. The double moon makes an appearance on Gérald Genta's Arena Tourbillon Perpetual Calendar Moon Phase, a composition in red, white, and black with completely visible discs, and on MB&F's Horological Machine N° 2, whose rectangular case has two dials: one on the right showing jumping hours and retrograde concentric minutes; one on the left displaying the retrograde date and moonphases for the two hemispheres. In the category of, "the moon here and elsewhere," we must also include Grande Lange 1 "Luna Mundi" from A. Lange & Söhne, two timepieces offered as a set: one watch in white gold with Ursa Major on the dial for the Northern Hemisphere moonphase; one in rose gold that features the Southern Cross for the

Southern Hemisphere. It is the first "geopolitically correct" moonphase! Another quirk: instead of advancing once or twice every 24 hours, the moonphases are linked to the hour wheel and progress incrementally and continually.

STARRING: THE MOON

As well as windows shaped like the traditional double-headed axe, there are also windows as round as the full moon; these systems are generally equipped with a movable cover-up whose movement reproduces that of the shadow the Earth casts on the moon, allowing the watch to represent the moon's changing faces throughout its synodic revolution. These round windows are used more and more often for very large displays that turn the moon into the star of the dial. Such is the case for Piaget's Emperador Coussin Grande Lune, one of the most noted creations of 2009. Equipped with the new in-house caliber 860P, this watch, with its very contemporary geometry, shows the moonphase in a round window with a diameter of 12mm. The moon disc is represented by a heat-formed crater-pocked white-gold plate; its hand-crafted creation means that each piece is one of a kind. The German watchmaker Martin Braun, now a part of the Franck Muller group, has also chosen to com-

THIS PAGE
TOP LEFT
***Andersen Genève**, Kamar*

TOP RIGHT
***Martin Braun**, Selene*

CENTER
***Sarpaneva**, Korona K3*

FACING PAGE
TOP LEFT
***Corum**, Romvlvs Perpetual Calendar*

TOP RIGHT
***Jaquet Droz**, Les Lunes*

CENTER
***Vincent Bérard**, Luvorene Four Seasons*

LEFT
***Richard Mille**, Planétaire-Tellurium*

RIGHT
***Ulysse Nardin**, Moonstruck*

bine poetry and realism on its Selene ("moon" in ancient Greek) model; a large round moon, based on a photograph, is alternately hidden and gradually revealed by a mobile cover. On its Kamar watch ("moon" in Arabic), Andersen Genève has designed a round window with a mother-of-pearl disc that includes a light moon and a dark moon, all on a dial in aventurine or in 22-karat guilloché blue gold. The extra-large display is quite majestic. The Finnish watchmaker Sarpaneva uses a circular window in its unusual Korona K3 collection, but the moonphase is displayed via a large central disc that has two human-faced moons that are visible through the openworked dial. Corum's Romvlvs Perpetual Calendar also boasts a round disc and circular window, with a rose-gold case and an exceptionally thin movement that is entirely skeletonized and decorated by hand.

NEW MOONS

Though clearly dominant, window-and-disc systems are not the only ways to show the phases of the moon. Some devices use hands. On its Les Lunes watch, with an annual date/day/month calendar, Jaquet Droz offers this type of display, which also boasts a retrograde mechanism: the hand follows the progression of the lunar cycle from one orb to the next (new moon, first quarter, full moon, last quarter), before jumping back to its original starting place. In Blancpain's Equation Marchante (See "Equation of Time" chapter), a retrograde hand indicates the moonphase on an arc between 10:00 and 11:00. On its new Luvorene Four Seasons watch, released in

four versions, each one devoted to a different season, Vincent Bérard also offers a pointer-type moonphase display.

Other horologers—still few and far between—give free rein to their imaginations, inventing brand-new ways of representing the moon-

the moon. On its caseback, this watch also presents a two-pusher system that allows the owner to speed up or slow down the functioning of the movement according to the rhythms of his life and personal style. Ulysse Nardin's Moonstruck, a worthy heir to the astronomical watches designed for the brand by Ludwig Oechslin (see "Grand Complications" chapter), continuously indicates the positions of the sun and the moon relative to any spot on the globe; the timepiece

THIS PAGE
TOP LEFT
***Zenith**, Class Lady Moonphase*

TOP RIGHT
***Patek Philippe**, Calatrava Ref. 4958*

CENTER
***F.P. Journe**, Octa Divine*

FACING PAGE
TOP LEFT
***Parmigiani Fleurier**, Luna Blu*

TOP RIGHT
***Audemars Piguet**, Millenary Ciel étoilé*

TOP FAR RIGHT
***Blancpain**, Blancpain Women "Orchidée" Annual Calendar Moonphase*

CENTER
***Girard-Perregaux**, Cat's Eye Bi-retro*

presented by Richard Mille and designed by Stephen Forsey, reproduces—with extreme precision—the movement of the planets around the sun, as well as that of the moon around the earth; it also features a perpetual calendar, a first for a watch of this type.

LADY LUNA

The last big trend to note: moonphase indications are becoming more and more common on models designed especially for women. As a tribute to its supposed "romanticism," the moonphase is considered by some to be the most "feminine" of complications (women being, it goes without saying, the most incorrigible romantics), and a good way to attract clients to marvels of mechanical watchmaking. Technically and aesthetically, the moonphases designed for the fairer sex present the same variety as those for men, with the added attraction of coming in sparkling, refined packages.

Equipped with an automatic Elite movement, Zenith's Class Lady Moonphase displays the moonphase in a large central window at 6:00, on a mother-of-pearl dial surrounded by diamonds; to preserve the purity of the rose-gold or steel case design, the correction of the moonphase display is done directly via the crown. The new Octa Divine—one of the few models by F.P. Journe set with diamonds—indicates its moonphase on an oblique axis at 7:00; as with all the brand's current models, it is powered by an 18-karat rose-gold movement. Playing with off-center displays on its Calatrava Ref. 4958, Patek Philippe combines small seconds and an astronomical moonphase in a window whose size is unusual for a ladies' watch; the diamond-set

gold case houses the brand's smallest complicated movement, and the dial features a guilloché center with a mother-of-pearl rim set with diamond indexes. This same careful refinement shows on the new "Bulgari Bulgari" Moon Phase: the moonphase at 9:00 stands out against a dial that blends mother-of-pearl, engraved decorations and diamond pavé in the shape of a crescent moon. A magnificent sight also awaits those admiring Audemars Piguet's haute jewelry watch Millenary Ciel Étoilé, with its oval case, off-center dark blue dial sprinkled with sparkling constellations, its moonphase window, and its white mother-of-pearl or diamond-pavé crescent moon. Girard-Perregaux also offers women moonphase indications on several models in its oval Cat's Eye collection, including the Cat's Eye Bi-retro, with retrograde displays for the seconds and the day of the week.

FEMININE REFINEMENT

The moon also shows up on ladies' watches that unite several complications—especially calendar displays. On its Toric Quantième Perpétuel Luna Blu, Parmigiani Fleurier displays the lunar months in both hemispheres; the blue lacquered dial in 18-karat gold sparkles with four diamond constellations. The Blancpain Women "Orchidée" Annual Calendar Moonphase shows a full moon with feminine facial features, complemented by a tiny beauty mark in the shape of a star, all crafted in white gold, mother-of-pearl and diamonds. Zenith offers women a brand new "Moon & Sunphase" display (previously discussed) on a special version of its very precious Starissime Tourbillon (see "Tourbillon" chapter), with a dia-

ANTOINE PREZIUSO
GENEVE

FACING PAGE
***Antoine Preziuso**, Starmoon*

THIS PAGE
TOP LEFT
***Perrelet**, Ladies' Moonphase, with a cushion-shaped dial*

TOP RIGHT
***Harry Winston**, Lady Z*

CENTER
***Maurice Lacroix**, Starside Sparkling Date*

mond star as the tourbillon bridge; the case is richly set with diamonds and the mother-of-pearl dial boasts large swirling numerals.

Occasionally the moon performs a one-woman-show on the dial. Available in a round or cushion-shaped version, Perrelet's Moonphase (which also includes a calendar with a hand) turns the spotlight toward a large window in a slightly slanted position between 7:00 and 1:00; the moon's cycle is depicted on a mother-of-pearl dial with diamond constellations. Equally glamorous is Antoine Preziuso's Starmoon, presented as the largest moonphase ever created, whose black ceramic dial shines with luminescent numerals, framed by a case set with starry diamonds and sapphires.

Watchmakers have also designed uniquely feminine ways of signaling the phases of the moon. In 2008, Maurice Lacroix showed off its originality and refinement by launching its Starside Sparkling Date. Besides its off-center hours and minutes, and its retrograde date display with a diamond cresting a small wave in the lower left corner of the dial, the timepiece stands out for its moonphase indication, in which the heavenly body plays hide-and-seek with a cabochon—carved from a moonstone. For its Lady Z, Harry Winston also innovates, drawing on mystery, sparkle and precious stones to propose a moonphase display marked by the comings and goings of two moons in aventurine, one white, the other black. Each moon is finished by a trail evoking the tail of a comet, set with diamonds and black sapphires.

BOVET

FLEURIER COMPLICATIONS: TRIPLE DATE

In the 42mm Fleurier self-winding, triple-calendar movement with moonphase and sweep seconds dress watch, BOVET shows how attractive clarity and precision can be while indicating seven scales of time—from running seconds to lunar months—on the dial. The Fleurier case is also an opportunity, even a requirement, to use BOVET's trademark serpentine hands. Three discs under the dial show the day, month and moonphase, and the dates circle the edge of the dial. Each indication has its pushpiece corrector in the caseband. The triple-calendar Fleurier watches with black or white dials and the signature appliqués in gold are the first of many varieties that are certain to be produced to specific customer order. This handsome and useful wristwatch will give a wider circle of collectors the opportunity to enjoy the quality and distinctive character of BOVET watchmaking.

BOVET

FLEURIER COMPLICATIONS: TRIPLE DATE

In the Fleurier 42mm dress watch, BOVET's designers show how attractive clarity and precision can be while indicating seven scales of time—from running seconds to lunar months—on the dial. Three discs under the dial show the day, month and moonphase, and the dates circle the edge of the dial. Each indication has its correcting pushpiece in the caseband and the self-winding movement—one of the finest in its category—delivers more than 70 hours of power reserve from twin barrels. In this watch, the movement is a BOVET livery of rhodium Côtes de Genève, blued steel screws, and a raised *fleurisanne* engraving on the 22K gold rotor.

DE BETHUNE

DB25 – REF. DB25LRS1V1

The heart of De Bethune's new DB25 collection is the new DB2105s caliber, fitted with a silicon balance wheel and available in three versions with different finishes and treatments. The 6-day power-reserve indicator is presented on the back of this watch. Beneath a hard (1800 Vickers), antireflective sapphire crystal, each silvered dial is unique, as the guilloché is hand applied by skilled artisans. The raised hour-ring sets off the central guilloché radiating in 12 sectors, as well as the barleycorn guilloché surrounding the dial. The three-dimensional moonphase display at 12:00 holds perfect accuracy for 122 years, when it will lose one lunar day. The sphere consists of two hemispheres, one in steel and the other in platinum. These hemispheres are fixed to each other and then polished and flame-blued by hand. The steel half becomes blued through the effect of oxidation while the platinum part preserves its natural color. This Ø 44.6x11.1mm watch is available in rose or white gold.

DE BETHUNE

DB25 – REF. DB25LWS1V1

The heart of De Bethune's new DB25 collection is the new DB2105s caliber, fitted with a silicon balance wheel and available in three versions with different finishes and treatments. The 6-day power-reserve indicator is presented on the back of this watch. From beneath a hard (1800 Vickers), antireflective sapphire crystal and encased in white gold, the dial portrays a blue sky dotted with gold stars and a three-dimensional moonphase indicator, which will hold perfect accuracy for 122 years, when it will lose one lunar day. Two hemispheres--one steel and one platinum--are fixed to each other and then polished and flame-blued by hand. The steel half is blued through oxidation while the platinum part preserves its natural color. It takes five different operations to illustrate the dial's skyscape: tiny holes are pierced into a metal sheet; the holes are enlarged into star shapes; little pieces of gold are pressed into the metal sheet; the sheet is polished and, finally, flame-blued. This piece measures Ø 44.6x11.1mm.

PIAGET

EMPERADOR COUSSIN LARGE MOON – REF. G0A34021

This model is a paragon of purity and understatement, featuring a generous 46.5mm case and an original and attractive moonphase display at 6:00. With its broad opening measuring 12mm in diameter, this large moon reveals a wealth of subtle craftsmanship exercised on a heated gold plate featuring reflections symbolizing moon craters. A mobile mask that gradually uncovers and re-covers the white-gold moon disc provides the moonphase indication. This display principle reproduces the natural interplay of the sun and the earth in relation to the moon. The complication beats to the rhythm of the new 860P caliber, a self-winding movement designed, developed and produced by the Manufacture de Haute Horlogerie Piaget. In addition to its approximately 72-hour power reserve, it features Piaget's signature finishes such as circular Côtes de Genève, a circular-grained mainplate, beveled bridges, and blued screws. Available in 18K white or pink gold, the case is fitted with a sapphire crystal caseback allowing one to admire the movement's finishing.

PIAGET

EMPERADOR TOURBILLON PHASE DE LUNE XL – REF. G0A31121

The Tourbillon Phase de Lune XL maintains the sophisticated lines and finishings of the Emperador watches, but offers a more powerful and masculine size. It houses the Piaget mechanical hand-wound Calibre 640P, the world's thinnest tourbillon movement at just 3.5mm thick. Admirably reflecting the mastery inherent to the manufacture, the carriage of this tourbillon—visible through a dial opening at 9:00—consists of 42 parts and weighs a mere 0.2 grams. A moonphase display appears at 6:00 on the rounded base of a delicately guilloché-worked surface. The lapis lazuli moonphase disc is enhanced by a golden moon and a pyrite star-studded dial.

VACHERON CONSTANTIN

KALLA LUNE – REF. 83630

The newest addition to the Kalla collection is the Kalla Lune complication. Its hand-wound mechanical movement, Caliber 1410, bears the prestigious Hallmark of Geneva. On the dial is the power-reserve display and moonphase display set with 14 diamonds (0.03 carat). The case is set with 158 baguette-cut diamonds (13.6 carats), and its winding crown is set with one diamond (0.1 carat). The dial is set with 170 baguette-cut diamonds and nine brilliant-cut diamonds (2.82 carats). Kalla Lune's 18K white-gold case measures 40.5mm in diameter, and its deployment clasp is set with eight baguette-cut diamonds (0.38 carat).

VACHERON CONSTANTIN

MALTE MOON PHASE AND POWER RESERVE – REF. 83080

The Malte Moon Phase and Power Reserve is available in a case of 18K white gold or 5N pink gold. The satin-brushed caseback is secured by screws and the dial is protected by a glareproofed cambered sapphire crystal. Guaranteed water resistant to a depth of 30 meters, this timepiece is fitted with a square-scale alligator-leather strap in black for the white-gold model and chestnut brown for the rose-gold model; each strap is equipped with a gold folding clasp matching the case.

VACHERON CONSTANTIN
TOLEDO 1952 – REF. 47300

This Toledo 1952 is crafted in 18K pink gold and houses the mechanical manual-winding Vacheron Constantin Caliber 1125. Beating at 28,800 vibrations per hour, the complicated movement is equipped with 36 rubies and offers 40 hours of power reserve. In addition to small seconds, the watch offers a full calendar (date, day, month, moonphase). The three-piece square case is fitted with a curved sapphire crystal, is water resistant to 3atm, and is secured with a hand-stitched alligator strap with pink-gold clasp.

ZENITH

CHRONOMASTER LADY MOONPHASE

Feminine interpretation of a traditional icon, the ChronoMaster Lady Moonphase offers an automatic chronograph with triple calendar indicators and moonphase display. The 410 El Primero caliber comprises 357 components, 31 jewels, provides approximately 50 hours of power reserve, and beats at the legendary 36,000 vibrations per hour. The dial reveals a subtle combination of mother-of-pearl and traditional Grain d'Orge pattern. The 37.5mm case can be set with 64 round diamonds. Shown in steel with a white dial, this timepiece is also available in rose gold with white dial and on a brown crocodile strap.

ZENITH

CLASS MOONPHASE EL PRIMERO

Housing the El Primero 4100 caliber, this timepiece offers the only automatic integrated column wheel manufactured chronograph with moonphase and complete calendar. The 357-part movement beats at 36,000 vibrations per hour and has 31 jewels. Water resistant to 50 meters, this Class Moonphase is crafted in stainless steel or in rose gold and is available in two different sizes (44mm or 40mm). Part of the "Nouveaux Classiques" the silver dial is decorated with Clous de Paris guilloché pattern.

ZENITH

CLASS MOONPHASE EL PRIMERO

Housing the El Primero 4100 caliber, this timepiece offers the only automatic integrated column wheel manufactured chronograph with moonphase and complete calendar. The 357-part movement beats at 36,000 vibrations per hour and has 31 jewels. Water resistant to 50 meters, this Class Moonphase is crafted in stainless steel or in rose gold and is available in two different sizes (44mm or 40mm). Part of the "Nouveaux Classiques" the silver dial is decorated with Clous de Paris guilloché pattern.

Ultra-complicated watches are to horology what Formula 1 racecars are to the automobile: the supreme manifestation of savoir-faire, and the best testing ground for technical innovations that will show up later on more common models. With hundreds of components, and a long gestation period that requires a considerable outlay of effort, these exceptional watches are produced in very small series, or even one at a time, and they largely serve as standard bearers for the prestigious manufactures to assert their mastery. Looking to seduce watch collectors and those who love rare pieces, watchmakers also offer a wide selection of multi-complications that are outfitted with a smaller number of functions, but keenly focused on ease of use, functionality and readability.

Zenith, *Class Traveller Open el Primero Multicity*
Jaeger-LeCoultre, *Hybris Mechanica à Gyrotourbillon*
Hublot, *Bigger Bang Tourbillon All Black*
Jaeger-LeCoultre, *Master Compressor Extreme*

Audemars Piguet, *Millenary*
Jean Dunand, *Shabaka*
Vacheron Constantin, *Kalla*

MULTI-COMPLICATIONS

A POCKETFUL OF RECORDS

If there is one name that stands out in the realm of ultra-complicated watches, it is Patek Philippe. Between 1925 and 1933, the Genevan manufacture created for Henry Graves, Jr. the Graves watch: a double-sided pocket watch with 24 complications, including a grande sonnerie with four bells and a map of the night sky as seen from New York. The title "most complicated watch in the world" has long been contested, however, by another complicated masterpiece, the Leroy 01 (1904), which laid claim to between 20 and 25 complications. In 1989, Patek Philippe finally put an end to the dispute by presenting the Calibre 89. With 33 complications and 1,728 components, this watch remains the most complicated portable watch in the history of horology. Besides the "classic" repertory of complications, (calendar, chronograph, sonnerie, astronomical complications, etc.), the Calibre 89 features some extremely rare functions, such as the so-called "secular" perpetual calendar (see "Perpetual Calendar" chapter) and an indication of the date of Easter. The timepiece is also equipped with a celestial map that portrays the Milky Way and 2,800 stars of the Northern Hemisphere, as well as their magnitudes.

In 2000, Patek Philippe once again distinguished itself by unveiling the double-sided Star Calibre 2000 pocket watch with 21 complications. The goal was not simply to assemble the greatest number of functions, but only those that "give time its most poetic representation," which usually means astronomical functions. Without trying to get into the *Guinness Book of Records*, other watchmakers have recently introduced ultra-complicated pocket watches that stand out for their sophistication.

FACING PAGE
TOP LEFT
Patek Philippe, *Graves*

TOP RIGHT
Louis Leroy, *Leroy 01*

BOTTOM
Patek Philippe, *Calibre 89*

THIS PAGE
TOP LEFT
Vincent Bérard, *Quatre Saisons Carrosse*

TOP RIGHT
Audemars Piguet, *Grande Complication Savonnette*

BOTTOM
Breguet, *Marie-Antoinette*

Audemars Piguet's Grande Complication Savonnette houses a perpetual calendar, a minute repeater, and a split-second chronograph in its yellow-gold case. Vincent Bérard has chosen to reinterpret "carriage" watches in the Quatre Saisons Carrosse, which has five complications, including a perpetual calendar, a quarter-hour repeater and a system of automata on the dial. The watch comes in four versions, each enameled to represent a different season.

Watchmakers have always pushed back the limits of their art by joining the greatest number of functions possible within the confines of a relatively narrow case. The most famous example is Breguet's Marie-Antoinette pocket watch, commissioned for or by the Queen of France in 1783 but not finished until 1827, long after her death. This masterpiece includes

automatic winding, a large independent second hand, a minute repeater, an equation of time, a power-reserve indicator, and a thermometer. It was stolen from a museum in Jerusalem in 1983, before resurfacing in 2007 under mysterious circumstances. The following year, Breguet presented an identical reproduction of this legendary timepiece, housed in a box crafted from the queen's favorite oak at Versailles.

WRIST WATCHING

The arrival of the wristwatch at the beginning of the 20th century forced watchmakers to use ever more ingenuity to miniaturize the mechanisms and join them in exceptional pieces. Since the mechanical renaissance of the 1980s, ultra-complicated timepieces have multiplied considerably, and the largest manufactures helped by the latest technology —have rejoined the race to create "the world's most complicated watch." In 1991, Blancpain introduced the 1735, which combines six major achievements of horology: an ultra-flat movement, moonphase, perpetual calendar, split-second chronograph, tourbillon, and minute repeater. In 1994, Gérald Genta launched its Grande Sonnerie with tourbillon, petite and grande sonnerie with a four-

FACING PAGE
LEFT
***Patek Philippe**, Sky Moon Tourbillon*

RIGHT
***Blancpain**, 1735*

THIS PAGE
***Vacheron Constantin**, Tour de l'Ile*

hammered Westminster carillon, minute repeater, perpetual calendar, second time zone, automatic winding with two barrels, and double display of both the movement and the carillon's power reserves all in an octagonal case that breaks definitively with the traditional aesthetic of multi-complications.

In 2001, Patek Philippe reaffirmed its preeminence by presenting the Sky Moon Tourbillon, a double-sided wristwatch that uniquely combined the 12 complications judged to be the rarest and most fascinating, including a minute repeater with cathedral chime, a tourbillon and a mobile skymap. In 2005, Vacheron Constantin celebrated its 250th anniversary by creating its Tour de l'Ile model. This double-sided timepiece contains no fewer than 16 complications in its 834-component movement. In 2006, Jaeger-LeCoultre raised the stakes by unveiling its Reverso grande complication à triptyque a watch that benefits from the brand's famous reversible case, created in 1932, in an unusual way. This exceptional timepiece has three faces for three dimensions of time. On the front can be read civil (mean) time, with a new escapement system and a titanium tourbillon. The back features sidereal time, with a map of the sky, a zodiacal calendar, equation of time and the times of sunrise and sunset. Within the Reverso carriage, on the "third face," resides a complete perpetual calendar. In all, the watch possesses an extraordinary record-breaking 18 complications.

MAîTRES du TEMPS
DATE
SWISS
MADE
SUNDAY
MONDAY

FACING PAGE
***Maîtres du Temps**, Chapter One*

THIS PAGE
LEFT
***Jean Dunand**, Grande Complication*

BELOW
***Franck Muller**, Aeternitas 8888 TQPS*

Among multi-complicated wristwatches, Franck Muller's Aeternitas 8888 TQPS with 15 complications in an elegant tonneau case must also be noted. The complications include a grand flying tourbillon and a "secular" perpetual calendar with retrograde date, astronomical moonphase, equation of time, and two supplementary time zones. Jean Dunand released in 2005 its Grande Complication, which boasted, among other functions, a monopusher split-second chronograph, tourbillon, hour repeater, quarter-hour repeater and minute repeater, and biretrograde (date and day) perpetual calendar, as well as various innovations or technical particularities. In 2008, three of today's greatest watchmakers Christophe Claret, Roger Dubuis and Peter Speake-Marin have joined forces under the name "Maîtres du Temps" and unveiled a masterpiece named Chapter One. This one-of-a-kind piece joins within its tonneau case a tourbillon, a monopusher column-wheel chronograph, a retrograde date, and a retrograde second time zone. Chapter One is also notable for its two rollers at 6:00 and 12:00, which display the day of the week and the moonphase, respectively.

EYE ON THE STARS

Ulysse Nardin, a brand famous for its marine timepieces, has explored the astronomical and astrological science of the Renaissance in its Trilogy of Time collection. The first piece, named Astrolabium Galileo Galilei, displays on its dial the functions of the astrolabe, a navigation tool used

THIS PAGE
TOP
Ulysse Nardin, *Tellurium Johannes Kepler*

LEFT
Ulysse Nardin, *Astrolabium Galileo Galilei*

RIGHT
Ulysse Nardin, *Planetarium Copernicus*

FACING PAGE
LEFT
Jaeger-LeCoultre, *Hybris Mechanica à Triptyque*

RIGHT
Jaeger-LeCoultre, *safe for the Hybris Mechanica 55*

in many astronomical discoveries. Most notably, it indicated the respective positions of the sun, the moon and the stars as seen from Earth. The Planetarium Copernicus displays the month and the Zodiac sign, as well as the astronomical positions of the planets in relation to the sun and the Earth, using a dial composed of seven rings. The brand's Tellurium Johannes Kepler, with its cloisonné enamel dial representing Earth as seen from the North Pole, displays the hours of sunrise and sunset (with light and dark areas), as well as solar and lunar eclipses. The universe is on your wrist!

SEEING TRIPLE

In 2009, Jaeger-LeCoultre made a splash once again, releasing a trio of timepieces baptized Hybris Mechanica 55 (from the Greek "hybris," meaning *excess*). These three watches feature a total of 55 complications some found in more than one model. The first of the trilogy, Hybris Mechanica Gyrotourbillon, pays tribute to the mechanical measure of time in its "spherical tourbillon," a feature introduced by Jaeger-LeCoultre on its Gyrotourbillon I and II (see "Tourbillons" chapter). The movement also contains a perpetual calendar with four retrograde hands and an equation-of-time display that is adjustable according to location all in a round case, inspired by the Master collection. The second piece, Hybris Mechanica à Triptyque, revisits the principle behind the brand's Reverso grande complication à triptyque mentioned above. The Hybris Mechanica à Grande Sonnerie highlights the magic of an aural indication of time with a 1,300-component movement that combines a flying tourbillon, a perpetual calendar with retrograde hands and a minute repeater sonnerie mechanism that includes numerous patented inventions (see "Minute Repeaters and Sonneries" chapter) all in a Duomètre case. The Hybris Mechanica 55 trilogy comes in a 1.5m-tall case with luxurious finishing, and only 30 examples will be produced between 2009 and 2014.

A. LANGE & SÖHNE

DATOGRAPH PERPETUAL – REF. 410.025

This model is driven by the manually wound Lange movement Caliber L952.1. It is a flyback chronograph with a precise jumping minute counter as well as perpetual calendar with outsize date, moonphase display, day-of-the-week, month, leap-year display, small seconds hand with stop seconds, and day/night indicator. The plates and bridges are made of untreated German silver and the balance cock is engraved by hand. The three-part platinum case features an antireflective sapphire crystal and caseback, main pushpiece for simultaneously advancing all calendar displays, as well as recessed pushpieces for separately advancing the calendar displays, and two chronograph pushpieces. The luminous two-part dial in rhodium-plated solid silver is marked with a tachymeter scale. The hand-stitched crocodile strap is secured with a solid-platinum buckle.

AUDEMARS PIGUET

JULES AUDEMARS SKELETON SELFWINDING GRANDE COMPLICATION

REF. 25996OR.OO.D002CR.01

The Jules Audemars Grand Complication houses the 2885 caliber, which contains more than 600 pieces. The watch possesses a perpetual calendar with 52-week indication, astronomical moon, a minute repeater and a split-seconds chronograph. It is housed in an 18K pink-gold 950 with five correctors with five correctors and a sapphire crystal and caseback revealing the engraving work on the movement. The 30-minute counter and day of the week are indicated at 3:00, the month and the four-year cycle are located at 6:00, small seconds and date are located at 9:00, while the moonphase and the week are read at 12:00. This timepiece is also available in 950 platinum or in titanium.

AUDEMARS PIGUET
ROYAL OAK GRANDE COMPLICATION – REF. 25865BC.OO.1105BC.01

The Royal Oak Grande Complication is powered by the 2885 caliber, a self-winding movement of 13.5''', which features a split-seconds chronograph, a minute repeater and a perpetual calendar. Seconds are displayed in a subdial at 9:00. Housed in an 18K white-gold case, the movement beats at 19,800 vibrations per hour. The dial displays 12 indications, including day, date, month, leap years and moonphase. The movement is comprised of 654 pieces.

BOVET

FLEURIER COMPLICATIONS: MINUTE REPEATER TOURBILLON AND REVERSE HAND FITTING

This single watch encompasses everything that BOVET is about. The 44mm case houses a minute repeater with tourbillon and a reversed hand-fitting, blackened movement (365 components) finished to the highest standards of Swiss watchmaking. The unique feature of this hand-wound caliber is that the movement is shown side up. This means that the hand-fitting has to be reversed so that the hands turn clockwise dialside. The inverted construction enables the main machinery of the watch to be displayed in new ways on the face of the watch. The BOVET minute repeater with tourbillon has two different cathedral chiming gongs, a low pitch to count the hours and a combination of high-low pitch gongs to chime the quarters and then the minutes.

BOVET

FLEURIER COMPLICATIONS: MINUTE REPEATER, TOURBILLON, TRIPLE TIME ZONE AND AUTOMATON

BOVET presents one of its most spectacular technical achievements in this hand-wound Minute Repeater, Tourbillon, Triple Time Zone and Automaton Fleurier 44mm wristwatch. The BOVET Haute Horlogerie movement made of more than 600 different components is visible on the backside of the case thanks to its transparent sapphire crystal glass. The cathedral gongs of the minute repeater have been attached to the case to provide a clearer sound to the fortunate owner of this magnificent piece of art. The handmade guilloché dial is adorned with two independent time zones offering to the traveler the indication of 40 cities. Fewer than 10 pieces of this model will be produced each year, in white gold or rose gold.

HUBLOT

KING POWER CHRONO TOURBILLON ALL BLACK – REF. 708.CI.0110.RX

The King Power Tourbillon All Black's flying tourbillon spins in a cage without ball bearings and raised 2.8mm above the base of the bottom plate. When the chronograph is stopped, the King Power Tourbillon All Black has a power reserve of 120 hours. The Ø 48mm case is crafted in Satin King Gold, and the bezel is coated in black rubber molding, with six black PVD-coated titanium H-shaped screws holding it in place. The chronograph hand is plated in Satin Gold, the hour and minute hands are brilliant black nickel with black SuperLumiNova, and the Satin Gold counter hand is coated with black SuperLumiNova. This is a limited edition of 28 pieces.

HUBLOT

KING POWER CHRONO TOURBILLON GOLD – REF. 708.PX.0180.RX

The King Power achieves a successful fusion of expressive power and emotionally charged luxury. Crafted in a new red-gold alloy developed exclusively for Hublot, King Power is redder and more resistant than ever. All of its parts have been redesigned: the case features sharp angles and straight edges with raised endpieces and screws; the pushpieces on the side of the case stand out more strongly than ever and the decorative tubes are inserted into black composite resin; the bezel looks decidedly different thanks to the rubber molding around the ceramic base; and its rubber strap features an embossed cutout motif that accentuates its rugged nature. This is chronograph-tourbillon is offered in a limited edition of 28 pieces.

IWC

GRANDE COMPLICATION – REF. IW377013

This IWC Grande Complication in shown in platinum on black crocodile leather strap. The watch features 659 mechanical parts (71 of them jewels) and 21 functions and displays including a perpetual calendar for the next 500 years, together with a perpetual moonphase display made of polished goldstone representing a star-studded sky. Working inside the highly complex case are a chronograph and a complicated minute repeater. This Grande Complication houses the 79091 caliber movement with 44 hours of power reserve and beating at 28,800 vibrations per hour. Also available on a platinum bracelet or in rose gold on a black crocodile leather strap or rose-gold bracelet.

IWC

GRANDE COMPLICATION – REF. IW377025

This IWC Grande Complication is shown in rose gold on black crocodile leather strap. The watch features 659 mechanical parts (71 of them jewels) and 21 functions and displays including a perpetual calendar for the next 500 years, together with a perpetual moonphase display made of polished goldstone representing a star-studded sky. Working inside the highly complex case are a chronograph and a complicated minute repeater. This Grande Complication houses the 79091 caliber movement with 44 hours of power reserve and beating at 28,800 vibrations per hour. Also available on a rose-gold bracelet or in platinum on a black crocodile leather strap or platinum bracelet.

JACOB & CO.

EPIC TOURBILLON

Crafted in stainless steel and black PVD, the Epic Tourbillon is also a multiple time-zone watch. The movement beats at 21,600 vibrations per hour and draws on 120 hours of power reserve. The multi-tiered dial, which has displays on six different levels, boasts signature Jacob & Co. geometric subdials and hands. Presented on a rubber strap, the 47mm Epic Tourbillon is also available in 18K rose gold.

MONTBLANC

EXOTOURBILLON CHRONOGRAPHE

The ExoTourbillon Chronographe masters the difficult task of combining two cherished complications: a chronograph function and a four-minute tourbillon boasting an unusual innovation: its balance is larger than the tourbillon's rotating cage, and placed outside it. A large minute hand and the elapsed-seconds hand of the chronograph share a central axis. On the dial, the tourbillon spins at 12:00, the 30-minute chronograph counter is at 3:00, the 24-hour second time-zone indicator sits between 4:00 and 5:00, the hours are at 6:00, and the small seconds are at 9:00. Just one platinum version will be produced, along with 18 pieces in 18K white gold and 18 pieces in 18K 5N red gold.

PARMIGIANI FLEURIER

TECNICA CHRONO SKELETON

This unique piece is a 43-jeweled manual-winding tourbillon that features a minute repeater with two cathedral chimes. According to the theme, the bridges are engraved by hand with chamfering, the backing is hand polished, and the steel is set lengthwise with stones. Beating at 21,600 vibrations per hour, the PF353 movement offers 48 hours of power reserve and other functions include hours, minutes, minute repeater and chronograph. The 44mm case is crafted in 950 platinum and is water resistant to 30 meters. Each watch is individually numbered on its back.

PARMIGIANI FLEURIER

TORIC CORRECTOR MINUTE REPEATER AND PERPETUAL CALENDAR

A world-premiere timepiece, this Toric houses the mechanical manually wound Parmigiani Fleurier caliber with retrograde perpetual-calendar module crafted entirely in-house. The 33-jeweled movement vibrates at 21,600 beats per hour and offers 45 hours of power reserve. The movement consists of hand-beveled bridges and the Côtes de Genève decorative motif. It offers hours, minutes, day, retrograde date, month, leap year and a high-precision moonphase indicator, as well as the minute-repeater mechanism that strikes on two gongs. The watch is offered in platinum or 18K pink gold with a pushpiece that instantly corrects all perpetual calendar and moonphase functions. The dial is silvered 18K gold with a barelycorn guilloché motif.

PATEK PHILIPPE

PERPETUAL CALENDAR MINUTE REPEATER – REF. 5074

This self-winding, 467-part movement with Geneva Seal (Patek Philippe caliber R 27 Q, R 27 PS base + calendar module) offers perpetual calendar (date, day, month, four-year cycle, moonphase) and minute repeater. The Ø 40mm case houses the repeater-perpetual movement realized by Patek Philippe long ago by combining the automatic base including a minute repeater (R 27 PS caliber without seconds) and the most classic calendar module with 24-hour indications. This model, presented in 2001 with only the repeater, is meant for connoisseurs. The case size assures a particularly clean amplification of the Cathedral sonnerie. The gong is realized with a special alloy and undergoes several rotations. The full and long-lasting sound thus obtained recalls the bells of ancient cathedrals. The special alloy used for the acoustic gongs, which assures an extraordinary resonance, was developed by Patek Philippe in cooperation with the metallurgy experts of the Federal Swiss Institute of Technology of Lausanne.

PATEK PHILIPPE

SKY MOON TOURBILLON – REF. 5002J

This manual-winding movement with Geneva Seal (Patek Philippe caliber RTO 27 QR SID LU CL) offers tourbillon, minute repeater, perpetual calendar, (retrograde date, day, month, four-year cycle, moonphase) and astronomic functions. On the sky map, the moon (with phases) and the Sirius star's sidereal positions are indicated on a 24-hour scale. The sidereal day is determined by two subsequent passages of a star on a meridian (here, the one of Geneva). The sidereal time indication is useful to determine the longitude from a certain place. The ellipsis moves and displays, at any moment, the part of the sky visible from that place (in this case, Geneva). The variations of astronomic indications by a few seconds each century are the slightest ones ever obtained by a mechanical watch.

ULYSSE NARDIN

GENGHIS KHAN – REF. 789-80

Within Genghis Khan's 42mm platinum case, Caliber UN-78 is equipped with a Westminster Minute Repeater Carillon Tourbillon. An animated Jaquemart adorns the Aventurine dial. Just 30 pieces of the Genghis Khan have been created.

ULYSSE NARDIN

MOONSTRUCK – REF. 1062-113

Moonstruck's Caliber UN-106 powers a scientifically accurate moonphase, representation of solar time, and indication of tides. Moonstruck is available in a 46mm, 18K red-gold or platinum case with a ceramic bezel and hand-painted mother-of-pearl dial. Each version is issued in a 500-piece limited edition.

VACHERON CONSTANTIN

MALTE OPENFACE RETROGRADE PERPETUAL CALENDAR – REF. 47032

This platinum Malte Openface Retrograde Perpetual Calendar houses the mechanical automatic-winding Vacheron Constantin Caliber 1126 QPR. The 36-jeweled movement beats at 28,800 vibrations per hour, has 38 hours of power reserve, is hand finished, and features a pink-gold mainplate. All of its parts have been hand chiseled and etched away for exceptional viewing. The perpetual calendar offers date, day, month, digital year indication, and four-year cycle. The dial consists of a sapphire crystal disc, luminescent peripheral date-ring, and white-gold hands. This piece is fitted on an alligator strap with platinum clasp.

VACHERON CONSTANTIN

MALTE PERPETUAL CALENDAR MINUTE REPEATER – REF. 30040/000R

Crafted and accented in 18K pink gold, this Malte Perpetual Calendar Minute Repeater offers a minute repeater and perpetual calendar with day, date, month, year, and moonphase. Powered by the extra-flat, mechanical manual-winding Vacheron Constantin Caliber 1755 QP, the model was released in a 30-piece limited edition. With a perpetual calendar module, the 30-jeweled movement measures 4.9mm thick, is finished and decorated by hand, and is visible through a sapphire caseback. The silvered dial is guilloché with a basket-weave pattern.

VACHERON CONSTANTIN

MALTE RETROGRADE PERPETUAL CALENDAR – REF. 47031

In this Malte model, Vacheron Constantin combines a perpetual calendar with a 31-day retrograde calendar. The Ø 39mm case, crafted in either platinum or 18K rose gold, houses the 1126 QPR automatic movement and offers hours, minutes, perpetual calendar, day and month indications via hands. Current year and leap year are displayed through a window. The retrograde crescent offers 31-day date and the movement beats at 28,800 vibrations per hour.

VACHERON CONSTANTIN

COLLECTION EXCELLENCE PLATINE: PATRIMONY TRADITIONNELLE CALIBRE 2253

REF. 88172

For 2010, Vacheron Constantin presents the Patrimony Traditionnelle Caliber 2253 watch in the Collection Excellence Platine. This model features a major astronomical complication in terms of technical application. Entirely constructed by Vacheron Constantin's engineering department and developed over thousands of hours, the new Caliber 2253 provides information derived from Earth's orbit around the sun, notably a perpetual calendar, the equation of time, and the times of sunrise and sunset. It has a tourbillon escapement as well. Such is the complexity and level of finish of this horological masterpiece, that it comprises no fewer than 457 parts in a movement only 9.6mm thick. Production is limited to just ten pieces.

VACHERON CONSTANTIN

PATRIMONY TRADITIONNELLE CALIBRE 2755 – REF. 80172

The Patrimony Traditionnelle Calibre 2755 belongs in the multi-complication category as a worthy heir of Vacheron Constantin's 250th anniversary masterpiece, the Tour de l'Ile, and as the ultimate demonstration of its unequalled skills. This incomparable timepiece harbors three of the most sophisticated complications in the universe of high-class watchmaking: the tourbillon, the perpetual calendar and the minute repeater. The Calibre 2755 beats at a frequency of 18,000 vibrations an hour and has a power reserve of approximately 55 hours. This watch is housed in a 44mm platinum case, giving the minute-repeater chime a remarkable resonance.

VACHERON CONSTANTIN

PATRIMONY TRADITIONNELLE CHRONOGRAPH PERPETUAL CALENDAR – REF. 47292

The Patrimony Traditionnelle Chronograph Perpetual Calendar Calibre 1141QP embodies the Vacheron Constantin convention in styling. It brings together a chronograph and a perpetual calendar driven by a highly regarded hand-wound movement. The Calibre 1141 is an exceptional design that has been used in some of the best chronographs. Experts consider it a model of highly complex chronograph construction.

VACHERON CONSTANTIN

QUAI DE L'ILE DATE SELF-WINDING – REF. 86050

Named for the brand's historic Geneva address, the new Quai de l'Ile line reveals the manufacture's pioneering character while drawing on more than 250 years of experience. The Quai de l'Ile Date Self-Winding makes an immediate impact with a semi-transparent dial, suspended displays, an appealing modern case, and an intriguing combination of materials. With a dial embodying the very latest security-printing technologies and a cushion-shaped case, the designers opted for a theme of transparency and avant-garde design. Visible through the dial, the movement is stamped with the prestigious Geneva Hallmark designed, developed and manufactured in-house. The rhodium-plated Caliber 2460QH displays the date via a disc and is housed in a 41mm 18K pink-gold case with gray dial. Also available in palladium with gray dial and rhodium-plated movement, and in titanium with dark dial and ruthenium movement, it is delivered with two straps: one in black or dark brown hand-stitched, saddle-finish, large square-scaled alligator leather; one in dark brown or black vulcanized rubber with a refined and elegant design.

VACHERON CONSTANTIN

QUAI DE L'ILE DAY-DATE AND POWER RESERVE SELF-WINDING – REF. 85050

The new Quai de l'Ile Day-Date and Power Reserve Self-Winding's fascinating semi-transparent dial embodies the latest security-printing technologies. Visible through the dial, the movement is stamped with the prestigious Geneva Hallmark designed, developed and manufactured in-house. Caliber 2475SC/1 displays the date, day of the week and power reserve via hands. Shown in a 41mm palladium case with gray dial and rhodium-plated movement, this watch is also available in 18K pink gold with gray dial and rhodium-plated movement, and in titanium with dark dial and ruthenium movement. There are two straps: one in black or dark brown hand-stitched, saddle-finish, large square-scaled alligator leather; one in dark brown or black vulcanized rubber. The brand has developed a personalization concept that is totally new in haute horlogerie: thanks to the Quai de l'Ile case's remarkable seven-piece middle, it is possible to choose from three metals, two dials and two different finishes on the movements to personalize the dream watch.

ZENITH

GRANDE CLASS TRAVELLER EL PRIMERO REPETITION MINUTES

Housing the new El Primero 4031 movement with minute repeater, alarm function (with vibrating alert or buzzer), dual time, large date and three power-reserve indicators at 6:00 (movement reserve level is shown on left side of aperture, alarm reserve on right; when the minute repeater's reserve is low, a red light comes on under the alarm indicator), this Grande Class Traveller Répétition Minutes contains 744 components and 63 jewels. Offering 50 hours of power reserve, it beats at 36,000 vibrations per hour and measures short time intervals to 1/10th of a second. The watch's 44mm 18K rose-gold case is water resistant to 50 meters and holds a curved sapphire crystal and sapphire crystal caseback.

TOURBILLONS

12
LUMINOR
PANERAI
pm
am
6
REG.
T.M.

CEO of Greubel & Forsey

Stephen Forsey

'These prizes are an honor for us, and a great sign of recognition.'

The year 2009 marked several milestones for Greubel Forsey. The brand won prizes at the Prix Gaïa, the Grand Prix d'Horlogerie Asia and the Grand Prix d'Horlogerie de Genève, as well as inaugurating its new headquarters.

FACING PAGE
Stephen Forsey

THIS PAGE
TOP LEFT
Exclusive Greubel Forsey movement

CENTER
Greubel Forsey's manufacture and headquarters

BOTTOM
Double Tourbillon Technique

Winners of prizes for Esprit d'entreprise at the Prix Gaïa, Best Complicated Watch at the Grand Prix d'Horlogerie Asia (for its Quadruple Tourbillon à Différentiel Sphérique), Haute Complication at the Grand Prix d'Horlogerie de Genève for its Double Tourbillon Technique, Robert Greubel and Stephen Forsey have certainly enjoyed the most fruitful year in their short history together. Having co-founded the Greubel Forsey brand in 2004, the two watchmakers are making an indelible imprint on the art of watchmaking.

These two exceptionally gifted men—Greubel is French, Forsey English—met in 1992 at Renaud & Papi (now Audemars Piguet (Renaud & Papi)). In 1999, the pair left that business to found CompliTime two years later. Within CompliTime, the watchmaking duo specialized in creating multi-complicated timepieces for various prestigious brands.

However, their true calling lay elsewhere. At BaselWorld 2004, after a long gestation period, the world came face to face with Greubel Forsey and its first timepiece: the Double Tourbillon 30°, which marked the launch of a stunning ascent. In 2005 the partners created GFPI, a company dedicated to the acquisition and administration of intellectual property rights. In 2006, convinced of the exceptional relevance and stability of the brand, the Richemont Group acquired a 20% stake

TOP
Robert Greubel - Emmanuel Vuille - Stephen Forsey

BOTTOM LEFT
Mouvement Double Tourbillon 30°

BOTTOM RIGHT
Mouvement Quadruple Tourbillon

in its capital. The same year, the entrepreneurial inventor-watchmakers created CT Design, followed in 2007 by CT Time, a company geared toward the development and production of more industrial movements for an exclusive clientele. Today the group employs 100 people, and Greubel Forsey produces and sells around 100 pieces per year (at prices ranging from $300,000 to $670,000), in approximately 30 retail outlets around the world.

The finishing touch for 2009 was undoubtedly the new group headquarters, recently inaugurated in La Chaux-de-Fonds and bringing the various companies under the same roof. A link between modernity and tradition, just like the Greubel Forsey brand itself, the complex joins a former farm listed on the national register of historic sites to an ultra-modern steel and glass building. Still riding high on his exceptional year, Stephen Forsey granted us an interview.

In 2009, you were recognized at the Gaïa Prize, the Grand Prix d'Horlogerie de Genève and the Grand Prix d'Horlogerie Asia. What an excellent year for Greubel Forsey...
Yes. These prizes are an honor for us, and a great sign of recognition. It is even more important this year, as we have assembled all our teams under the same roof within new premises in La Chaux-de-Fonds. These distinctions bring certain renown to the brand, which really motivates our teams. I am also happy for the collectors and watch lovers who have purchased our watches: this proves that they were right!

You have actually created an entirely new site, joining an old farmhouse to an ultramodern building. Is this what you dreamed of, or were you operating under some constraints?
A little of both! The farm had fallen into disrepair, and we had the chance to bring it back to life. In this region where the first watchmakers were in fact farmers, this very farmhouse might well have given rise to the Greubel Forsey brand itself. In this sense, it is a perfect match for our horological adventure and provides us with a highly suitable working environment.

As a whole, is the new building a simple production tool, or also a symbol of grandeur?
It is a showcase, but also a reminder! All of horological tradition was born here, in the mountains of Neuchâtel. This site is useful for high-quality production, but also serves as a compass to help us stay the course.

Where do you get your inspiration?
It's very difficult to determine. Robert Greubel and I have a very strong background in watchmaking. We come from different places—he's French, I'm English—and that makes us complementary. We can tackle anything new with confidence, because we know what we're dealing with. We also appreciate nature and other true values, so this background

LEFT
Tourbillon 24 Secondes in 5N gold

RIGHT
Quadruple Tourbillon in 5N red gold

is useful for taking on new challenges and not getting sidetracked or led in the wrong direction.

You and Greubel are called "kings of the tourbillon." Are you thinking of moving on to other complications in the future?

We thought that the tourbillon deserved particular attention, but as watchmakers, we are naturally interested in other experiments. We would love to start integrating other developments into our watches, but we don't want to create for the sake of creating—it must be useful. That doesn't make the challenge any easier!

Where do you get your motivation?

From exchanging ideas! Since we've brought everyone to the same place, we can now build an ideal horological culture!

What does an ideal horological culture mean for you?

It's what I call the Watchmaking Spirit! It's a blend of shared expertise, traditions to be respected, challenges to overcome and personal development—we spend a third of our lives at work, so we might as well make it pleasant. We are also concerned to ensure that this art endures; we must remember that we have gone from a phase in the 1970s when everything almost disappeared, to the incredible boom we are currently experiencing, even if it has now slowed down somewhat.

Are you affected by the global crisis?

We're lucky to have a very limited production—just 110 watches a year—so demand is still exceeding supply. We've gotten very good at handling the situation, but we have international partners working in markets that are changing very rapidly, and we have stepped up our efforts to support them.

Are you going to increase your production in the next few months to respond to this demand?

No, we're not equipped to do that, and our new manufacturing facility was not designed with that in mind. We have about 65 people working here, and we're not going to increase our watchmaking teams. However, we are planning on developing our communications department.

You were at SIHH for the first time this year, having previously participated in the BaselWorld Fair. Was this a strategic choice?

It's part of our natural evolution. We were very happy at Basel among the independents. But we've gotten to a point where we didn't have enough space, and the possible solutions didn't really work for us. In 2006, the Richemont Group acquired a 20% stake in our company, which certainly facilitated our entry into the SIHH.

CEO of Richard Mille

Richard Mille

'I created an ultra-light watch for Rafael Nadal'

With its headquarters in Brittany, offices in Paris, and manufacture in Switzerland Richard Mille is like no other brand—and it never has been. Upon its release in 2001, the company's first watch, the RM 001, triggered a figurative earthquake in the watch industry, and an avalanche of envy for its creator. Ten years later, that success has proven that it was but a taste of great things to come. The latest creation was unveiled this spring: an ultra-light watch, created especially for professional tennis player Rafael Nadal.

FACING PAGE
Richard Mille

THIS PAGE
TOP
RM 016 Plasma

BOTTOM
RM 004 Felipe Massa

Richard Mille—the man as well as his company—is like a shooting star. He is always on his way from one airplane to another, conveying his passion for horology in the few free minutes he has, while still apologizing for not being more available. No stranger to stratospheric success, in 2009 the brand saw a 22% rise in sales, while other brands experienced a similar decrease! Richard Mille's secret: technique in the service of aestheticism.

You were at SIHH for the first time this year. Was it everything you expected?
It was great, just incredible! I expected it to be, but not to this point. SIHH is a beautiful machine that has made our lives enormously easier.

Did you get a lot of orders?
Surprisingly, we did get many more orders!

Did you see it as a kind of recognition, being admitted into the Holiest of Holies?
We first applied for this three years ago. Not hearing anything back for all that time, I had sort of given up on the idea, rationalizing it away. On the other hand, I didn't want to spend the rest of my life squatting in Geneva's luxury hotels to present my new products every year. My biggest concern was finding a place to host journalists. So when the news of our admission to SIHH came in October, it was really a blessing!

How did 2009 end for you?
Altogether, the year went fairly well! I released nine new products, which helped us get through the crisis. Also, geographically, I have a lot of potential for development. Right now, Richard Mille watches are not sold in Germany nor Scandinavia, Canada, India, Australia...So now that Spain and the United States are starting to cool down, there are plenty of other places to go!

Did you open any new markets last year?
Some, but not many! In 2009, our sales rose by 22% despite our problems with meeting demand, especially with the RM 019—the ladies' model—and the Hommage à Boucheron model. Those problems slowed us down somewhat, but we didn't ship any fewer watches: in 2008, we shipped 2,022 pieces. In 2009, it was a little under 2,500, and in 2010, it should be around 2,900 watches.

How many watches have you created since your start in 2001?
A little under 10,000, I think.

While other brands focus solely on their new models, at SIHH, you presented all your models, new and old. Is the notion of "novelty"—not to be confused with "innovation"—secondary for you?
I like the idea of having new models every year, but there has got to be a coherent concept behind it. Each new watch must bring its own stone to the construction, and find its place in the collection while still making its own argument.

Besides which, from following your releases over the years, it seems as though you have only one collection, despite the disparate character of your pieces...
Exactly! At the same time, you have to know how to excite interest and desire—the clientele is more and more demanding. That reduces the lifespan of a watch. For example, I make 200 or 300 tourbillons per year. But in my conception of a watch, the tourbillon represents only 10 or 15% of the interest of a piece. It's almost beside the point. If haute horology wants to leave its ghetto, it's got to get in gear!

But does it really want to leave?
It's in its own best interest to get out of the ghetto! The industry must be more open to the world, to art, to architecture, to lifestyle—it has to leave behind its esotericism...

Its esotericism?
You know, the thirty-sixth hand that indicates the thirty-sixth function, or whatever. People are tired of it.

Is that where you're different?
Our specialty is using technique in the service of aestheticism. The honeycomb design of the RM 022—I had dreamt of that for ten years, but the technology didn't exist to produce it until 2010! The RM 012, where we removed the bottom plate, that was a technical accomplishment. The result is very architectural, but it does not improve the performance. The Hommage à Boucheron was a deliberately provocative model. Everyone was expecting a diamond-set piece, and instead I came

FACING PAGE
RM 022

THIS PAGE
FROM LEFT
RM 007 B1
RM 018
RM 017
RM 25

out with wheels carved out of precious and semi-precious stones. Even if I haven't yet managed to deliver any, that's not too serious...

Oh really?

Right now, over 95% of those wheels have to be thrown out. But what I love is to go from one theme to another, without being tied down.

What is the Richard Mille watch that represents you the best?

If I said, "the next one," that would be a cliché. But it's the truth, because I am extremely involved in its creation.

Which one is that?

It is an ultra-light model for Rafael Nadal. The goal is for him to wear it in a tennis match. The watch is coming out in March—it's very different from the others, but it definitely has its place in the collection.

Over the long term, how will you evolve your brand?

In Mexico, they have the Institutional Revolutionary Party. It's not a joke! I want to be a little like them—just because I am at SIHH now doesn't mean that I'm going to stop making revolution. My credo is, "limited volume, limited distribution, limitless creativity."

When you launched your first model in 2001, you met with immediate success, so completely had you overturned the codes everyone was then following in haute horology. Was that intentional or calculated?

Yes, it was intentional! I was spending my life working on taking care of brands for others. I was tired of it. So I wanted to create a product that would derive its claim to fame solely from the exceptional character of its conception. I didn't do any studies of the market, or of the competition, just some research on positioning. I made the watch that I had dreamt of, and didn't think of the price until I was done. That is heresy in marketing, but that's what made my brand so successful. I knew there would be clients for my watches—I just didn't know how many! Today, people say I'm a genius, but listen: at the time, I was never in danger. I was always extremely careful. If I sold a few dozen pieces, I was ahead of the game!

Your current projects include a book: "Technical Individuals, Human Individuals" (Individus techniques, individus humains) tells the story of the specialists who make your watches. Where did this idea come from?

I wanted to show that my watchmakers are like surgeons before a difficult operation: they have doubts, fears, worries. I wanted to show the "dramatic" side of this approach.

You live in a château in Brittany. Do you feel like a lord of the manor?

Yes, it's a château, but basically it is just a Breton home: very austere, square, granite, in the middle of nowhere. It's the opposite of how I am, but overall, it's pretty nice...

invented in the early 19th century to compensate for the effects of gravity on the workings of pocket watches, the tourbillon remains one of the most ingenious mechanisms in horological history. With its tiny mobile cage that weighs less than a gram and consists of up to 70 pieces, the complication is also one of the best manifestations of artisanal virtuosity. For several years, the tourbillon has been a star among complications, the “open sesame” for any brand looking to become a major player in this ultra-competitive industry. This new popularity brings with it the danger of becoming banal, to be sure, but also the risk of obscuring the complication’s original function: increasing precision. To keep the tourbillon among horology’s nobility, the best watchmakers are reinventing not only the way it looks, but also the way it works. We are also seeing new construction—multiple, multi-axis or vertical tourbillons—that are more suited to wristwatches.

Bell & Ross, *BR 01 Instrument Tourbillon*
Richard Mille, *RM 009 Felipe Massa*
Piaget, *Polo Tourbillon*
Breguet, *Tourbillon Messidor*

Audemars Piguet, *Royal Oak Hand-Wound Tourbillon Watch with Chronograph*
Zenith, *Academy Tourbillon El Primero*
Hublot, *Bing Bang Gold Mat Big Date*

TOURBILLONS

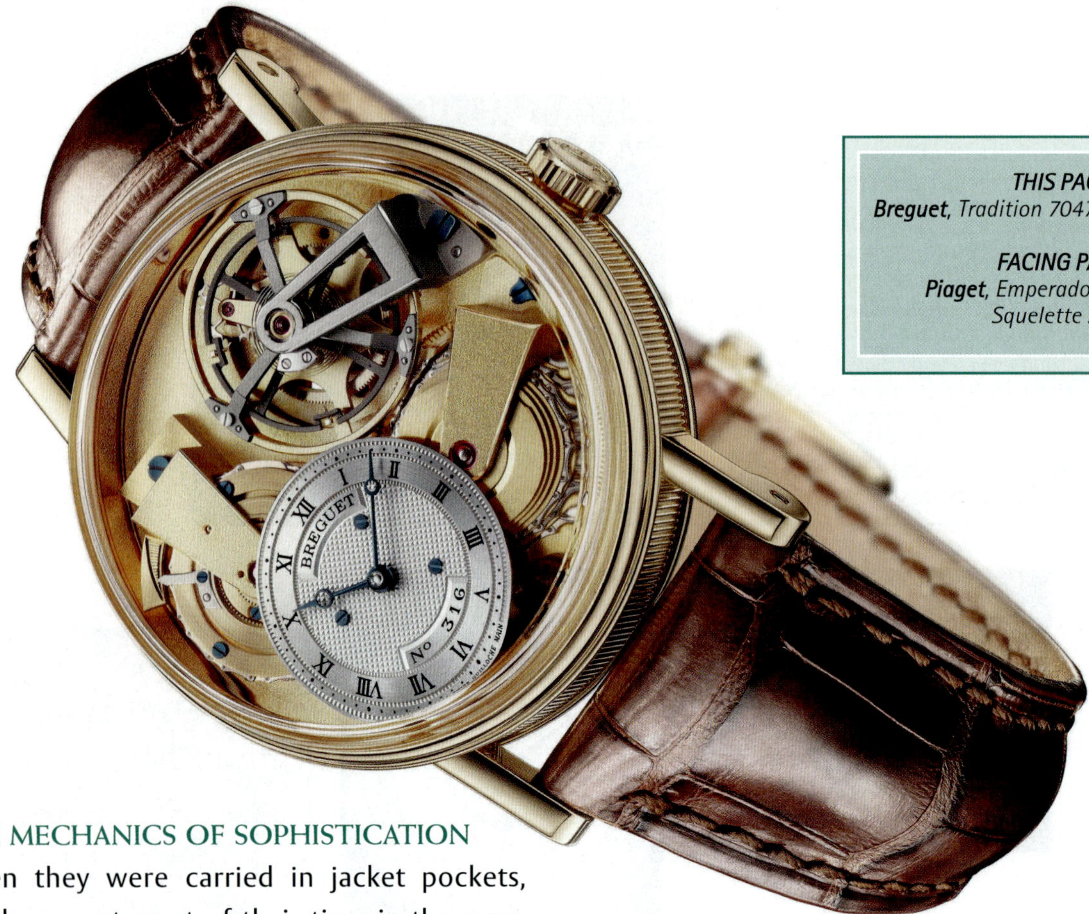

THIS PAGE
***Breguet**, Tradition 7047 fusée tourbillon*

FACING PAGE
***Piaget**, Emperador Tourbillon Squelette Serti*

THE MECHANICS OF SOPHISTICATION

When they were carried in jacket pockets, watches spent most of their time in the same vertical position. The force of gravity exerted a negative influence on the functioning of the watch, especially on the oscillations of the balance and the balance spring, two organs that largely determine the watch's precision. To avoid the irregularities that gravity caused to the mechanism, Abraham-Louis Breguet (1747-1823) enclosed the "heart" of the movement (balance, balance spring and escapement) in a small mobile cage rotating once a minute on its axis. By successively adopting every vertical position, the balance allowed the deviations in the rate to cancel each other out. The triumph of the wristwatch in the 20th century could have signaled the total demise of the tourbillon, as the mechanism loses much of its reason for being when the watch moves in all directions with the wrist. But the renaissance of mechanical horology in the 1980s propelled the tourbillon back to the top of horological complications as the supreme incarnation of Swiss savoir-faire.

A NEW BEGINNING

Since the turn of the millennium, we have seen a true tourbillon craze. More than 50 Swiss brands offer them in their collections, which is a little odd when you consider that only a handful of artisans are truly capable of producing the mechanism. Confronted with the (relative) banalization threatening the tourbillon, the most reputed horological brands have offered their own variations of the tourbillon with novel solutions. Breguet has given a place of honor to this choice aspect of its heritage in the Tradition collection. One timepiece in this line unveils a spectacular fusée tourbillon, with a fusée-chain transmission device that optimizes the regularity of the movement. For its rectangular Emperador collection, Piaget created the flattest tourbillon movement in the world (3.5mm thick); for its Emperador Tourbillon Squelette Serti, the brand has created an ethereal version

PIAGET

THIS PAGE
TOP LEFT
Chopard, *L.U.C Tourbillon Tech Steel Wings*

ABOVE
Blancpain, *Carrousel Volant Une Minute*

LEFT
Harry Winston, *Tourbillon Glissière*

FACING PAGE
Montblanc, *Grand Tourbillon Heures Mystérieuses*

of the mechanism, with diamonds and sapphires set directly onto the movement. Chopard has earned accolades for its L.U.C 1.02 caliber with four barrels providing an eight-day power reserve; this movement powers the L.U.C Tourbillon Tech Steel Wings. On Harry Winston's Tourbillon Glissière, a novel winding system uses two sliding weights and a winding ratchet. Blancpain recently showed its innovative side with the launch of the first wristwatch equipped with a carrousel. An alternative to the tourbillon, the carrousel is set apart (or could be set apart—the topic is controversial) by the double train of wheels that connects it to the barrel—the first transmits the energy needed for the functioning of the escapement, and the second controls the speed of the cage's rotation. In tackling this complication, invented in 1892 but having more or less faded into obscurity since then, Blancpain has also accelerated the carrousel's speed of rotation, which is now 60 seconds, as opposed to several minutes on a traditional carrousel.

REVEALING SOPHISTICATION

With its mobile cage turning on an axis like a tiny planet, the tourbillon makes for a fascinating spectacle that most brands reveal through an opening on the dial. At 6:00 on its new Master Grande Tradition Tourbillon à Quantième Perpétuel (see "Perpetual Calendars" chapter) Jaeger-LeCoultre exposes a 78-piece, 0.28-gram titanium tourbillon cage for all to admire. The complication takes the spotlight in the upper

part of Montblanc's Grand Tourbillon Heures Mystérieuses' dial with a bridge that forms two figure eights—the symbol for infinity. This highly stylish timepiece, created in the Minerva manufacture (now a part of Montblanc) also stands out for its hour/minute display, which seems suspended in midair, thanks to two crystal discs. Other brands go further still in the quest for beautiful displays: Girard-Perregaux sets the tone with its famous Tourbillon with three gold Bridges;

Ulysse Nardin's Royal Blue Tourbillon's sapphire crystal bridges and bottom plate give the impression of a floating tourbillon cage; for the Regulus, Vincent Calabrese devised a flying tourbillon that also seems to float completely unsupported; and MB&F's Horological Machine N° 1 gives place of honor to the tourbillon in a novel three-dimensional design, which features two separate dials for the hours and minutes, as well as four barrels that provide a seven-day power reserve.

THIS PAGE
TOP LEFT
***Girard-Perregaux**, Tourbillon with three gold Bridges (skeletonized version)*

TOP RIGHT
***Vincent Calabrese**, Regulus*

CENTER
***Ulysse Nardin**, Royal Blue Tourbillon*

BOTTOM
***MB&F**, Horological Machine N° 1*

FACING PAGE
***Breguet**, Marine 5837 Tourbillon Chronograph*

NEW TECHNOLOGY FOR AN AGE-OLD ART

For the last several years, joining forces between innovative constructions, high-tech materials and new digital technologies has rejuvenated the tourbillon. Richard Mille is an influential pioneer in the use of innovative alloys. With both case and movement crafted in avant-garde materials, the RM 009 Felipe Massa takes the title of the lightest wristwatch in the world (less than 30 grams). The Breguet 5837 Marine Tourbillon Chronograph joins a balance spring, escapement wheel and pallet-lever made entirely in silicon with a tourbillon featuring a bridge and pillars in titanium. Jaeger-LeCoultre sparked a true revolution with its Master Compressor Extreme Lab, the first mechanical watch to perform accurately and reliably without lubrication. This feat was made possible by a new balance-wheel configuration, new lighter materials and a cutting-edge tourbillon in a magnesium cage. A worthy inheritor of the advances made by Freak (2001), in which the whole movement rotated like a tourbillon cage, Ulysse Nardin's InnoVision also needs no lubrication, employing ten technological innovations in silicon.

SPIN DOCTORS

The last few years have also bred a new generation of tourbillons, equipped with several axes of simultaneous rotation and/or rotating at different speeds from the classic one turn per minute. The objective is to offer constructions suited to wristwatches, and to increase their precision—mostly by multiplying the number of positions that the balance wheel can occupy. For Parmigiani Fleurier's Pershing Tourbillon 30 Second Ajouré, a product of the brand's partnership with the prestigious Italian yacht maker, the horologers chose a rotation speed that is twice as fast as normal—displayed in a skeletonized movement that provides seven days of power reserve. Jaeger-LeCoultre's Gyrotourbillon 1 features two cages, one inside the other. The exterior cage makes one rotation in 60 seconds; the interior cage is placed at a 90° angle to the first and takes 18.75 seconds to make a full rotation. This concept of a "spherical" tourbillon was reintroduced in 2008 on the Gyrotourbillon 2, housed in Jaeger-Coultre's double-sided Reverso case. The Bi-Axial Tourbillon from Girard-Perregaux also combines two concentric cages, turning on their respective axes in 45 seconds and one

FACING PAGE
TOP LEFT
Ulysse Nardin, *InnoVision*

TOP RIGHT
Jaeger-LeCoultre, *Master Compressor Extreme Lab*

THIS PAGE
TOP LEFT
Parmigiani Fleurier, *Pershing Tourbillon 30 Second Ajouré*

TOP RIGHT
Jaeger-LeCoultre, *Gyrotourbillon 2*

CENTER LEFT
Harry Winston, *Opus 6*

CENTER RIGHT
Girard-Perregaux, *Bi-Axial Tourbillon*

BOTTOM
Greubel Forsey, *Double Tourbillon Technique*

minute and 15 seconds. A similar double-cage principle (but at a 30° angle) inspired Harry Winston's Opus 6, designed by Robert Greubel and Stephen Forsey. These two watchmakers have also developed under their own line many innovative constructions that play on angles and speeds of rotation. The Double Tourbillon 30°, reinterpreted in 2009 in the completely transparent Double Tourbillon Technique, possesses an interior cage that rotates in one minute and an exterior cage that rotates in four minutes.

TOP LEFT
***Thomas Prescher**, Round Watch with Three-Axis Tourbillon*

TOP RIGHT
***Panerai**, Luminor 1950 Tourbillon GMT*

BOTTOM
***Greubel Forsey**, Invention Piece 3*

In the Tourbillon 24 Seconds Incliné, which is the base of the Invention Piece 3 model, the cage angled at 25° rotates two and a half times faster than an ordinary tourbillon and required special conical gearing as well as customized alloys. Thomas Prescher went one step farther, multiplying the angles of rotation by creating a round watch with a triple-axis tourbillon. To sidestep the controversy over the usefulness of a tourbillon (designed for vertical positions) in a wristwatch (which goes through multiple positions), certain brands are innovating by placing their tourbillons vertically. In the Luminor 1950 Tourbillon GMT by Panerai, the cage turns at a right angle to the balance's axis of oscillation, rotating twice per minute; a small indicator at 9:00 reveals the tourbillon's rotation, hidden by the dial. Concord turned heads in 2009 with its C1 QuantumGravity, which features an unusual bi-axial vertical tourbillon outside of the movement (in a manner of speaking) and linked to the bottom plate by a system of cables evocative of suspension bridges. Zenith, in its Defy Xtreme

TOP LEFT
***Concord**, C1 QuantumGravity*

TOP RIGHT
***Piaget**, Polo Tourbillon Relatif*

CENTER
***Jean Dunand**, Tourbillon Orbital*

BOTTOM
***Zenith**, Defy Xtreme Tourbillon Zero-G*

Tourbillon Zero-G (for zero gravity) has chosen another path, using a "gyro-gravitational" tourbillon with a "gyroscopic" cage that includes an escapement mounted on cardan joints, much like marine chronometers.

MERRY-GO-ROUNDS

Jean Dunand sticks to two dimensions with its Tourbillon Orbital, but offers a sophisticated system in which the tourbillon turns on its axis in one minute while completing a revolution around the dial in one hour. The same double-revolution principle is explored in the Piaget Polo Tourbillon Relatif, released in 2009 in a maritime version in a case with grand feu enamel, with an engraving of sails and boats on the case-sides and a compass on the dial. Suspended at the end of the minute hand, the mobile tourbillon cage appears independent from the movement that it regulates: a beautiful alliance between mechanical prowess and visual magic. The Blu Majesty T3 model invents a new way of telling time by combining three different

THIS PAGE
***Greubel Forsey**, Quadruple Tourbillon à Différentiel*

FACING PAGE
TOP LEFT
***Blu**, Blu Majesty T3*

TOP RIGHT
***Harry Winston**, Histoire de Tourbillon 1*

CENTER
***Breguet**, Double Tourbillon tournant*

BOTTOM LEFT
***Antoine Preziuso**, 3Volution*

rotational speeds. The tourbillon turns on its axis in one minute; it is housed in a cage that completes one rotation per hour and acts as a minute hand; and the cage spins around the dial in 12 hours, its position indicating the hour.

TRIPLE TOURBILLON THREAT

Another option is to increase the number of tourbillons on the same watch. Breguet's Double Tourbillon tournant features two independent tourbillons linked by differential gearing and mounted on a bottom plate that completes one rotation in 12 hours. These two mechanisms compensate for each other's small differences in rate, offering a superior level of precision. The Histoire de Tourbillon 1 from Harry Winston (the first taste of a new collection featuring five limited editions of 20 pieces each, with all devoted to this complication) is housed in a white-gold and Zalium case, and presents two ultra-light tourbillons that are inclined at 25° angles and complete a rotation in 36 seconds. For its 3Volution, Antoine Preziuso invented a plate that completes a revolution in two minutes and fifteen seconds and bears three one-minute tourbillons. The proximity of the tourbillons creates a resonance that makes the balance-springs less sensitive to position variations, and more accurate. In 2008, after five years of development, Greubel Forsey presented its Quadruple Tourbillon à Différentiel with two double, asymmetrical tourbillons linked by a spherical differential, much like the differential in a car.

THIS PAGE
TOP LEFT
Parmigiani Fleurier, *Kalpa XL Tourbillon Diamants*

TOP RIGHT
Zenith, *Star Tourbillon El Primero*

ABOVE
Richard Mille, *RM 019 Celtic Knot Tourbillon*

LEFT
Audemars Piguet, *Jules Audemars Lady Chronograph Tourbillon*

FACING PAGE
Chopard, *L.U.C Tourbillon Lady*

A FEMININE TOURBILLON

Wedding haute horology to fine jewelry, the biggest watchmaking houses have released tourbillon watches designed especially for women. The Star Tourbillon El Primero from Zenith features a diamond star as the tourbillon bridge; the watch is set with more than 280 diamonds, and the mother-of-pearl dial is decorated with large whirling numerals. Parmigiani Fleurier's Kalpa XL Tourbillon Diamants combines a one-week power reserve with a cage that rotates twice per minute. Audemars Piguet's Jules Audemars Lady Chronograph Tourbillon sparkles with the light reflected from 251 brilliant-cut diamonds and 68 baguette-cut diamonds. The Piaget Polo Tourbillon's precious mechanism resides beneath inlaid mother-of-pearl and a geometric design of round- and baguette-cut diamonds. Chopard takes an innovative step by crafting a ladies' watch within which beats a proprietary L.U.C movement. The L.U.C Tourbillon Lady also boasts a tourbillon, 9-day power reserve, chronometer certification and Poinçon de Genève, and its case is set entirely with baguette diamonds and the tourbillon bridge is decorated with the Chopard "C." Richard Mille joined the movement with its RM 019 Celtic Knot Tourbillon, with a black onyx bottom plate and a bridge that illustrates the mysterious ancient symbol for which it is named.

A. LANGE & SÖHNE

LANGE 1 TOURBILLON

The Lange 1 Tourbillon houses the manual-winding L961.2 caliber, which contains 381 components and is largely decorated and assembled by hand. Its three-quarter plate is crafted in untreated German silver, and the side of the movement is engraved by hand. The 38.5mm case is made of honey-colored gold, as are the hands. The solid gold, argenté, guilloché dial displays hours, minutes, small seconds, a Lange large date, a 72-hour power-reserve indicator, and reveals a one-minute tourbillon with patented stop seconds. This Lange 1 Tourbillon, released in a limited edition of 150 watches, is mounted on a hand-stitched, red-brown crocodile strap with Lange prong buckle in solid honey-colored gold.

ARTYA

UNIQUE ARTPIECE TESLA SQUELETTE TOURBILLON 1/1

Each member of the Artpiece 1/1 collection is one of a kind. The automatic movement, entirely manufactured and assembled by master watchmakers in Switzerland, oscillates at 28,800 vibrations per hour. Tesla coils were used to sculpt the satin-finished case crafted in grade-316 stainless steel and treated with black PVD (physical vapor deposition). Water resistant to 50 meters, this featured piece is available on a hand-sewn strap of high-tech rubber combined with processed calfskin or tanned toad skin.

AUDEMARS PIGUET

JULES AUDEMARS MINUTE REPEATER TOURBILLON WITH CHRONOGRAPH

REF. 26050PT.OO.D002CR.01

The Jules Audemars Tourbillon Minute Repeater Chronograph houses the manual-winding 2874 movement. It boasts a minute-repeater mechanism that sounds the hours, quarter-hours and minutes upon request with a two-note chime, as well as a chronograph with 30-minute counter and small seconds on the tourbillon axis. This watch is also available in 18K pink gold.

AUDEMARS PIGUET

ROYAL OAK CHRONOGRAPH TOURBILLON – REF. 25977ST.OO.1205ST.02

Presented in stainless steel, this Royal Oak Tourbillon Chronograph houses the manual-winding 2889 caliber. The 25-jeweled movement beats at 21,600 vibrations per hour and offers 70 hours of power reserve. Fitted with a sapphire caseback, the watch indicates the hours and the minutes, and has a chronograph function. This watch is also available in yellow gold.

BELL & ROSS

BR 01 INSTRUMENT TOURBILLON

The mechanical manual-winding BR 01 TOURBILLON movement contains carbon-fiber mainplates and a black-gold tourbillon carriage. It is housed inside a 46mm XXL case, crafted in glass-bead-blasted titane with DLC (Diamond-Like Carbon) virtually scratchproof coating. The dial is in black carbon fiber; the numbers, hands and indexes have photoluminescent coating for nighttime reading. Hours can be read in a counter at 12:00, a trust index is positioned at 3:00, and the 120-hour power-reserve indicator is at 9:00. A central hand displays the minutes. The timepiece is fitted on a rubber or alligator leather strap and is water resistant to 100 meters. Limited edition of 60 pieces.

BELL & ROSS

BR 01 INSTRUMENT TOURBILLON PHANTOM

Created in a limited edition of just 18 pieces, the BR 01 INSTRUMENT TOURBILLON PHANTOM has a black carbon-fiber dial and is encased in glass-bead-blasted titanium with DLC. It is powered by a mechanical manual-winding BR 01 TOURBILLON with carbon-fiber mainplates and a black-gold tourbillon carriage. The hours are shown in a counter at 12:00, the trust index is positioned at 3:00, and the 120-hour power-reserve indicator is at 9:00. A central hand displays the minutes. Water resistant to 100 meters.

BELL & ROSS

INSTRUMENT BR 01 TOURBILLON GOLD (ALUMINUM + PINK GOLD)

The polished rose-gold case houses a manual-winding mechanical movement. The watch displays a trust index at 3:00, a 120-hour power-reserve indicator at 9:00, an hour counter at 12:00 and a central minute hand. The BR 01 Tourbillon in gold features carbon-fiber bottom plates and a tourbillon cage in black gold. The dial is in black aluminum fiber, with indexes and hands treated with photoluminescence for easy nighttime reading. The case boasts a large 46mm diameter and sapphire crystals on the front and back. Water resistant to 100 meters, the watch is available on a rubber or alligator strap.

BELL & ROSS

INSTRUMENT BR 01 TOURBILLON GOLD (PINK GOLD + TITANIUM)

The BR 01 Tourbillon Gold features a mechanical movement with manual winding that powers its various displays: minutes on a central hand, hours in a subdial at 12:00, a trust index at 3:00, and a 120-hour power-reserve indicator at 9:00. The hands and indexes feature photoluminescent coating for easy night reading. The case, water resistant to 100 meters, is crafted in 18K pink gold and measures an extra-large 46x46mm.

BELL & ROSS

INSTRUMENT BR MINUTEUR TOURBILLON

This tourbillon is powered by a manual-winding mechanical movement and its bridges are in rose gold and anodized aluminum. The watch displays the hours, minutes, small seconds, a 3-day power-reserve indicator and a flyback function (two counters: 60 minutes and 10/10ths of an hour), which features a zero-setting and quick restart. The case is in polished rose gold and measures 44x50mm. The black dial possesses hands and an index treated with photoluminescence for easy nighttime reading. Water resistant to 100 meters, the watch is available on a rubber or alligator strap.

BELL AND ROSS

INSTRUMENT BR MINUTEUR TOURBILLON

This tourbillon is powered by a manual-winding mechanical movement and its bridges are in aluminum and anodized aluminum. The watch displays the hours, minutes, small seconds, a 3-day power-reserve indicator and a flyback function (two counters: 60 minutes and 10/10ths of an hour), which features a zero-setting and quick restart. The case is in polished aluminum and measures 44x50mm. The black dial possesses hands and an index treated with photoluminescence for easy nighttime reading. Water resistant to 100 meters, the watch is available on a rubber or alligator strap.

BOVET

FLEURIER MANUALLY WOUND 8-DAY TOURBILLON LIMITED EDITION

This model was designed to celebrate BOVET's 185th anniversary, in combination with the acquisition of DIMIER 1738, Manufacture of Haute Horlogerie Artisanale. For better reliability and performance, the tourbillon cage was lightened and framed in a solid, yet harmonious and rounded bridge. The back of the movement becomes a true piece of art, with its main plate entirely hand-engraved in BOVET's *fleurisanne* style. This "Hunter Case" version is in white gold with the dial and front cover fully hand-engraved in *fleurisanne* style. Also available with automatic movement.

BOVET

FLEURIER COMPLICATIONS: TOURBILLON WITH BUTTERFLY-SHAPED BRIDGES

The tourbillon embodies all the ingenuity, precision and beauty of fine horology—qualities that Bovet honors in this magnificent piece. The butterfly structure reveals the astonishing workmanship of an original tourbillon construction: wolf's teeth and curved spokes on every wheel, serpentine jumper springs in blued steel, blue jewels, and the entire surface of the movement's 18K gold structure is blackened and engraved in *fleurisanne* style. The hand-wound haute horology movement has a power reserve of 110 hours.

BREGUET

CLASSIQUE GRANDE COMPLICATION – REF. 5347PT/11/9ZU

This Classique Grande Complication wristwatch is crafted in platinum and houses a hand-wound movement, featuring a center plate engine-turned by hand including two apertures for the tourbillons, which rotates in step with the passing hours, and Breguet overcoils. Its ring-shaped dial forms a flange in silvered 18K gold and displays a chapter ring with Roman numerals. The hour hand is an extension of the bridge supporting the two tourbillon carriages. The water-resistant case has a sapphire caseback, bearing a hand-engraved drawing representing the solar system.

BREGUET

CLASSIQUE GRANDE COMPLICATION – REF. 5359BB/6B/9V6 DD00

This Classique Grande Complication is crafted in 18K white gold and houses a hand-wound movement featuring a tourbillon with small seconds on the tourbillon shaft and a compensating balance-spring with Breguet overcoil. Its silvered gold dial is hand-engraved on a rose-engine and paved with 356 diamonds (approximately 0.5 carat). The bezel, lugs and caseband are paved with 134 baguettes (approximately 10.37 carats) and the case is water resistant.

CHANEL

BLACK J12 TOURBILLON

Created in a 38mm case of high-tech ceramic and white gold, this J12 Tourbillon houses the manual-winding Chanel movement 0.1-T.1. It offers 100 hours of power reserve and is water resistant to 50 meters. Vibrating at 21,600 rotations per hour, it is equipped with 17 rubies. This J12 Tourbillon is adorned with baguette-cut diamonds (5.3 carats). Only five pieces will be produced and each bears its edition number engraved on the back of the case.

CHANEL

BLACK J12 TOURBILLON – CASEBACK

A world premiere, both aesthetically and technically: a black ceramic bottom plate.

CONCORD

C1 QUANTUMGRAVITY REF. 0320071

The C1 QuantumGravity is presented in an 18K white-gold and titanium case measuring Ø 48.5mm and 22mm thick. A rubber-coated titanium ring protects five spectacular sapphire crystals, which literally emerge from the case. The structural, skeletonized, and three-dimensional dial displays various subdials and time-measurement indications, superimposed to create a sense of perfectly mastered space. This timepiece holds a mechanical hand-wound movement—Concord Caliber C104—with a three-day power reserve indicated vertically via a mobile glass column filled with a liquid featuring green phosphorescent nanoparticles. The seconds are displayed on an external vertical wheel, while the bi-axial tourbillon is fitted outside the movement and case, but connected to the rest of the mechanism by a horizontal pinion and held in place by cable-stayed bridges. This intense timekeeper is water resistant to 3atm.

F.P. JOURNE

TOURBILLON SOUVERAIN WITH INDEPENDENT SECONDS

This platinum world-exclusive tourbillon timepiece is fitted with the manually wound F.P. Journe caliber FPJ1403 with tourbillon, power-reserve indicator, hours, minutes and an independent seconds subdial. It is equipped with a remonitoir, or constant force device, and is now enriched with the independent, or deadbeat seconds dial. In a deadbeat seconds watch, the seconds hand remains motionless for as long as the second has not actually elapsed. The hand only indicates the second once it has passed. In the Tourbillon Souverain with Independent Seconds, the watch is equipped with a natural deadbeat seconds device mounted on one of the wheels of the constant-force device. The movement beats at 21,600 vibrations per hour with a dedicated four-arm balance with inertia adjustment.

FREDERIQUE CONSTANT

MANUFACTURE TOURBILLON MOONPHASE DATE 24

Frédérique Constant presents its Manufacture Tourbillon Moonphase Date 24. Based on its award-winning Heart Beat Manufacture Calibre, Frédérique Constant developed its tourbillon watch with silicium escapement wheel and lever entirely in-house. This technical masterpiece is limited to 188 pieces in rose gold with a black dial and 88 pieces in white gold with a silvered dial.

GREUBEL FORSEY

TOURBILLON 24 SECONDES

In the continuing race against gravity, Inventor-Watchmakers Robert Greubel and Stephen Forsey have come up with their third invention seeking to neutralize the possible positional discrepancies through maximum efficiency and optimal performance. Using a 25°-inclined tourbillon cage with a high-velocity rotation of 24 seconds, this unique timepiece takes the exploration of a tourbillon regulator into a whole new dimension. To counter the inertia of the system, Forsey and Greubel came up with a compact 88-part inclined tourbillon weighing only 0.39 grams, optimizing the amount of mechanical energy needed to drive it. Admired through a lateral sapphire crystal window and the dial opening, the angular velocity of the tourbillon cage provides a cherished view of the qualities inherent in a Greubel Forsey timepiece.

GREUBEL FORSEY

INVENTION PIECE 3

Paying homage to their third invention—Tourbillon 24 Secondes—Robert Greubel and Stephen Forsey redefine the frontiers of technical accomplishment with an unprecedented architectural setting combining complex and highly innovative techniques. The tourbillon at 8:00 takes center stage over the concentric 24-hour and minute display in 18K white gold with red and blue indicators. Four sublimely engraved gold plates unveil a teasing introduction to the inventors' personal message. These features are all balanced with the power-reserve indicator at 2:00 and the subseconds at 5:00. A lateral convex sapphire crystal further enhances the aesthetic link between the two sides and a view into the tourbillon cage. The personal message consisting of some 1,300 characters from the watchmakers to the collector is engraved on a crescent-shaped hand-finished 18K gold plate, fully revealed with the aid of the special magnifying glass provided.

GUY ELLIA

TOURBILLON ZEPHYR

With a movement created by Swiss manufacturer Christophe Claret, the Tourbillon Zephyr symbolizes transparency with excellence. Caliber GES 97 features a 110-hour power reserve and winding ring set with 36 baguette-cut diamonds (1.04 carats), or engine turning and one-minute tourbillon movement. The latter beats at 21,600 vibrations per hour within an entirely hand-chamfered cage. The convex case with 950 platinum sides has a transparent back cover and hearth engraving. Mounted on an alligator strap with a folding buckle, this model is also available in platinum and titanium.

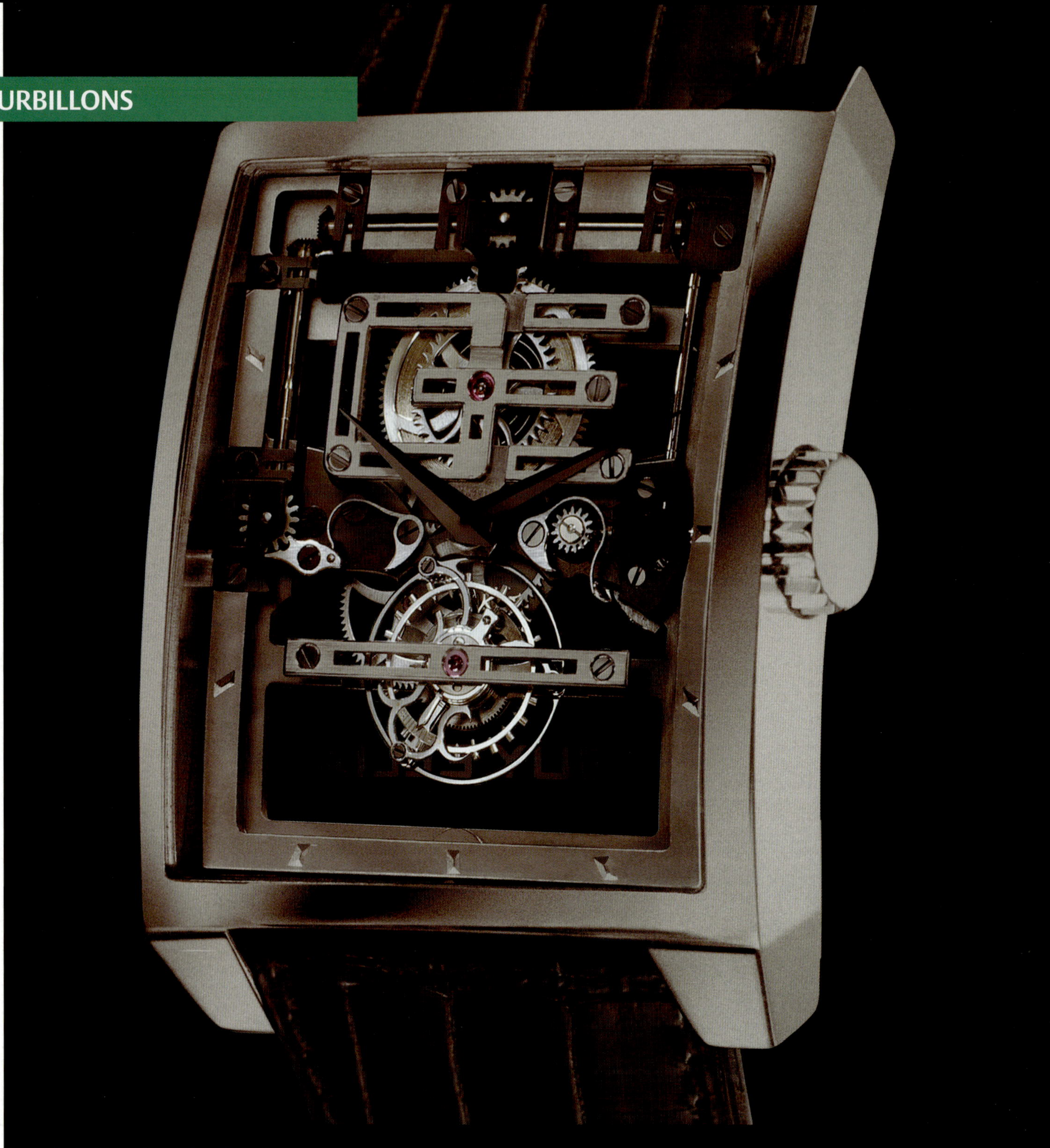

GUY ELLIA

TOURBILLON MAGISTERE TITANIUM

Designer Guy Ellia presents the titanium version of his famous skeletonized mysterious-winding tourbillon. The Time Square Tourbillon Magistere's Caliber TGE 97 was created by Swiss manufacturer Christophe Claret and features a 110-hour power reserve, one-minute tourbillon, and a titanium bottom plate and bridges. The movement beats at 21,600 vibrations per hour within an entirely hand-chamfered cage.

GUY ELLIA

TOURBILLON MAGISTERE II

Guy Ellia has renewed its collaboration with Christophe Claret to present their latest timepiece enhanced with a tourbillon escapement: the Tourbillon Magistère II. Inside its distinctive case, an elongated rectangle (44.2x36.7mm), the skeleton movement has a mysterious winding and features an "invisible" dial, whose main hands display the hours and minutes while seeming to float in space. In fact, the technical genius of this watch, produced in a limited edition of 12 pieces for each version, lies in the inversion of its bridges compared with a classic tourbillon timepiece. Hence the location of the winding crown at 6:00 and the use of the crown positioned at 12:00, while maintaining pressure on the security pushpiece at 10:00 to set the time. This piece is for lovers of fine watchmaking in search of the unusual.

HUBLOT

GUMMY BANG ALL BLACK TOURBILLON – REF. 305.RX.1910.RX

The Gummy Bang All Black sits in a case crafted from titanium and coated in black rubber, which is water resistant to 10atm. The titanium dial also features a black rubber molding, with an opening at 6:00 over the tourbillon cage. Beneath the dial, the hand-wound tourbillon HUB6000 movement beats at 21,600 vph. The Gummy Bang All Black, which boasts a flying tourbillon with cage without ball bearings, is fitted on an adjustable smooth black natural rubber strap with Hublot's logo. This timepiece is available in a limited edition of 28 pieces, numbered from 01/28 to 28/28.

HUBLOT

ONE MILLION $ BLACK CAVIAR – REF. 302.WX.9104.RX.00

Hublot presents the quintessence of "invisible visibility" in a uniform range of black tones. Hublot and setting workshop Bunter SA have developed a world's first with a completely invisible setting, using only black diamonds in a technological and artistic achievement. The dream of combining key Hublot concepts—invisible visibility, "All Black," watchmaking tradition and state-of-the-art technology—has become reality thanks to the creativity and ingenuity of its designers. Its setting is very complex. The difficulty resides in the unusual lines of the Big Bang case—round but with sharp angles. The white-gold one-piece construction of the case does not reveal any gold, and the diamonds, cut in mysterious ways, seem to hold together as if by magic. VVS TW-IF quality baguette diamonds (544 of them) adorn the watch's case, dial, crown and deployant clasp. Inside, the mechanical manual-winding proprietary movement powers a tourbillon and holds 120 hours of power reserve, displayed between 9:00 and 12:00.

IWC

PORTUGUESE TOURBILLON MYSTERE – REF. IW504207

Housed in the Portuguese case, the Tourbillon Mystère is powered by the IWC 50900 caliber with 7-day power reserve. The watch features an elevated tourbillon that makes it appear to move freely and entirely independent of any other drive-elements. This watch is a limited edition of 250 watches in 18K white gold. It offers a minute tourbillon, Pellaton automatic-winding mechanism, power-reserve display and small seconds at 9:00.

JACOB & CO.
CRYSTAL TOURBILLON

The Crystal Tourbillon is powered by the manual-winding Jacob & Co. 7 Caliber movement, skeletonized and set with 1.6 carats of baguette diamonds. The tourbillon movement can be seen through both the transparent dial and the exhibition caseback. The 47mm case, crafted in 18K white gold, is set with 17.48 carats of baguette-cut diamonds. Mounted on a crocodile strap, the watch also bears 2.22 carats of baguette-cut diamonds on its buckle.

JACOB & CO.

QUENTTIN

The most technically advanced in the Jacob & Co. family and arguably throughout the timepiece world, this limited edition, Swiss made, technically sophisticated instrument melds movement and state-of-the-art craftsmanship. The Quenttin, housing a vertical mechanical movement with manual-winding escapement, is the first ever 31-day power reserve supplied by the energy of seven spring barrels. Due to the unique configuration of this revolutionary tourbillon, the hours, minutes and power reserve are indicated by vertical discs assembled coaxially. Only 135 pieces of this innovative timepiece will be created; 99 pieces in 18K white gold, 18 pieces in 18K rose gold, and 18 pieces in magnesium.

JAEGER-LECOULTRE

MASTER GRAND TOURBILLON

Encased in Ø 43mm of 950 platinum, the Master Grand Tourbillon's mechanical automatic-winding Jaeger-LeCoultre Caliber 978 beats at 28,800 vph and holds 48 hours of power reserve. The watch features a 24-hour second time-zone indicator and an innovative date indicator, which jumps between 15 and 16 so as not to spoil the view of the impressive technical feat that is the main highlight of the dial: the tourbillon. For the feather-like tourbillon (0.28 grams), Jaeger-LeCoultre's engineers designed a carriage from an ultra-light, precision-enhancing titanium alloy prized for its exceptional hardness. The cambered escapement bridge cleverly follows the curve of the carriage and the single-piece oscillating weight in 22K pink gold is embellished with a stamped medallion motif with relief engravings. The seconds display appears within the circular tourbillon opening with a three-arm hand including an arrow-tipped spoke that indicates the passing seconds in step with the revolving tourbillon carriage.

LEVIEV

"DOUBLE EAGLE" TOURBILLON

The LEVIEV "Double Eagle" Tourbillon is handcrafted in Switzerland by Christophe Claret, is COSC certified, and holds a 110-hour power reserve. The "Double Eagle" Tourbillon's Ø 43mm platinum case is set with LEVIEV diamonds and is attached to a blue saddle-stitched alligator leather strap, which fastens with a triple-folding platinum clasp. The crown is also adorned with a LEVIEV diamond. This watch is produced in a limited edition and each piece is engraved with an individual serial number.

MONTBLANC

GRAND TOURBILLON HEURES MYSTERIEUSES

The MBM65.60 that powers the Grand Tourbillon Heures Mystérieuses is manually wound, has a 50-hour power reserve and consists of 281 meticulously hand-finished components. In front of the mirror-finished dial rotate two highly transparent, wafer-thin sapphire glass discs, one embossed with the hour hand, the other the minute hand. This feature provides the "mysterious hours" of the watch's name. The case is available in 950 platinum, 18K white gold, or 18K 5N rose gold.

PANERAI

RADIOMIR TOURBILLON GMT – REF. PAM00330

A faithful reproduction of the very first watches of its kind, the Radiomir Tourbillon GMT 48mm in pink gold is powered by the caliber P.2005 with tourbillon, representing the sophistication of Officine Panerai's manufacturing skill. Not only does the cage make a full rotation in 30 seconds instead of every minute, it is also the only existing tourbillon to place the rotating balance wheel inside a cage that is perpendicular to the base of the movement. This unusual feature better compensates for any positional inaccuracies the watch may assume while being worn on the wrist. Made up of 239 components and featuring a six-day power reserve, this structurally complex and highly innovative hand-wound movement is revealed through the sapphire crystal caseback and stealthily indicated by the luminescent dot at 9:00. This piece is water resistant to 10 bar.

PARMIGIANI FLEURIER

KALPA XL TOURBILLON – REF. PF013512.01

This limited edition Kalpa XL Tourbillon is created in 25 18K rose-gold and 25 platinum pieces. The unique tourbillon features a cage with a 30-second rotation, making two complete revolutions in one minute. The watch houses the manual-winding PF50002 caliber with eight days of power reserve. Beating at 21,600 vibrations per hour, the 28-jeweled movement offers a power-reserve indicator and Côtes de Genève decoration. This Kalpa XL is water resistant to 30 meters and features sapphire crystals with antireflection treatment.

PARMIGIANI FLEURIER

KALPA TONDA TOURBILLON – REF. PF600695

This limited edition Kalpa Tonda Tourbillon is created in 100 18K rose-gold and 100 platinum pieces. Its unique tourbillon features a cage with a 30-second rotation, making two complete revolutions in one minute. The watch houses the manual-winding PF510 movement with 8 days of power reserve and beats at 21,600 vibrations per hour. The 28-jeweled movement features the Côtes de Genève decoration and hand-chamfered bridges; Côtes de Genève also decorates the dial. This watch is water resistant to 30 meters and features sapphire crystals with antireflection treatment on the back. Each watch is also individually numbered on its back.

PIAGET

PIAGET ALTIPLANO TOURBILLON GOUSSET IN WHITE GOLD – REF. G0A32063

Piaget now revives the tourbillon pocket watch, interpreted in a highly contemporary square form characteristic of the brand, that of the Altiplano collection. The 40mm white-gold case houses the Piaget mechanical hand-wound Calibre 600P, the world's thinnest tourbillon movement at just 3.5mm thick. Admirably reflecting the mastery inherent to the manufacture, the carriage of this tourbillon—visible through a dial opening at 9:00—is made of 42 parts and weighs a mere 0.2 grams. Like all vintage Piaget models, the caseback is engraved with the brand's coat of arms. To provide a variety of manners of wearing it, this refined and elegant watch comes with a white-gold chain as well as a leather cordlet.

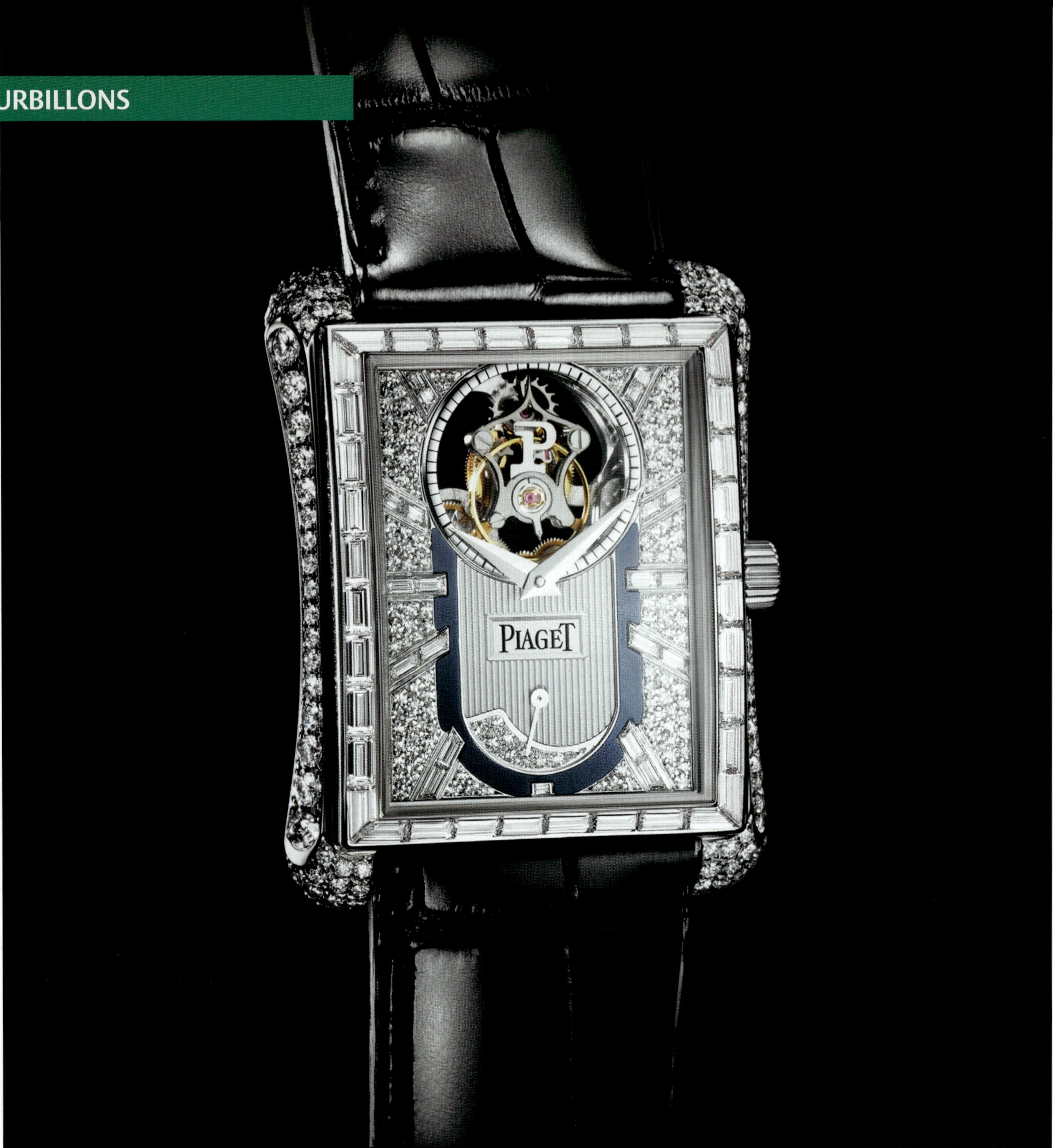

PIAGET

PIAGET EMPERADOR TOURBILLON HAUTE JOAILLERIE – REF. G0A30018

Equipped with the mechanical manual-winding Piaget 600P shaped caliber, this high-jeweled Emperador Tourbillon is equipped with 24 jewels and 40 hours of power reserve. The three-piece case is crafted in 18K white gold and bedecked with 153 brilliant- and baguette-cut diamonds weighing 3.3 carats. Its dial is also ensconced in diamonds. The three bridges of the tourbillon are crafted in titanium and the movement is decorated with the Côtes de Genève pattern.

PIAGET

PIAGET POLO TOURBILLON IN WHITE GOLD – REF. G0A30111

A wonderful rendition of an iconic timepiece, this Piaget Polo Tourbillon is equipped with the shaped 600P caliber. The mechanical manual-wind movement consists of 24 jewels and offers 40 hours of power reserve; the bridges of the tourbillon are created in titanium. The case is crafted in 18K white gold and set with fancy-cut diamonds.

PIAGET

PIAGET POLO TOURBILLON RELATIF IN WHTE GOLD – REF. G0A31123

Suspended from one end of the minute hand, the flying tourbillon carriage appears to be disconnected from the base movement driving it. The hours are read off a central disc, while the tourbillon carriage is swept along in the rotation of the minute hand. Expressing the magic of perfect equilibrium, the Piaget Polo Tourbillon Relatif marks off time to the rhythm of the new proprietary Calibre 608P, a mechanical hand-wound flying tourbillon movement. Composed of 42 parts, the carriage—which spins on its axis once per minute, in addition to the hourly rotation around the dial—weighs a mere 0.2 grams! The tourbillon movement, Piaget Calibre 608P, beats at a frequency of 21,600 vibrations per hour (3 Hz) and is endowed with a 70-hour power reserve.

RICHARD MILLE

RM 017 TOURBILLON 'ULTRA FLAT'

The new RM 017 is a world premiere for 2010, with a total thickness comprising a mere 8.7mm and whose manual-winding movement is among the thinnest tourbillon constructions ever created. The RM 017 uses a movement base plate in carbon nanofiber, a major innovation. Via a special pusher in the crown for the separate Winding, Neutral and Hand-setting functions, the RM 017 adds a quick setting capability for time-zone changes, the setting "S," allowing one to change the hour hand independently of the minute hand. The RM 017 combines cutting-edge technology with elegance and exceptional lines, useful functionality and unmistakable recognition: the RM 017 Tourbillon 'Ultra Flat' typifies everything that Richard Mille Watches stands for.

RICHARD MILLE

RM 019 LADIES' TOURBILLON 'BLACK ONYX'

Dating back to about the fifth century, the most emblematic and identifiable artwork in Celtic history must be considered the Celtic knot. With its unlimited and returning pathway, the Celtic knot symbolizes an uninterrupted life; it is both an emblem of longevity and the never-ending cycle of our existence. Brought to haute horology, this eternal symbol takes on a new relationship with the timelessness of time itself. The base plate of the watch has been created of black onyx, a gemstone able to deflect and channel harmful energy towards the Earth, thus providing stability. Adding a refined visible touch to the back view of the base plate, a Celtic triquetra knot turns a complete revolution once every minute.

RICHARD MILLE
RM 020 TOURBILLON POCKET WATCH

This manual-winding tourbillon pocket watch is the first built using a base plate structure created from carbon nanofiber, completely befitting the first radically new tourbillion pocket-watch design of the 21st century. It provides hours, minutes, a power-reserve indicator (approximately 10 days of power via a double-barrel system) and function indicator for Winding, Neutral, and Hand-setting operations. The PVD-treated variable inertia free-sprung balance wheel with overcoil spring and Zircon endstones for the tourbillion cage provides optimal chronometric results and excellent long-term wear capability. It is supplied with a titanium watch chain comprising a new design of fast release/attach mechanism, and in the tradition of fine pocket watches of the past, it can also be used as a "pendulette de bureau" with a specially designed stand in complementary style.

RICHARD MILLE

RM 021 TOURBILLON 'AERODYNE'

Continuing the expansion and application of truly unique materials to watchmaking, the RM 021 Tourbillon 'Aerodyne' is the first watch created with a composite base plate utilizing a titanium exterior framework in combination with honeycombed orthorhombic titanium alumide and carbon nanofiber. This material was originally the subject of research by NASA for application as a core material of supersonic aircraft wings. This new tourbillon provides hours, minutes, indicators for power reserve (approximately 70 hours), torque indicator, and function indicator for Winding, Neutral, and Hand-setting operations. The PVD-treated variable inertia balance wheel with overcoil spring and ceramic endstone for the tourbillon cage offers optimal chronometric results and excellent long-term wear capability.

STÜHRLING ORIGINAL
KING'S COURT TOURBILLON

The King's Court Tourbillon is powered by a 26-jeweled double-barrel tourbillon movement that boasts 72 hours of power reserve. The movement is decorated with Côtes Circulaires and fixed with blued screws. The case is crafted in 18K yellow gold, measures 40mm in diameter, and is mounted on a crocodile strap. The Roman numerals are individually applied, and the screw-down exhibition caseback reveals the workings of the movement. Available in a limited edition of 14 pieces.

ULYSSE NARDIN

FREAK DIAMOND HEART – REF. 029-80

The 44.5mm Freak Diamond Heart is encased in platinum studded with 284 diamonds. Visible through an exhibition caseback, the Caliber UN-201 features a carrousel-tourbillon, a 7-day power reserve, and the patented "Dual Ulysse" escapement in diamond. This Freak model is limited to 99 pieces.

ULYSSE NARDIN

ROYAL BLUE – REF. 799-90

Measuring 43mm, this Royal Blue is crafted in platinum and houses Caliber UN-79 with flying tourbillon, a circular rack winding mechanism, and sapphire bridges and mainplate. Limited to 99 pieces, the Royal Blue is also available on a bracelet.

VACHERON CONSTANTIN
OPENWORKED MALTE TOURBILLON

Housed in a stunning 18K pink-gold tonneau case, this Malte Tourbillon is powered by the hand-wound 1790 mechanical caliber with tourbillon regulator. It offers a 31-day analog date calendar, 55 hours of power reserve, and is completely openworked and beveled. The dial features baton hands and a crown signed with the embossed symbol of Vacheron Constantin.

VACHERON CONSTANTIN

MALTE TOURBILLON REGULATOR – REF. 30080

For this Malte Tourbillon Regulator's large, perfectly balanced tonneau case, Vacheron Constantin's master watchmakers designed a mechanical movement that fits perfectly into this geometric shape: Caliber 1790R. This movement is equipped with the tourbillon, which remains one of the most emblematic complications of the art of watchmaking and is the distillation of all the savoir-faire possessed by the brand's master watchmakers; and the regulator display offering a vertical reading of the time on the tourbillon cage. Five different finishings (snailing, guilloché, opaline, vertical satining, and circular satining) ensure that each indication is extremely easy to read. Water resistant to 100 feet, the case is enhanced with a domed sapphire crystal that prolongs the lines of the bezel. The Malte Tourbillon Regulator is available in 950 platinum or 18K pink gold on a dark blue (for the platinum version) or brown (for the pink-gold version) hand-stitched, saddle-finish alligator strap with a folding clasp and polished half Maltese cross.

ZENITH

ACADEMY TOURBILLON ZERO G EL PRIMERO

The Tourbillon Zero G is a world premiere from Zenith and a revolution in mechanical watchmaking. A self-regulating gyroscopic module guarantees a flat positioning of the regulating organ—whatever the position of the wearer—and therefore ensures greater accuracy. Named El Primero 8800, the caliber is composed of 318 components, 160 of which are in the Zero G module! With its breathtaking design, reminiscent of the terrestrial globe, it has an exenterate axis of time and four front sapphire glasses. The 45mm case is made of 18K rose gold and mounted on a black crocodile leather strap lined with silky Alzavel calfskin. This is an individually numbered edition.

ZENITH

STARISSIME TOURBILLON EL PRIMERO

This Starissime Tourbillon houses the El Primero 4029 automatic chronograph movement. The 292-part tourbillon movement consists of 35 jewels, features a central rotor on ball bearings and a 22K white-gold oscillating weight with 0.3 carat of diamonds. El Primero 4029 beats at 36,000 vibrations per hour and offers 50 hours of power reserve. The 30-minute and 12-hour counters are each symbolized by a Zenith star. The 18K white-gold case, bezel and horns are set with 112 baguette-cut diamonds weighing 8.8 carats. The dial is 18K gold and mother of pearl, set with diamonds, and positioned on a black galuchat strap.

CHRONOGRAPHS, SPLIT-SECOND AND FLYBACK CHRONOGRAPHS

TACHYMETRE
ZENITH
CHRONOGRAPH
AUTOMATIC
El Primero
SWISS MADE
SWISS MADE

CEO of Zenith

Jean-Frédéric Dufour

'Everyone should have a Zenith as a first watch!'

Jean-Frédéric Dufour, the CEO of Zenith since mid-2009, has planned no end of projects for the LVMH group. Among the extensive offerings are new neo-retro models and a mechanical chronograph accurate to one-tenth of a second, displayed by a central jumping second.

Jean-Frédéric Dufour was named CEO of Zenith on June 1, 2009, after his predecessor Thierry Nataf left the company to pursue his career outside the LVMH group. A graduate of the University of Geneva in business, Dufour was employed by Swatch Group, Ulysse Nardin and Chopard, taking on more and more responsibility in the brands' industrial, commercial, marketing and managerial capacities. From 2001 to 2009, he directed product development for watches and jewelry at Chopard.

How do you see the chronograph's role in the universe of horological complications?

The chronograph is often much more complicated than we imagine, and many people—even watch lovers—underestimate its complexity. It also acts as a base for quite a few other complications. Since winning its first prize in 1896 at the Swiss National Exposition in Geneva, Zenith has had a formidable reputation in the chronograph world. This reputation was assured forever in 1969, with the launch of the El Primero Calibre.

Ah yes, the El Primero movement—what is its role in the history of chronograph movements?

It is a legend, a cornerstone in the edifice of Swiss horology. Nicolas Rieussec invented the first chronograph in 1822. The second date to remember in the history of chronograph movements is

FACING PAGE
Jean-Frédéric Dufour

THIS PAGE
TOP
Zenith Chronograph Automatic El Primero

BOTTOM
El Primero movement

Pop Art depiction of the iconic Zenith Chronograph Automatic El Primero

chronograph movement, as opposed to another movement from the same family that came out the same year, which used an additional module.

The El Primero has already been released in many different versions over the past few years. Will there be more developments in that direction?

The heart of El Primero beats at a high frequency of 36,000 beats per hour. This allows it to mechanically indicate times to a precise one-tenth of a second. This is why we worked on developing a central jumping second, to achieve this precision. We also wanted to publicize Zenith's reputation in the chronograph field. The brand has filed an estimated 170 patents in 145 years of existence. It has also won 1,565 awards, and equipped armies and navies around the world in the days when the chronograph was an essential work tool. Zenith has put all its energy at the service of precision, and continues to do so. We want anyone who is thinking of chronographs to think of Zenith!

The many components of the El Primero movement

What are your priorities since arriving at Zenith?

I want to position Zenith among the manufactures that count. And when I say, "manufacture," understand that Zenith is one of just a handful of manufactures in Switzerland. All Zenith watches are equipped with Zenith movements. We want to be one of the principal actors in the very high-end watch industry. But we will not get stuck in the past—we are going to be creative, bringing new aspects to a traditional universe. The best parallel I can make is the Mini Cooper. The latest models are equipped with all the newest automotive technological advances: antilock brakes, airbags, GPS, etc. But once you're inside, you've immediately gone 40 years back in time.

What has your predecessor left you that you are going to keep?

Zenith has become somewhat trendy as a brand; I want to bring it back to something more classic. We're going to move away from the Open concept, except for the El Primero ChronoMaster collection, which will still feature it. From 808 different models, I took it down to 130-140. I want to refocus on four collections: Elite, El Primero, Defy and Academy.

You recently announced that you would like to lower Zenith's prices and offer a model for less than 3,000 €...

We are not going to lower the prices of our current models. However, we are indeed planning on expanding to a new price point. It's a trend to which we must adapt. We hope to expand production volume, which currently stands at several dozen thousand pieces per year. But a watch for 3,000 € is still a high-end product.

What do you see as the strong points of 2010?

We are going to launch new El Primero models, as it is the king of all it surveys! We'll bring out a Captain model, which is a very elegant watch, and a Pilot model, which is a military and pilot's watch. These models were already Zenith products, but we are updating them for today's tastes.

Are you worried about running out of steam with this "new vintage" trend?

Zenith is not some kind of marketing artifact. The manufacture has been at the same address for 145 years! It has never been closed; the electricity has never been cut off. Zenith is one of the few, or perhaps even the only brand that can say this! Zenith has launched over 50 movements—over 600,000 examples of the El Primero movement have been produced over the past 40 years, with less than 1% being returned for repairs! Our reputation is outstanding. So, to answer your questions, no, we're not worried about running out of steam by showing what we can do. All watch lovers should have Zenith in their collections, and every teenager should have Zenith as a first watch!

CEO
of Hublot

Jean-Claude Biver

'Hublot had a record year in 2009!'

Jean-Claude Biver never ceases to subvert expectations—and to exceed them. While the other watchmaking brands were flying their flags at half-mast, Hublot's charismatic director announced that 2009 was a banner year for the brand. 2010 is shaping up to be even better.

After putting Blancpain back on the rails and breathing new life into Omega, Jean-Claude Biver took the reins at Hublot in 2004. In just six years, Biver increased Hublot's sales by a factor of ten and, just as the rest of the world was stepping on the brakes, he was hitting the accelerator. In 2008 LVMH purchased Hublot, in 2009 the brand inaugurated of a brand new manufacture, and 2010 will see the commercial release of the brand's in-house Unico movement. All of that is due to Hublot's one and only iconic collection: the Big Bang!

How did 2009 end for Hublot?

It was a record year! December was Hublot's best month ever. And that's not all: November was our second best month ever, and October was our fourth best!

What is your secret?

We never let up: our investments in marketing, in events, in sponsoring, in research and development have not stopped. When everyone else was slowing down, we sped up: we built a manufacture and hired 25 people. This allowed us to win over new segments of the market and to be the first to take advantage of the rebound.

You announced in September that 2009 would end with 20% less in sales for Hublot. Did that happen?

No! We were almost at the same level as the year before. It was phenomenal!

FACING PAGE
Jean-Claude Biver

THIS PAGE
TOP
Hublot's boutique on Rue Saint-Honoré, Paris.

CENTER
The new Big Bang Gold King Tourbillon GMT

You are seen as a marketing genius. But if you are the focus of so much attention, does that push the actual product into the background?
Everything comes from the product: for Euro 08, we had a Big Bang Euro 08; for our partnership with Manchester United, we came out with a Big Bang Manchester; the same for Morgan, Senna, and Alinghi. There is always a product behind the marketing—certain people even criticize me for having so many. But I like it that way!

Hublot was acquired by LVMH in 2008. What has changed in the past two years?
Nothing at all! LVMH purchased a company that was self-financed, profitable, with an iconic product and a solid team. What would you want to change about that?

The following year, in 2009, you opened a brand new manufacture. Is it the tool you imagined it would be?
It's much better!

You have saved a little extra room to grow, but that floor space has been given over to Chaumet, another LVMH brand. Will that slow your growth?
Not at all! We had always planned on renting that space, which measures 600 square meters. Hublot has 6,000 square meters, which is plenty of room for the five years to come. And if we really need the space, they'll leave!

Your in-house chronograph movement Unico will be released for the first time at this year's BaselWorld. How do you think it will be received?
I hope to sell 5,000 of them!

Will the Unico power a specific collection?
Yes, of course: these watches will have a place to themselves in the Hublot collection, with a new recognizable dial. They will be at the higher end of our range.

Do you see another model ever joining Hublot's Big Bang?
It's impossible to say—I have no answer to that! If you asked Ferdinand Porsche if he thought he would one day produce a 4x4, I'm sure he would have said no! It's the market that decides—the way people's habits evolve and change. It's not something we can decide in advance.

What surprises do you have for us in 2010?
In terms of products, the Unico is already a huge deal. But 2010 will also mark Hublot's arrival on New York's Madison Avenue, next to Hermès, as well as on Paris's Place Vendôme, between Patek Philippe and Chaumet. We're on the ball, ears perked up, and ready to take action!

So things are looking up this year?
It won't be easy, because we are trying to replicate 2009's performance, but with more competition.

FACING PAGE
TOP
The Hublot-sponsored Alinghi

CENTER
Hublot's tower clock

RIGHT
Big Bang King Power Alinghi

THIS PAGE
Big Bang Ayrton Senna 2

What do you mean?
All the other watch brands basically came to a standstill in 2009. I'm proud to have been able to take advantage of the slowdown. But these companies are starting to rev back up, and we won't have the market to ourselves anymore. We'll have to defend the market segments we won over during the crisis.

How much longer will you stay at Hublot?
Ideally, I would love to stay here forever. But my age and my health will eventually get the better of me. I will stay on as long as there is passion and pleasure in the work.

Are you preparing for what will come after you—for your retirement?
Every day! I have a fantastic team, headed by Ricardo Guadalupe, who is extremely competent.

Is Hublot without Jean-Claude Biver even imaginable?
Who remembers Enzo Ferrari? And people also said that Chanel without Coco was impossible. Those two examples prove that Hublot without Biver is completely possible, because Hublot is not just me, but a whole team! We have increased sales by a factor of ten since 2004; I would never have been able to do that alone. We began in a Salvation Army office and ended up in a brand-new $20 million dollar manufacture—I wasn't alone! And if there's a team, it's easy to imagine that another director could take up the reins of the whole project.

You're not just a watchmaker, you're also a farmer...
All watchmakers are farmers!

But you actually have a farm in Tour-de-Peilz, in Switzerland. How many cows do you have?
Including heifers, I have 100 animals.

Is that how you make ends meet at the end of the month?
(Laughs) It's a passion that I discovered at the same time as horology. It was the watchmakers in the Vallée de Joux, back when I was getting Blancpain back up to speed, who introduced me to Alpine pasture cheese. They helped me discover that cows from Alpine pastures gave cheese a different taste than cows that eat hay. They taught me that morels don't grow under red firs, only under white firs!

You never pass up a chance to offer people your own cheese, and every year you invite your friends and the press as you walk your cows down from the mountains for the winter—is that what being Swiss means to you?
It's the culture, the tradition, the heritage. People may make fun of it, but it is really something that we need to honor, cherish and perpetuate. On the other hand, Switzerland also stands for high technology, the Ecole Polytechnique Fédérale de Lausanne—which is very cutting edge—or Alinghi. The two sides are interconnected—if the farmers of the Vallée de Joux had not been so patient and meticulous, they would not have been able to embrace horology as they did centuries ago.

CEO of Bell & Ross

Carlos Rosillo

'The skull conveys bravery, force and invincibility.'

Traveling at supersonic speeds, pilots rely on an aircraft's flight instruments to deliver essential information at a glance. Legibility is at a premium, especially when a split-second decision could mean the difference between life and death. That instant readability is one of the principles upon which Bell & Ross was founded more than 15 years ago. It's also one of the reasons Bell & Ross has earned the trust of so many with high-risk professions who rely on the company's precision instruments.

Bell & Ross CEO Carlos Rosillo says aviation's influence on the brand has been profound, noting that an aircraft's dashboard inspired the BR01, the company's first watch. "The square shape of the watch with its round face and the simple, bold numbers on the dial are all reminiscent of the instruments found in a cockpit."

While the look is distinctive, Rosillo says function, not style, is the design's guiding principle. "Pilots need to read information under extreme conditions. Our black cases minimize light reflection. Our dials are highly readable during daytime, while the numbers, index marks and hands are covered with a photoluminescent coating for night reading."

The Instrument BR 01 Airborne, one Bell & Ross's latest, pays tribute to soldiers and their selfless willingness to face of death in service of a greater cause. Dubbed the Talisman watch, the Airborne takes its design from the skull and crossbones adopted by paratroopers as their ensign. "The skull is a talisman that conveys bravery, force and invincibility," Rosillo explains. "It is also a reminder to each soldier that death is always around the corner."

Despite the stylized look of the skull-shaped dial and sword-shaped hands, Rosillo says the BR 01 Airborne conforms to the company's core principle of functionality. "It is a tribute watch," he says, "but first and foremost, it is an instrument watch."

FACING PAGE
Carlos Rosillo, Bell & Ross CEO.

THIS PAGE
TOP RIGHT
BR01 Airborne 415 Shadow.eps
Limited to 99 pieces, the BR 01 Airborne 415 uses 156 black and 259 white diamonds to form its signature skull and crossbones.

CENTER
Instrument BR01 Airborne 672 Shadow.pdf The BR 01 Airborne 672's carbon-coated case (46mm) is paved with 413 black diamonds. More than 4.5 carats of diamonds are used to create its dazzling design.

BOTTOM
Airborne night-close-up.eps
A luminescent coating makes it possible to read the BR 01 Airborne in the dark, reflecting Bell & Ross's fundamental attention to legibility.

A carbon scratch.eps
Worn by pilots in the French Air Force, the Instrument BR 03 Type Aviation integrates a digital readout. This limited edition includes 250 pieces in black carbon coated (shown) and 250 pieces in steel.

Bell & Ross enhances the spirit of the Talisman watch with Airborne 415 and Airborne 672, two limited editions with gem-set cases and dials. The skull-shaped dials of both are set with white diamonds, while black diamonds are used to outline the Airborne 415's bezel and completely cover the Airborne 672's case.

The unusual combination of military symbolism and haute joaillerie takes its inspiration from military tradition, Rosillo says. "It pays tribute to those moments of glory and celebration, like when a soldier's dress uniform is decorated with shiny medals."

The Airborne joins a number of limited edition, military-influenced watches by Bell & Ross, including the Instrument BR 03 Type Aviation. Created at the behest of the French Air Force, its mix of analog and digital displays is tailored to the needs of fighter pilots. When engaged, the digital readout can display one of the following: time, chronograph, alarm, second time zone, timer, perpetual calendar, or seconds with date.
"A digital display enables us to put more functions and a large amount of pertinent information in a single, small, legible space," Rosillo explains. "The smaller digital display also allows the case size to be more compact."

To optimize reliability, the watch is outfitted with a silver-oxide battery that enables it to run up to 35 months, depending on how often the alarm and

TOP
The Instrument BR Heritage's vintage style embodies the look of the 1940s. Its leather strap, printed with the Bell & Ross logo, complements the dial's khaki accents.

CENTER
Bell & Ross offers two versions of the Type Aéronavale, one equipped with ultra-rounded synthetic glass (shown) and the other with a sapphire crystal.

chronograph are used. As an added safety feature, the digital display blinks to warn when the battery should be changed.

Bell & Ross produces two versions of the Type Aviation, one exclusively for Air Force personnel adorned with the Air Force logo and the other without the logo for civilians.
Where the Type Aviation's design visually references the instruments in a modern aircraft cockpit, Bell & Ross turns back the hands of time to the 1940s for the look of its Instrument BR Heritage.

Its vintage appeal evokes the WWII-era with classic-style hands and numerals. The dial's khaki color scheme is echoed by the leather strap's natural color. The modern world, however, does make a subtle appearance in the form of the case's carbon-powder coating. Available in 42mm or 46mm models, the BR Heritage is powered by an automatic ETA movement.

Bell & Ross returns to the here and now with the Type Aéronavale. Designed to meet the French Naval Air Force's specifications, this chronograph is well suited for aerial navigation. The watchmaker offers two versions, one with a sapphire crystal over the dial and the other with domed acrylic glass. The latter was popular in watches made during the '50s.

"Like all Bell & Ross designs, not only is the acrylic glass an homage to the past, it is functional as well," Rosillo says. "Acrylic glass is often used in military watches because it is shatterproof, an important feature on dangerous missions. The material is also lightweight, another key factor."

Bell & Ross employs a clean dial design for the Type Aéronavale, upholding its dedication to legibility. Luminescent hands and indexes are instantly readable at night on the matte black dial.

Like the Type Aviation, Bell & Ross will produce two versions of the Type Aéronavale, one for the general public and the other emblazoned with the French Naval Air Force's logo and available exclusively to military personnel.

To create these professional-grade timepieces, Bell & Ross looked to the sky for inspiration, finding it in the lives of pilots and soldiers who face danger every day. Designed to meet their extreme needs, these uncompromising instruments exceed the needs of the Earth-bound majority.

CEO of
TAG Heuer

Jean-Christophe Babin

'The Calibre 1887 was designed to be accurate and reliable.'

From the new Monaco V4 and the Calibre 1887, to the newest products of 2010 and the 150th anniversary of the brand, TAG Heuer's CEO reflects on a year full of excitement.

FACING PAGE
Jean-Christophe Babin

THIS PAGE
TAG Heuer's Monaco V4

Jean-Christophe Babin, CEO of TAG Heuer, is coming off of a decisive year for the Swiss brand: after five years of research and development, the brand unveiled its striking Calibre V4, whose barrels and transmission belts are arranged in a "V" shape. TAG Heuer also has an eye on assuring its legacy with the production of Calibre 1887, a chronograph movement that can be mass-produced.

Your new chronograph movement is called Calibre 1887. Where did that name come from?

We developed Calibre 1887 from a base developed by SII (Seiko Instruments Inc.), to which TAG Heuer had acquired intellectual property usage rights. But our Research & Development team totally industrialized the caliber and reconstructed certain major components around an ensemble of high-end Swiss-made components to increase accuracy and reliability. Among other things, we equipped it with a redesigned version of our rotating pinion, patented in 1887. So the name is a tribute to one of our major horological inventions.

Will this movement replace another?

No! This new automatic movement will join the 11 and 12 calibers (developed with Dubois Dépraz), the 16 and 17 calibers (created on Valjoux and ETA 2894 bases), the 36 caliber (provided by Zenith) and the 360 (our own in-

THIS PAGE
TAG Heuer Silverstone Automatic Chronograph

FACING PAGE
LEFT
TAG Heuer's CAL. 1887

CENTER
TAG Heuer's CAL. 11

RIGHT
TAG Heuer's 1933 Hervue Pair

house movement, precise to one-hundredth of a second). The Calibre 1887 will simply join the ranks, completing a fleet of seven mechanical chronograph movements—the most extensive range of any luxury watchmaker.

Why did you decide to produce a new chronograph movement?

We needed a model that could be mass-produced. The industrial aspect of the project is one of the major difficulties of the project, which involves several constraints. The goal is to produce ten thousand units at a time.

What makes this movement unique?

We weren't trying to innovate for the sake of innovation. The Calibre 1887 was designed to be accurate, reliable, somewhat simple and not too expensive to produce, easy to maintain, and versatile, so that it can support any future additional complications. It beats at 28,800 vibrations per hour, measures 29.3mm in diameter, and includes 39 jewels along with 320 functional components. It is a chronograph equipped with a column-wheel, as well as regulators imported from the V4.

Yes, the Calibre V4—that was a great innovation...

It's probably the greatest horological complication ever created!

Why?

For four centuries, mechanical horology rested on three essential pillars: the escapement (which transforms a linear force into segments of time); the gears (which transmit the force); and the barrel (which provides the power reserve). For the V4, we went straight for the central pillar: the gears! By inventing the first horological transmission belts in history, we were breaking away from all existing movement constructions in the watch industry.

How many transmission belts are there?

There are five belts per movement, each possessing about 200 teeth and measuring 0.07mm—less than a hair's breadth! They are produced by a company in France that heats the material to 180° Celsius and injects it at high pressure (3000 bar) into a 600kg steel mold. The watch's chain's three belts are made of three different viscoplastic polymers, and the two belts on the barrel chain—pushed to every possible limit—are reinforced by a central steel section.

The transmission belts are not the only innovation…

The Calibre V4 is equipped with a linear oscillating weight, a unique system that confronted our team of developers with no end of challenges. The distance that the weight covers is actually quite restricted, so we had to reduce its volume as much as possible, while still keeping it sufficiently heavy! It will equip two pairs of barrels arranged at a 13° angle, linked and mounted in parallel. That is also a first.

Do all these inventions weaken the movement?

The Calibre V4 is the first fine watch movement able to withstand 5000G collisions. It is extremely reliable! We took as long as we needed to make sure of that.

How long was that?

The Calibre V4 was presented for the first time at BaselWorld 2004. At that point, it was a concept watch. Up until 2006, we had only explored theories and performed calculations. Then we moved on to the test stage. It took us five years in all.

Where is the Calibre V4 produced?

Apart from the oscillating weight and the transm,ission belts, everything is made at our La Chaux-de-Fonds production site. It is assembled in our Grandes Complications workshop. It takes five hours for our master watchmaker to mount it, and another five hours to perform all the adjustments.

Is this the beginning of a new era for TAG Heuer?

The V4 is the marriage of science and artisanship. But of course that does not detract from the beauty of the work! On the contrary, it allows us to rethink the future: we will produce versions of the V4 using elements like its components (such as the transmission belts or the ball bearings on the oscillating weight) and its principles (such as the 100% ISO certification, and the absence of lubrication).

Are there any other surprises in store for 2010?

The Silverstone Chronograph Calibre 11. It is one of our historical models, launched by Heuer in 1974. For the 150th anniversary of TAG Heuer, we decided to reissue this legendary watch in a nearly identical version, adding only qualitative elements from the 21st century: the Calibre 11, with a module by Dubois Dépraz, has been improved, the glass has been replaced by a sapphire crystal, and the caseback is now transparent.

Has the design been updated?

The crown is still at 9:00—when it was initially released, Jack Heuer, who had designed it, wanted it to be very clear that the piece did not need winding. The shape of the case is still the same, somewhere between round and square. The Silverstone Chronograph Calibre 11 is available with a brown or blue dial.

The chronograph is not the most exclusive function, nor the most difficult to build, but it is undoubtedly a rising star among complications, essential in any self-respecting collection. Its success can be explained largely by its technical, sporty appeal, a reflection of the wearer's dynamic lifestyle. To rise to this unprecedented demand, brands are coming up with ever more innovations in design, materials, mechanisms and performance. They are also increasingly developing in-house chronograph movements a guarantee that the buyer is getting a timepiece with an original "motor."

***Cartier**, Rotonde Central Chronograph*
***Rolex**, Cosmograph Daytona*
World Chronograph
***F.P. Journe**, Centigraphe Souverain*

***Zenith**, Baby Doll Star*
Open Sea Décentrique GMT
***Porsche Design** Indicator by Eterna*
***IWC**, Pilot's Watch Double Chronograph*

CHRONOGRAPHS, SPLIT-SECOND AND FLYBACK CHRONOGRAPHS

THIS PAGE
TOP LEFT
***Omega**, Speedmaster Professional Moonwatch Apollo 11 40th Anniversary*

TOP RIGHT
***Zenith**, Grande ChronoMaster Open El Primero*

FACING PAGE
***TAG Heuer**, re-release of the 1969 Monaco*

A MODERN COMPLICATION

Other than the multiple-time-zone watch, the chronograph is the youngest of all the complications in the classic repertory. Before measuring short times, watches needed to attain a certain level of precision. Watchmakers also had to perfect a system that would stop and restart a hand without disturbing the functioning of the movement. The first chronograph worthy of the name was created by Rieussec in 1822. To indicate times to one-fifth of a second, the hand deposited a drop of ink on the dial, giving the complication its name. (In Greek, chronos means "time," and grapho means "writing.") The function of sending the hands back to zero appeared around the middle of the 19th century.

The first chronograph-wristwatches entered the scene in 1915. They were equipped as were pocket watches with a single pusher (in the crown) for all three functions. Breitling would give the chronograph its current configuration in 1915 by creating the first independent pusher. In 1934, Breitling would also introduce the second pusher for a return to zero. In 1937, Dépraz & Cie (now Dubois Dépraz) presented a chronograph movement that was controlled by cams. This was less expensive and easier to make than the traditional column-wheel mechanism. The chronograph continued its glorious career with the introduction of several classics, including the Speedmaster by Omega, which accompanied American astronauts on their first trip to the moon in July 1969, earning it the nickname "moonwatch." To celebrate the event's 40th anniversary, Omega presented two special editions in 2009 called Speedmaster Professional Moonwatch Apollo 11 40th Anniversary. The small seconds subdial is adorned with a medal depicting the Apollo 11 logo, with an eagle

clutching an olive branch in its talons next to an inscription reading 02:56 GMT.

SUMMER OF '69

1969 was also marked by the creation of the first automatic chronograph movements. The one developed by Breitling/Buren/Heuer-Leonidas in collaboration with Dubois Dépraz was the Chrono-Matic caliber, a cam-based modular mechanism with an off-center microrotor. The famous El Primero, introduced by Zenith, featured a column-wheel chronograph integrated within the movement, and a central rotor. Beating at a frequency of 36,000 vibrations per hour, the El Primero was also the first mechanical chronograph movement capable of measuring time to one-tenth of a second. Besides the Zenith models that it powered, the movement later also graced some of the watch world's most prestigious timepieces by the most beloved brands. To name just one, the legendary Cosmograph Daytona housed the El Primero, at least before Rolex created its own chronograph movement at the turn of the third millennium. Zenith also honored its invention by creating (among other pieces) the Grande ChronoMaster Open El Primero, with an opening in the dial revealing the watch's beating heart. In 2009, the brand celebrated 40 years of El Primero by creating the New Vintage 1969 – The Originals, inspired by the first chronograph equipped with El Primero. TAG Heuer re-released its famous 1969 Monaco (one of the first models powered by the Chrono-Matic Caliber), a watch that entered into history on the wrist of Steve McQueen in the film *Le Mans*. For its part, Breitling is proposing two limited editions with quadrennial or perpetual calendar of its historic Chrono-Matic, which returned to Breitling's collections several years ago.

CREATING CHRONOGRAPHS IN-HOUSE

The advent of more precise quartz movements almost dealt a fatal blow to the rise of the mechanical chronograph, but when mechanical watchmaking enjoyed a renaissance in the 1980s, chronographs came along for the ride. We must remember, however, that for a long time, it was very rare for a brand or even a manufacture to produce its own chronograph movement, and that a large part of the mechanical chronographs offered by many different brands all house the same ETA 7750 Valjoux movement, reworked to a greater or lesser extent, and sold with differences in prices that are sometimes hard to justify... But the times, they are a-changing. A better-informed public will gladly pay a premium for a high-end chronograph, but only if it contains an exclusive movement or at least a slightly original one. The announcement that Swatch Group would end deliveries of ETA movements on January 1, 2011 also spurred competing brands to take alternative measures. For some years, we have seen an increase in development of "in-house" chronographs featuring interesting innovations. Patek Philippe introduced its Annual Calendar Chronograph Ref. 5960 with a vertical disc clutch that allows the chronograph hand to be used for the running seconds, and a single counter for the hours and minutes. Chopard unveiled a movement with column-wheel, vertical clutch, instant restart and 60-hour power reserve, which powers the L.U.C Chrono One. Piaget created the 880P caliber, with a second 24-hour time zone and flyback function; it proudly inhabits the new Polo FortyFive collection, launched in 2009 to celebrate the 30th anniversary of the Polo model, with a sporty chic look that joins titanium, steel

FACING PAGE
CLOCKWISE FROM LEFT
***Patek Philippe**, Annual Calendar Chronograph Ref. 5960R (new 2009 version in rose gold)*
***Chopard**, L.U.C Chrono One*
***Vulcain**, Vulcanographe*
***Eberhard & Co**, Chrono4*
***Parmigiani Fleurier**, Kalpagraph*

THIS PAGE
TOP LEFT
***Audemars Piguet**, Tourbillon Chronographe MC12*

TOP RIGHT
***Breitling**, Chronomat B01*

BELOW
***TAG Heuer**, Carrera Calibre 360*

and rubber. Parmigiani Fleurier made its grand entrance in the sports watch universe when it introduced the Kalpagraph, powered by an in-house movement. Vulcain, master of the alarm watch, renewed ties with the chronograph when it created the Vulcanographe, equipped with an automatic column-wheel movement. In 2009 Breitling reaffirmed its independence by presenting its first completely in-house chronograph movement; the B01 Caliber, fabricated according to a revolutionary industrial process that completely revamps traditional movement assembly, was launched in a newly redesigned version of the brand's flagship model, called Chronomat B01.

A NEW ATTITUDE

For a long time, chronographs were distinguished by their rather classic aesthetic, with three small symmetrically placed counters. This traditional look has now been swept aside by many models that reinvent the ways of telling time. Eberhard & Co set the tone by launching the Chrono4, with four counters aligned horizontally or vertically. Chronographs with retrograde displays have gained in popularity, such as the Arena Chrono Quattro Retro from Gérald Genta. The chronograph universe has also been marked by the appearance of new materials that allow the watches to become lighter, more robust or more technically sophisticated, as well as shaking up long-established aesthetic codes. One fine example is Audemars Piguet's Tourbillon Chronographe MC12, marrying high-tech materials with a daring automotive-inspired design. The AMVOX2 Chronograph Concept by Jaeger-LeCoultre even sparked a small revolution on the commands: the traditional pushers are replaced by a case middle that pivots slightly on a horizontal axis. To start or stop the chronograph, the wearer presses on the crystal at 12:00, and a push at 6:00 triggers the return to zero.

ONE ONE-HUNDREDTH OF A SECOND

In high-performance watches, TAG Heuer made quite the splash when it introduced the prototype of its Calibre 360 Concept Chronograph, the

first mechanical wrist-chronograph accurate to one one-hundredth of a second. This feat was achieved thanks to the fusion of two independent movements, the second of which (the one powering the chronograph) beats at 21,600 vibrations per hour. F.P. Journe repeated the accomplishment, taking a different path (a single balance beating at 21,600 vibrations per hour) on the brand's Centigraphe Souverain. The hundredths of a second can be read using a hand that makes a complete revolution in one second its tachymetric scale allows measurement of speeds up to 360,000 kilometers per hour!

MONOCOUNTER MADNESS

Leaving behind the concept of separate small counters for minutes and hours, many watchmakers have opted for a monocounter with both indications, following the example set by Patek Philippe. The goal: to allow for a simpler, faster reading of longer times, as one might read the time on one's watch. This is the case with IWC and its Da Vinci Chronograph, equipped with a tonneau-shaped case and a proprietary movement. In its Duomètre à Chronographe, Jaeger-LeCoultre proposes a new concept of movement construction, with two independent mechanisms, one for the hour (with golden hands), the other for the chronograph (with blue hands), synchronized by the same regulating organ. The hour and minute counters are shown on a single subdial at 2:30 and a flying seconds hand at 6:00 allows measurement of times as short as one-sixth of a second. Pierre DeRoche, on its SplitRock, goes even further in emphasizing readability by offering a chronograph with the hour, minute and second hands on the same axis; the watch is equipped with an exclusive Dubois Dépraz caliber. On the new Cartier Rotonde Central Chronograph, the chronograph indications are grouped in the center of the dial, with a seconds hand and an arced counter for the 30-second totalizer; the hour and minute are displayed around the edges, indicated by two hands that never obstruct the view of the chronograph, because only their tips are visible.

FACING PAGE
TOP LEFT
***Jaeger-LeCoultre**, AMVOX2 Chronograph Concept*

TOP CENTER
***Pierre DeRoche**, SplitRock Full Black*

TOP RIGHT
***Jaeger-LeCoultre**, Duomètre à Chronographe*

CENTER
***IWC**, Da Vinci Chronographe*

RIGHT
***Maurice Lacroix**, Mémoire1*

THIS PAGE
TOP
***Christophe Claret**, DualTow*

FAR LEFT
***Ebel**, 1911 BTR*

LEFT
***Blancpain**, Villeret Monopusher Chronograph*

Other pioneering brands use the same hands for the chronograph and for time indications, for example the new Aquaracer Calibre S from TAG Heuer, with a quartz movement. The three central hands display the classic hours/minutes/seconds, the elapsed hours/minutes/seconds, or the minutes/seconds left in the "regatta" countdown. These three functions can be selected by a push on the crown. Maurice Lacroix released the Mémoire1, the first mechanical watch with memory, in 2008. It features two hands (seconds and minutes) as well as a disc for the hour display. When the wearer presses a button in the crown, the watch switches from "time" mode to "chrono." Another push brings back the time display. The switch between functions is possible even when the chronograph is running.

THE DAYS OF DISCS

To spice up the looks and vary the ways of telling time, watchmakers are also turning to disc displays. On the Porsche Design Indicator by Eterna, the hours and minutes of elapsed time are displayed digitally using rotating discs in a window at 3:00. The titanium Grand Carrera Calibre 17 RS2 by TAG Heuer a gem in a collection characterized by its Rotating System presents two disc indications, one for the small seconds, the other for the chronograph minute counter. The displays are equally original on Ebel's automatic chronograph 1911 BTR, equipped with the exclusive 139 caliber. To enhance readability, the traditional minute counter has been replaced by a window shaped like a 120° arc at 12:00, with a three-armed red hand. The hours are counted off in a window at 6:00 with a disc marked from 1 to 12 that rotates beneath the dial.

THE MONOPUSHER CHRONOGRAPH

The list of chronograph specialties has expanded to include the "monopusher" chronographs, whose sophisticated construction entails a single pusher that successively controls start, stop, and reset to zero. Among these gems is

THIS PAGE
TOP LEFT
***Officine Panerai**, Luminor 1950 Chrono Monopoussoir*

TOP RIGHT
***Montblanc**, Grand Chronographe Régulateur*

BOTTOM
***TAG Heuer**, Grand Carrera Calibre 17 RS2*

FACING PAGE
TOP LEFT
***A. Lange & Söhne**, Tourbograph Pour le Mérite*

TOP CENTER
***A. Lange & Söhne**, Lange Double Split*

TOP RIGHT
***Girard-Perregaux**, Vintage 1945 XXL Foudroyante Split-seconds Chronograph*

CENTER
***Patek Philippe**, Split-Second Réf. 5959*

Blancpain's Villeret Monopusher Chronograph. The Chronographe Monopoussoir Hommage La Chaux-de-Fonds 1738 by Jaquet Droz is the first timepiece of its kind to feature an hour counter as well as an offcenter hour/minute indication. Panerai has created, among other exclusive movements, the caliber P.2004 eight-day manual-winding monopusher chronograph with time zone. Montblanc confirmed its rise to the high end with the Grand Chronographe Régulateur, developed and produced by the prestigious Minerva manufacture. This monopusher chronograph boasts a regulator-style dial, with hours at 12:00 and a large central minute hand. Christophe Claret, one of the most prestigious providers of complicated movements, celebrated the manufacture's 20th anniversary with a spectacular "planetary" monopusher chronograph with sonnerie and tourbillon, under a first for the brand its own name. This model, DualTow, is notable for its "planetary gear" chronograph system (with gears for seconds, minutes and hours), which limit the variations in the balance's amplitude, leading to greater precision.

A SPORTY COMPLICATION FOR SPORTY WOMEN

Another strong trend at the beginning of the third millennium is the expansion of the range of models specifically designed for women. Chronographs are decorated in soft colors, crafted dials and even diamonds. On its Baby Doll Star Open Sea, with El Primero movement, Zenith combines mother-of-pearl, pearls, galuchat and star decorations. Girard-Perregaux has also offered a wonderful combination of beauty and brains with its ladies' automatic Petit Chronographe with column-wheel.

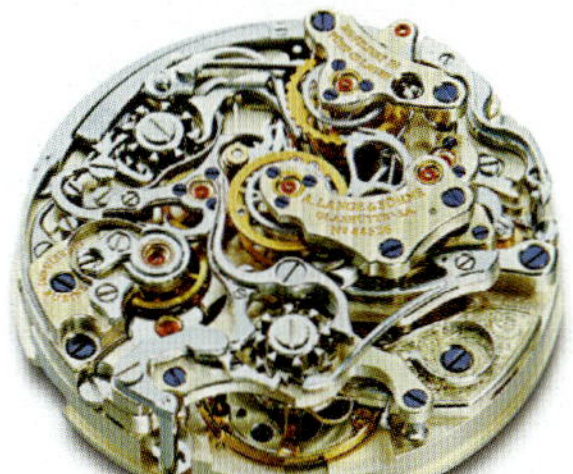

SPLIT-SECOND CHRONOGRAPHS

Split-second chronographs are equipped with an additional seconds hand, which can be stopped independently to measure an intermediary or reference time. Activating the pusher is all that is needed for the split-second hand to catch up with the main chronograph hand. The ultra-sophisticated clutch work makes the split-second chronograph one of the most difficult complications to achieve, every bit the equal of the tourbillon or the minute repeater.

The split-second chronograph, invented in 1838, is one of the greatest demonstrations of horological savoir-faire. All of the most prestigious brands have offered this kind of complication in their collections. In its Ref. 5959, Patek Philippe presented the flattest (5.25mm) column-wheel split-second chronograph ever produced, with a two-pusher system (instead of the usual three), and several patented features. In its Tourbograph Pour le Mérite, A. Lange & Söhne combines the split-seconds chronograph with two of the most complex mechanisms ever invented for improving the precision of movements: the tourbillon and the fusée-chain, which delivers regular torque to the escapement. The German brand has also innovated with its Lange Double Split, the first wrist-chronograph with two split hands, one for the minutes counter and one for the chronograph seconds. Girard-Perregaux equipped its Vintage 1945 XXL Foudroyante Split-seconds Chronograph with a "flying seconds" hand that goes around the dial in one second, which allows measurement of times as brief as one-eighth of a second. On its Pilot's Watch Double Chronograph, IWC has placed the split-seconds chronograph within a scratch-resistant high-tech ceramic case equipped with an antimagnetic shield of soft iron. Blancpain created new challenges for itself and its Villeret collection by adding a Monopusher Split-seconds Chronograph with two column wheels: one for the chronograph, the other for the split-second function. Panerai has enriched its line of in-house movements, presenting the split-seconds P.2006 Caliber, which is also based on a monopusher system.

SIMPLIFIED SPLIT-SECONDS

Created in 1946 by Georges Dubey, cofounder of the brand Dubey & Schaldenbrand, the Index Mobile is a simplified form of the split-seconds function that is limited to measuring times of less than one minute. The two second-hands of the chronograph are linked by a spiral spring visible on the face of the watch. The split-seconds hand stays stopped as long as there is pressure on the pusher; when the pusher is released, that hand joins the other, pushed by the spring. Dubey & Schaldenbrand ushered this original system back into the spotlight, notably in its Spiral-Sixty model.

AUDEMARS PIGUET

MILLENARY CARBON ONE TOURBILLON CHRONOGRAPH

REF. 26152AU.OO.D002CR.01

Audemars Piguet Caliber 2884 is an oval hand-wound movement developed and crafted entirely by Audemars Piguet. It is a complex movement equipped with a tourbillon, an ultra-efficient column-wheel chronograph mechanism and twin barrels. This watch's case is in forged carbon with a black ceramic bezel, crown and pushbuttons, a cambered glareproof sapphire crystal, and blackened titanium caseback fitted with sapphire crystal. Limited edition of 120 pieces.

AUDEMARS PIGUET

ROYAL OAK OFFSHORE CHRONOGRAPH – REF. 26170TI.OO.1000TI.01

When first created in 1972, the Royal Oak overturned existing fine watchmaking codes and asserted itself as the first high-end sports watch. Twenty years later, the famous octagon was reinterpreted in an extreme sports version that became the Royal Oak Offshore collection—the first chapter in an ongoing success story. The latter is now enhanced with new dials in unusual colors and equipped with the exclusive self-winding Caliber 3126/3840. The case is crafted in titanium, and the watch's matching bracelet has an AP triple-blade folding clasp. Also available in stainless steel on bracelet or hornback crocodile leather strap.

AUDEMARS PIGUET

ROYAL OAK OFFSHORE CHRONOGRAPH – REF. 26176FO.OO.D101CR.01

Powered by the self-winding chronograph Caliber 3126/3840, this bold chronograph features the small seconds at 12:00, date at 3:00, a 12-hour counter at 6:00, and a 30-minute counter at 9:00. It also boasts a forged carbon case, ceramic bezel, engraved caseback, and a titanium AP folding clasp. The watch is protected against magnetic fields and water resistant to 100 meters.

AUDEMARS PIGUET

ROYAL OAK OFFSHORE GRAND PRIX COLLECTION – REF. 26290IO.OO.A001VE.01

The Royal Oak Offshore Grand Prix Collection embodies the powerful ties between the horology and automobile industries. Powered by an in-house self-winding 3126/3840, this watch's forged carbon case is detailed with a forged carbon and black ceramic bezel, a blackened titanium crown, black ceramic and titanium pushpieces, titanium pushpiece guards, and a titanium exhibition caseback fitted with a sapphire crystal. The version presented here is released in a limited edition of 1,750 pieces; models are also available in 18K pink gold (650 pieces) and 950 platinum (75 pieces).

BOVET

SPORT*STER*: SAGUARO GIBEON METEORITE

In 2009, the 46mm Saguaro chronograph model meets the stars with a variety of exclusive Gibeon iron meteorite dials—whether black, white or rose, they are an invitation to dream. Each meteorite fragment is unique and comes from molten planetary cores that were broken apart. This unusual, rare and timeless material transforms the edgy Saguaro into a unique watch where infinity meets time. The large date, Art Deco numerals, and the tachymeter and pulsometer scales demonstrate that functionality need not compromise stylishness. Water resistant to 300 meters, this Saguaro is certified by Chronofiable and has a rubberized and waterproof strap.

GUY ELLIA
JUMBO CHRONO

The Jumbo Chrono, the first round men's watch created by GUY ELLIA, is based on an interesting technological approach demonstrating that it is possible to combine aesthetic balance with masculine detail and a fine mechanical movement. The Jumbo Chrono boasts an exceptional Ø 50mm size that is rarely seen in the world of luxury watches. The Jumbo Chrono's rhodium-plated rotor is unique and the impressive discovery dial reflects a strong graphic design: sweep-seconds chronograph in the center, hour and minute at 12:00, date at 2:00, 30-minute counter at 3:00, seconds at 6:00, and 12-hour counter at 9:00. This model is shown in black gold, but also available in white gold and pink gold.

IWC

AQUATIMER CHRONOGRAPH – REF. IW376701

Sporting the attributes of the new Aquatimer family, such as the external rotating bezel and the quick-change bracelet system, the Aquatimer Chronograph is available in stainless steel on either a stainless steel bracelet or coordinating rubber strap and with two dial variants: the Aquatimer signature colors of black and yellow, or in the striking color combination of blue and coral red. The Ø 44mm case is pressure resistant to 12 bar and houses the 79320 caliber chronograph movement that records aggregate times up to 12 hours on rhodium-plated inner dials. In addition to the date, it also has a day display and a 44-hour power reserve.

*The Aquatimer quick-change bracelet system was developed by IWC under a patent license from Cartier.

IWC

AQUATIMER CHRONOGRAPH – REF. IW3769

Of the diver's chronographs, the sportingly elegant Aquatimer Chronograph in red gold stands out in both visual and horological terms. It is the first watch in the Aquatimer family to be equipped with the IWC-manufactured 89360 caliber. It is distinguished by its flyback function and the two-hand display of the long stop-times on a single inner dial. The 89360 caliber, automatically wound by the IWC double-pawl system, is currently regarded as one of the most modern mechanical movements with a stop function, which is observed through the sapphire glass back. This watch is pressure resistant to 12 bar and available only in a Ø 44mm red-gold case with a black rubber strap.

IWC

AQUATIMER CHRONOGRAPH EDITION GALAPAGOS ISLANDS – REF. IW376705

The Aquatimer family has undergone an eye-catching transformation with the newly developed external, unidirectional rotating diving bezel with indexing in one-minute intervals. In contrast to the inner rotating bezel, which is adjustable via a crown, the non-slip external bezel offers two advantages: easier operation when wearing gloves and far better brilliance and luminosity. Its measurement scale is a 4mm-wide sapphire crystal ring, printed underneath, which fits with the surface of the bezel. The ring's underside is coated with a thick layer of SuperLumiNova, which shines through the non-printed surfaces or numerals. This "evolutionary" innovation contributes to safety. This chronograph with a pressure resistance to 12 bar, a 44-hour power reserve and aggregate time recording up to 12 hours is equivalent in technical terms to its predecessor, the Aquatimer Chrono-Automatic.

*The Aquatimer quick-change bracelet system was developed by IWC under a patent license from Cartier.

IWC

DA VINCI CHRONOGRAPH – REF. IW376402

For the Da Vinci Chronograph, IWC developed its first proprietary chronograph movement and gave it a modern interpretation with an incomparable analog time display. The manufacture's 89360 caliber boasts a 68-hour power reserve, an IWC double-pawl automatic-winding system, and is actuated via a classic column wheel. The Da Vinci Chronograph is available in platinum, rose gold or steel.

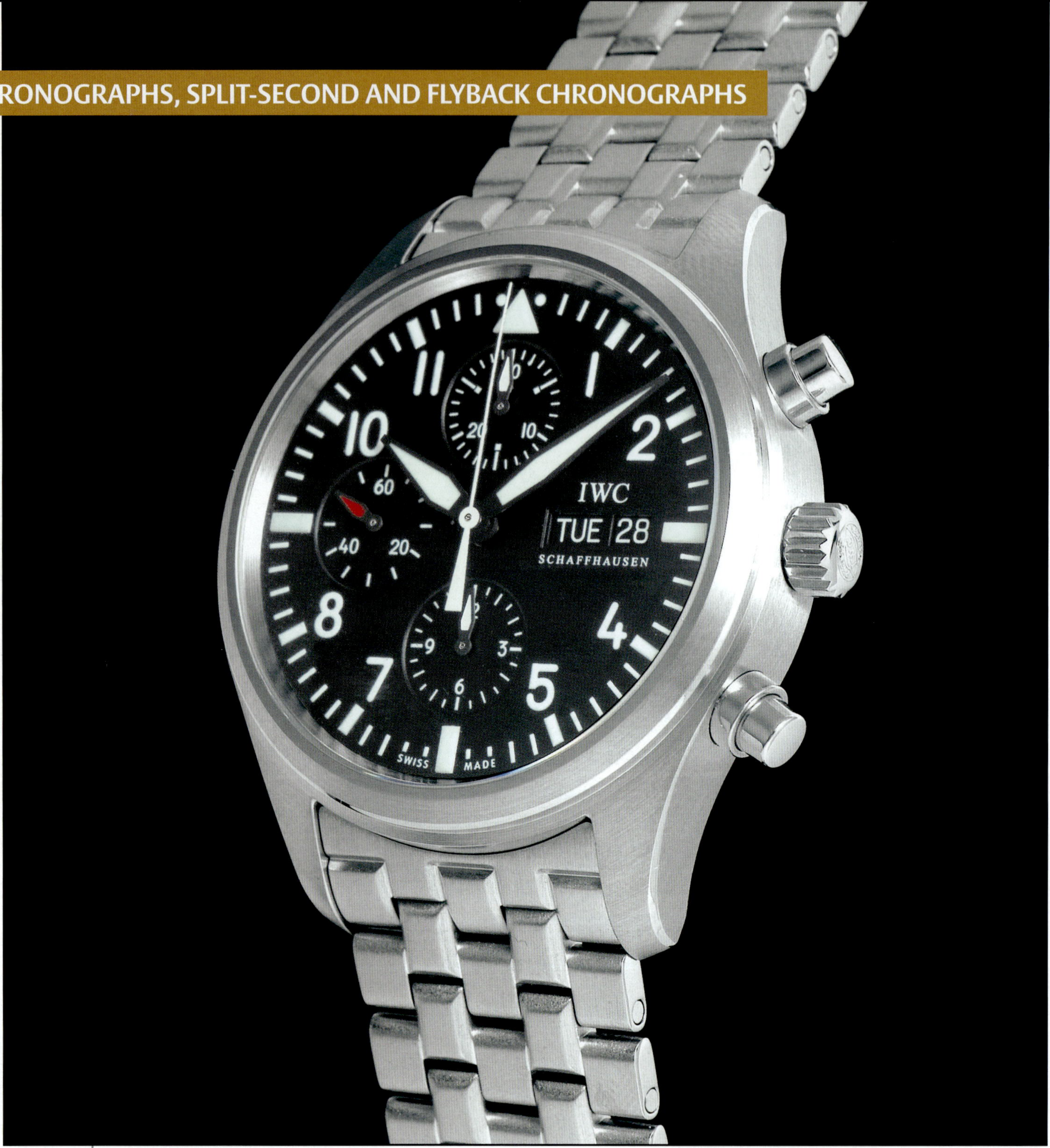

IWC

PILOT'S WATCH CHRONO-AUTOMATIC – REF. IW371704

The Pilot's Watch Chrono-Automatic features a robust mechanical chronograph with day and date indicator. It houses the IWC 79320 caliber with 25 jewels, 44 hours of power reserve and features a soft inner iron case to protect against magnetic fields. With its cockpit look, this watch has outstanding readability.

IWC

PORTUGUESE CHRONO-AUTOMATIC – REF. IW371431

This 18K white-gold Portuguese Chrono-Automatic features the classic pocket-watch format on the wrist. It features a mechanical chronograph movement and a small seconds hand with stop function. This watch houses the IWC 79350 caliber with 31 jewels and 44 hours of power reserve.

JAEGER-LECOULTRE

AMVOX2 CHRONOGRAPH CONCEPT

One of Jaeger-LeCoultre's most dramatic innovations, the Amvox2 Chronograph Concept driver's watch features a patented technical breakthrough: the vertical-trigger chronograph. This mechanism makes it possible to start, stop and reset the chronograph simply by pressing on the sapphire crystal, eliminating the need for pushbuttons. Available in a limited series, the titanium and steel watch houses the recently developed chronograph Caliber 751B, a 41-jeweled movement consisting of 272 parts. Starting is achieved by pressing the crystal at 12:00, reset at 6:00. The watch incorporates a ball-joint system that enables the case and bezel to pivot away from the shoulders of the watch, thereby activating a series of levers that transmit impulses to control the chronograph. There is also a three-position cursor that locks the column-wheel chronograph so it is not triggered by the wearer's normal arm motions.

JAEGER-LECOULTRE

DUOMETRE A CHRONOGRAPHE

Positioned upon this prestigious Ø 42mm watch's finely grained dial are two large subdials: one on the left for the conventional hour and minute and the other for the chronograph hour and minute, in which a disc indicates the minute units 0 to 9—a new display for which a patent has been filed—and jumping seconds are positioned at 6:00. Duomètre's new case is distinguished by polished welded lugs and a satin-brushed caseband, and houses the Jaeger-LeCoultre 380 'Dual-Wing' with two independent barrels, which may be admired through a sapphire crystal. As the first model in this prestigious line, Duomètre à Chronographe will be issued in pink gold and 950 platinum, as well as a 300-piece limited edition in 18K yellow gold.

JAEGER-LECOULTRE

MASTER COMPRESSOR CHRONOGRAPH

The Master Compressor Chronograph houses the automatic Jaeger-LeCoultre Caliber 751 with 272 parts and 41 jewels. Beating at 28,800 vibrations per hour, it offers 72 hours of power reserve. The chronograph features an hour and minute counter and has a center second readout and offers date, and a tachymetric scale on the inner bezel; the case features the 1000 Hours Control seal on the caseback.

JAEGER-LECOULTRE

MASTER COMPRESSOR DIVING CHRONOGRAPH LADY

Equipped with Caliber 751D with a 65-hour power reserve, this Ø 38mm Master Compressor Diving Chronograph Lady is topped with a Jaeger-LeCoultre diving bezel set with diamonds and featuring characteristic touches of color. The hours and minutes as well as the chronograph seconds are indicated by central hands, whereas the other chronograph functions are displayed in two subdials on the opaline dial: an hour counter at 9:00 and a 30-minute counter at 3:00, complete with the two-tone wind rose, which is the signature feature of the Master Compressor Diving Line. The date appears through an aperture between 4:00 and 5:00 on a disc bearing turquoise transferred numerals against a white background. This ladies' chronograph is water resistant to 30atm and available on a white articulated rubber-molded metal-frame strap, triple-link steel bracelet, or white alligator leather strap.

JAEGER-LECOULTRE

MASTER COMPRESSOR EXTREME WORLD CHRONOGRAPH

This Master Compressor Extreme World Chronograph houses the mechanical automatic Jaeger-LeCoultre Caliber 752, which is crafted, assembled and decorated by hand. It beats at 28,800 vibrations per hour, offers 72 hours of power reserve and consists of 279 parts and 41 jewels. The chronograph indicates hours, minutes, date, running indication and simultaneous indication of the 24 time zone. The dial is black for the titanium-and-steel version, gray for the 200 titanium-and-platinum pieces. The crown, equipped with a compression key, starts the watch and adjusts the date. This Master Compressor is water resistant to 100 meters, equipped with a shock absorber and features the 1000 Hours Control seal on the caseback.

LEVIEV

CHRONOGRAPH 18K WHITE GOLD BAGUETTE DIAMONDS

This watch features the self-winding mechanical LEVIEV LL 101 (base: A. Schild caliber 5008 with Lajoux-Perret complications), featuring bridges and bars with circular graining, a bi-directional oscillating weight, engraved and decorated with the Côtes de Genève pattern, blued screws, and an Incabloc shock-protection device. The chronograph has a 42-hour power reserve and beats at 28,800 vibrations per hour. The Ø 43mm case is composed of 18K white gold, set with 57 LEVIEV baguette-cut diamonds with a total weight of 3.9 carats, and fitted with a glareproof sapphire crystal. The ebony dial is in 18K gold and decorated with 96 LEVIEV baguette-cut diamonds (2 carats) and 18K white-gold indexes. The date is located at 3:00, second time zone at 6:00, small seconds at 9:00, and 30-minute counter at 12:00. The watch is water resistant up to 30 meters (approximately 99 feet) and the black alligator leather strap is saddled-stitched by hand and fastened with an 18K white-gold triple-folding clasp. Each watch is handmade in Geneva, where it is engraved with an individual serial number and produced in a limited edition.

LEVIEV

GMT CHRONOGRAPH 18K WHITE GOLD

This GMT Chronograph houses the LEVIEV LL 101, a self-winding mechanical movement (base: A. Schild caliber 5008 with complications by Lajoux-Perret) with bridges and bars with circular graining, a bi-directional oscillating weight, engraved and decorated with the Côtes de Genève pattern, blue screws, and an Incabloc shock-protection device. This LEVIEV GMT Chronograph has a 42-hour power reserve with a rate frequency of 28,800 vibrations per hour. The case measures 43mm in diameter, is composed of 18K white gold and fitted with a sapphire caseback and a glareproof sapphire crystal. The watch is water resistant up to 30 meters (approximately 99 feet) and its black alligator leather strap is saddled-stitched by hand and fastened with an 18K white-gold triple-folding clasp. Each watch is handmade in Geneva, Switzerland, where it is engraved with an individual serial number and produced in a limited edition.

LEVIEV

GMT CHRONOGRAPH MEGA YACHT®

This piece is powered by the self-winding mechanical LL 101 (base: A. Schild caliber 5008 with complications by Lajoux-Perret), which features bridges and bars with circular graining, a bi-directional oscillating weight, engraved and decorated with the Côtes de Genève pattern, blue screws, and an Incabloc shock-protection device. The GMT Chronograph MEGA YACHT® has a 42-hour power reserve with a rate frequency of 28,800 vibrations per hour. Its Ø 43mm 18K 6N red-gold case features a crown set with a LEVIEV diamond (0.25 carat), and is fitted with a glareproof sapphire crystal and a sapphire caseback. The ebony dial is in 18K gold and decorated with a guilloché pattern and 18K white-gold indexes. The date is located at 3:00, second time zone at 6:00, small seconds at 9:00, and 30-minute counter at 12:00. The MEGA YACHT® fastens to the wrist via a LEVIEV personalized natural rubber strap with an 18K 6N red-gold triple-folding clasp. Each LEVIEV MEGA YACHT® watch is crafted in Geneva, Switzerland, where it is engraved with an individual serial number and produced in a limited edition.

MONTBLANC

METAMORPHOSIS

The face of the Metamorphosis changes from a traditional hours-minutes-seconds display to a chronograph with the push of a slide. On the original dial, a regulator-style subdial with Roman numerals indicates the hours at 12:00, while a retrograde minute hand covers the area between 8:00 and 4:00 from the center of the dial. A central seconds hand and date-display hand at 6:00 complete the dial. When the wearer pushes on the slide on the side of the case, the timepiece transforms into a chronograph, a process that takes approximately 15 seconds and relies upon a unique mechanical function that operates a bit like an elevator, with "wings" on the dial that open and recede to allow the chronograph face to rise.

PANERAI

LUMINOR CHRONO DAYLIGHT – REF. PAM00250

The Panerai Luminor Chrono Daylight is a high-performance sports watch fitted with the Panerai OP XII caliber, a COSC-certified movement with chronograph functions on three counters. Two chronograph pushpieces on the three-part, 44mm brushed steel case are integrated into the patented device protecting the crown, which ensures the piece is water resistant to 10 bar. The "Daylight" inscription at 12:00 brings back to the limelight a name reserved by Officine Panerai for Sylvester Stallone, who starred in the successful film of the same title.

PANERAI

LUMINOR 1950 8 DAYS CHRONO MONOPULSANTE GMT – REF. PAM00317

Innovative yet traditional, the Luminor 1950 8 Days Chrono Monopulsante GMT has an avant-garde movement fitted inside a 44mm black ceramic case that is unmistakable for its original and functional qualities. The P.2004 caliber, executed exclusively by Officine Panerai, consists of 329 components and features a second time zone with a 24-hour indicator, seconds reset and an 8-day power reserve, which is displayed via a linear indicator on the dial. Visible through the sapphire crystal caseback, the bridges are treated with a special hard black coating. This watch stands out among other sports chronographs due to reliability, water resistance to 10 bar, and its single pushpiece controlling all functions.

PANERAI

LUMINOR 1950 8 DAYS RATTRAPANTE – REF. PAM00319

Representing the latest and most sophisticated development of the P.2004 caliber, the P.2006/3 split-seconds chronograph caliber made of 350 components is executed entirely by Officine Panerai. This exceptional hand-wound movement is contained in a classically elegant 47mm case, which is water resistant to 10 bar and crafted of brushed 18K pink gold. With an 8-day power reserve and just two pushpieces to control all of its functions (rather than the usual three), this rattrapante model is extremely rare in a limited edition of 300 pieces.

PANERAI

RADIOMIR CHRONOGRAPH – REF. PAM00288

The Radiomir Chronograph, fitted with the COSC-certified Panerai OP XII caliber, is a classic model with its own sports character. It has two chronometer pushpieces perfectly incorporated into the design of the 45mm polished steel case (at 2:00 and 4:00). These "pump" type pushpieces, coupled with the screw-down winding crown, ensure the watch's perfect water resistance to a depth of 10 bar.

PARMIGIANI FLEURIER

KALPAGRAPH – REF. PF 003912.01

Shown in polished steel on a Hermès calfskin strap, the 53.4x39.2mm Kalpagraph is powered by the automatic-winding PF Caliber 334.01 with 50-hour power reserve, 68 jewels, and beating at 28,800 vph. (The gold versions have a 22K gold oscillating weight.) The snailed chronograph counters are at 3:00 (small seconds), 6:00 (12-hour) and 9:00 (30-minute). The dial is decorated with velouté and satin sun finishes, applied indexes and luminescent delta-shaped hands. Each sapphire crystal caseback is individually numbered. Versions are available on rubber straps and in rose gold or 950 palladium.

PIAGET

LIMELIGHT EXCEPTIONAL PIECE – REF. G0A33144

This model combines luxury hand-wound watchmaking technology with fine jewelry craftsmanship. The Limelight Exceptional Piece coussin shape is set with 518 brilliant-cut diamonds (approx 2.3 carats) and 116 baguette-cut diamonds (approx 8.6 carats). The sapphire caseback reveals the 880P caliber, designed and developed entirely in-house. In addition to its chronograph and flyback functions, this movement displays the hour and minute functions, along with a 30-minute counter at 3:00, small seconds at 6:00, a second 24-hour time zone at 9:00, and date at 12:00. This 5.6mm-thick self-winding mechanical movement has two barrels and a large screw balance, and offers a 50-hour power reserve when the chronograph mode is engaged. With its column wheel and vertical coupling-clutch, the 880P caliber has all the qualities of a fine chronograph movement.

PIAGET

PIAGET POLO FORTYFIVE – REF. G0A34002

The Piaget Polo FortyFive chronograph is made of titanium, a first for the brand. It reinterprets the original aesthetic in a case that is watertight to 100 meters, extended by a strap made of injection molded rubber, and expanded to a diameter of 45mm. The case has been given a new curve that ensures a good fit to the wrist. The sapphire caseback reveals the 880P caliber, which was designed and developed entirely in-house. In addition to its chronograph and flyback functions, the movement displays the hour and minute functions, along with small seconds at 6:00, a 24-hour second time zone at 9:00, and the date at 12:00. The 5.6mm-thick self-winding mechanical movement has two barrels and a large screw balance, and offers a 50-hour power reserve when the chronograph mode is engaged. With its column wheel and vertical coupling-clutch, the 880P caliber has all the qualities of a fine chronograph movement.

RICHARD MILLE

RM 008-V2 FM TOURBILLON SPLIT SECONDS CHRONOGRAPH

Representing a totally new design of spilt-seconds chronograph movement with tourbillon escapement, the RM 008-V2 FM was the result of many years of development. Built on a gray carbon nanofiber base plate, it offers hours, minutes, seconds at 6:00, a 30-minute counter, split seconds, a power-reserve indicator and a torque indicator in dNmm. The column wheel and other parts of the movement are crafted from titanium; the exceptional movement can be seen through the sapphire glass caseback. This limited edition version dedicated to Felipe Massa sports interior flanges of green and yellow with green-filled hour and minute hands, topped off with a red Alcryn collared crown. Its unusual pushbutton arrangement is designed to optimize practical use of the chronograph and its split-seconds function.

RICHARD MILLE

RM 025 TOURBILLON CHRONOGRAPH DIVER'S WATCH

The unique case, water resistant to 300 meters, uses torque screws that can be individually and precisely tensioned with high accuracy around the exterior circumference of the case with the additional integration of the lugs into the case's torque screw system, as well as a screwed crown construction and newly designed watertight pushers. The bezel is constructed of three layers, connected with 24 screws, and turns unidirectionally following ISO 6425 norms in order to avoid timing miscalculations. In addition, the entire bezel system is screwed to the case, making it absolutely stable as well as impossible to inadvertently dislocate or loosen. Within ticks the RM 025 caliber, a carbon nanofiber tourbillon chronograph based upon the famed RM 008 caliber, which is one of the major and uniquely novel chronograph designs of the 21st century.

TAG HEUER

1911: THE TIME OF TRIP

This is the first dashboard chronograph, patented by Heuer in 1911, designed for aircraft and automobiles. With an 11cm diameter, it fits into all types of dashboards. The large hand at the center of the dial indicates the hour. The pair of small hands located at 12:00 gives the duration of the trip not exceeding 12 hours. The same pushpiece starts, stops and resets the watch to zero. A small window at 3:00 indicates whether the instrument is working correctly. Private collection of TAG Heuer museum.

TAG HEUER

1916: THE MICROGRAPH

The Micrograph, the world's first stopwatch accurate to 1/100th of a second, was patented in 1916. This model revolutionized timing, notably in Olympic sprint competitions and technical research. Private collection of TAG Heuer museum.

TAG HEUER

1933: HERVUE PAIR

In 1933 Heuer began offering the Time of Day Clock called the Hervue and the Twelve-Hour Timer called the Autavia mounted together on a double back-plate. In the late 1950s, Heuer began to refer to the Master Time clock and Monte Carlo stopwatch as the "Rally-Master" pair. Private collection of TAG Heuer museum.

TAG HEUER

1965: CARRERA DATE 45

After the launch of the Carrera series in 1964, Jack Heuer created the Carrera Dato 45 in 1965. It was one of the first chronograph models to feature a date disc (at 9:00). Previously, the date had been indicated by a hand. Private collection of TAG Heuer museum.

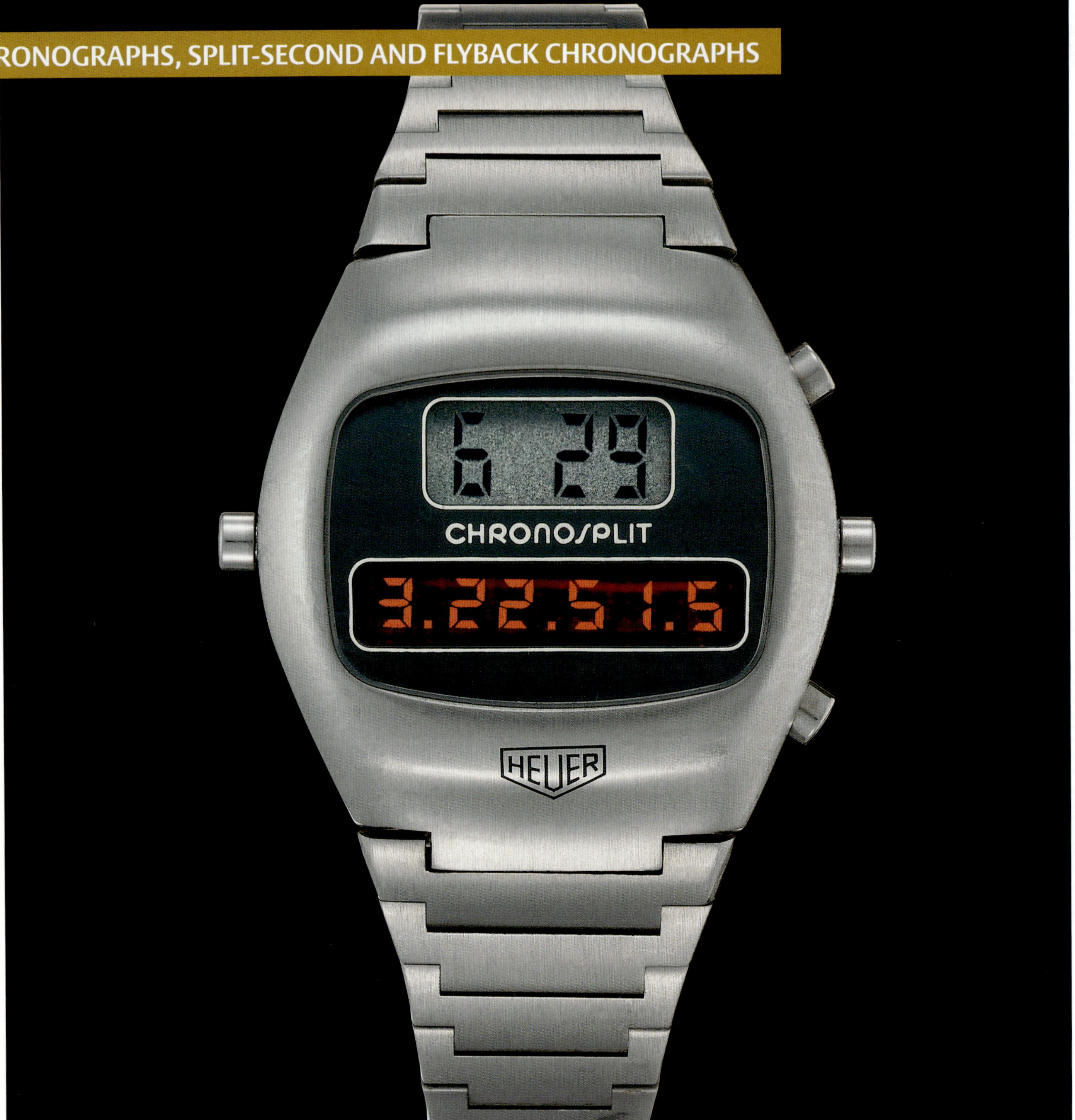

TAG HEUER

1975: THE CHRONOSPLIT

The Chronosplit is the world's first quartz wrist-worn chronograph with double digital display—LED and LCD; it is accurate to 1/100th of a second. Private collection of TAG Heuer museum.

TAG HEUER

2005: THE CALIBRE 360

The Calibre 360 beats ten times faster than the most precise mechanical wristwatch movements on the market today. It is like being endowed with two hearts—two sets of escapement mechanisms are allowed to cruise at a regular speed (28,800 oscillations/hour) under normal conditions and then accelerate to immense speed (360,000 oscillations/hour) in chronograph mode. For a movement to be this incredibly precise, it requires more than 230 components, a lightened and miniaturized hairspring and escapement mechanism (26% smaller in diameter than an ordinary balance wheel), and, finally, no fewer than three exclusive worldwide patents: 1. 1/100th-of-a-second display on a mechanical wrist-worn chronograph; 2. Bi-directional crown and rewind system: The single crown controls the automatic watch and the mechanical chronograph, as well as the watch's hour and date settings. When turned counter-clockwise, it rewinds the automatic watch; when turned clockwise, it rewinds the manual chronograph; 3. Transmission of the date from the base of the movement to the upper dial.

TAG HEUER

2006: THE CARRERA CALIBRE 360 ROSE GOLD LIMITED EDITION (500 PIECES)

At BaselWorld 2005, TAG Heuer presented the Calibre 360 Concept Chronograph, the first mechanical wrist-worn chronograph to measure and display time to 1/100th of a second. At BaselWorld 2006, privileged collectors looking for the most accurate mechanical timepiece ever made had their first glimpse of the Carrera Calibre 360 Rose Gold, in a special limited edition of only 500 pieces. Private collection of TAG Heuer museum.

TAG HEUER

2006: MONACO CALIBRE 360 LS CONCEPT CHRONOGRAPH

At BaselWorld 2006, TAG Heuer introduced the next evolutionary phase of its 1/100th of a second chronograph technology: the Monaco Calibre 360 LS (Linear Second) Concept Chronograph, a daring new timepiece with an all-new architecture proudly exposing the unparalleled Calibre 360 LS precision technology within. Private collection of TAG Heuer museum.

TAG HEUER

2007: GRAND CARRERA CALIBRE 17 RS CHRONOGRAPHE

In 2007, TAG Heuer introduced a new premium collection of sophisticated timepieces inspired by the spirit of modern GT cars. Among its many premium features is the ingenious Rotating System. This makes it possible to replace conventional hands by a disc displaying functional information even more clearly on the dial and which enables the user to read small seconds and chronograph time effortlessly, intuitively and instantaneously. Launched worldwide in 2008.

TAG HEUER

2008: TAG HEUER GRAND CARRERA CALIBRE 36 RS CALIPER CHRONOGRAPH

TAG Heuer pulled off yet another world first: powered by a column-wheel movement, the Grand Carrera Calibre 36 RS Caliper Chronograph is the only automatic chronograph capable of measuring and displaying 1/10th of a second! Visible through a tinted double sapphire crystal, the COSC-certified movement oscillates at an astonishing 36,000 vibrations per hour. This enables the central seconds hand to tick off 1/10th second intervals, giving at-a-glance readings of an unparalleled exactitude—an engineering feat of the highest level. The breathtaking creation has a stylish 43mm carbide-coated black titanium case, a Calibre 36 RS movement with a power reserve of about 50 hours, and two "Black Gold" Rotating Systems indicating the chronograph minutes at 3:00 and the chronograph hours at 6:00. It also features a linear second at 9:00. Another principle design innovation is the way in which it displays this information. TAG Heuer has developed an exclusive Rotating Scale that permits a precise reading of 1/10th of a second—magnified 10X! The new titanium carbide-coated and rubber bracelet with folding buckle is another stunning innovation.

TAG HEUER

2010: THE TAG HEUER MONACO V4

For its 150th anniversary, TAG Heuer brings to the commercial market its boldest breakthrough innovation since the 1/100th-of-a-second mechanical chronograph. The first advanced integrated mechanical movement of the third millennium, TAG Heuer Monaco V4 represents a complete break with tradition and the audacious next step in mechanical movement engineering. This belt-driven wonderment, first unveiled as a Concept Watch at BaselWorld in 2004, is now industrialized and entirely hand manufactured in TAG Heuer's workshop in an exclusive luxury edition of only 150 platinum pieces. Until the V4, all modern mechanical movements, regardless of their complications, were generally based on "classic" watchmaking components, most of which date back to the 18th and 19th centuries: an energy reserve via one or several springs; a transmission using gears; and a regulatory function usually organized around a recoil escapement. For gear transmission and automatic rewinding, the V4 team set these aside and started from scratch. The result is a complete paradigm shift, two worldwide patents, and a new generation of mechanical movements.

ULYSSE NARDIN

MAXI MARINE CHRONOGRAPH – REF. 353-66/355

Presented in stainless steel, the Maxi Marine Chronograph's 41mm case houses Caliber UN-35, which is visible through the exhibition caseback and equipped with an exclusive 45-minute register. The small-seconds register is positioned at 3:00 and the date is viewed at 4:00. This Maxi Marine Chronograph is also available in 18K rose gold, on a bracelet or leather strap, and with various dial combinations.

ULYSSE NARDIN

MAXI MARINE CHRONOGRAPH – REF. 356-66-3/354

Shown in 18K rose gold, the Maxi Marine Chronograph's 41mm case houses the Caliber UN-35, which is visible through the exhibition caseback and equipped with an exclusive 45-minute register. The small-seconds register is positioned at 3:00 and the date is viewed at 4:00. This Maxi Marine Chronograph is also available in stainless steel, on a bracelet or leather strap, and with various dial combinations.

ULYSSE NARDIN

MAXI MARINE DIVER CHRONOGRAPH – REF. 8003-102-7/91

This Maxi Marine Diver Chronograph is presented in a 42.7mm, stainless steel case and topped with a unidirectional rotating bezel. Caliber UN-800 is visible through the exhibition caseback and the chronograph features central seconds and a small-seconds register at 9:00. The watch is also available in 18K rose gold, on a rubber and titanium strap, and with various dial combinations.

ULYSSE NARDIN

MAXI MARINE DIVER CHRONOGRAPH – REF. 8006-102-3A/92

This diver chronograph is presented in a 42.7mm, 18K rose-gold case and topped with a unidirectional rotating bezel. The chronograph features central seconds and a small seconds register at 9:00. Caliber UN-800 is visible through the exhibition caseback. The Maxi Marine Diver Chronograph is available in stainless steel, on a bracelet, and with various dial combinations.

VACHERON CONSTANTIN

MALTE CHRONOGRAPH – REF. 47120

The timeless classic Malte Chronograph features a hand-wound mechanical movement, Caliber 1141, with column-wheel chronograph mechanism with telemetric tachymetric scale, 30-minute totalizer and subdial for the running seconds. Its dial is engine-turned by hand and graced with applied hour markers in 18K gold. Case diameter measures 41.5mm and features a transparent caseback with sapphire crystal. The Malte Chronograph is water resistant to 100 feet and available in 18K white or pink gold.

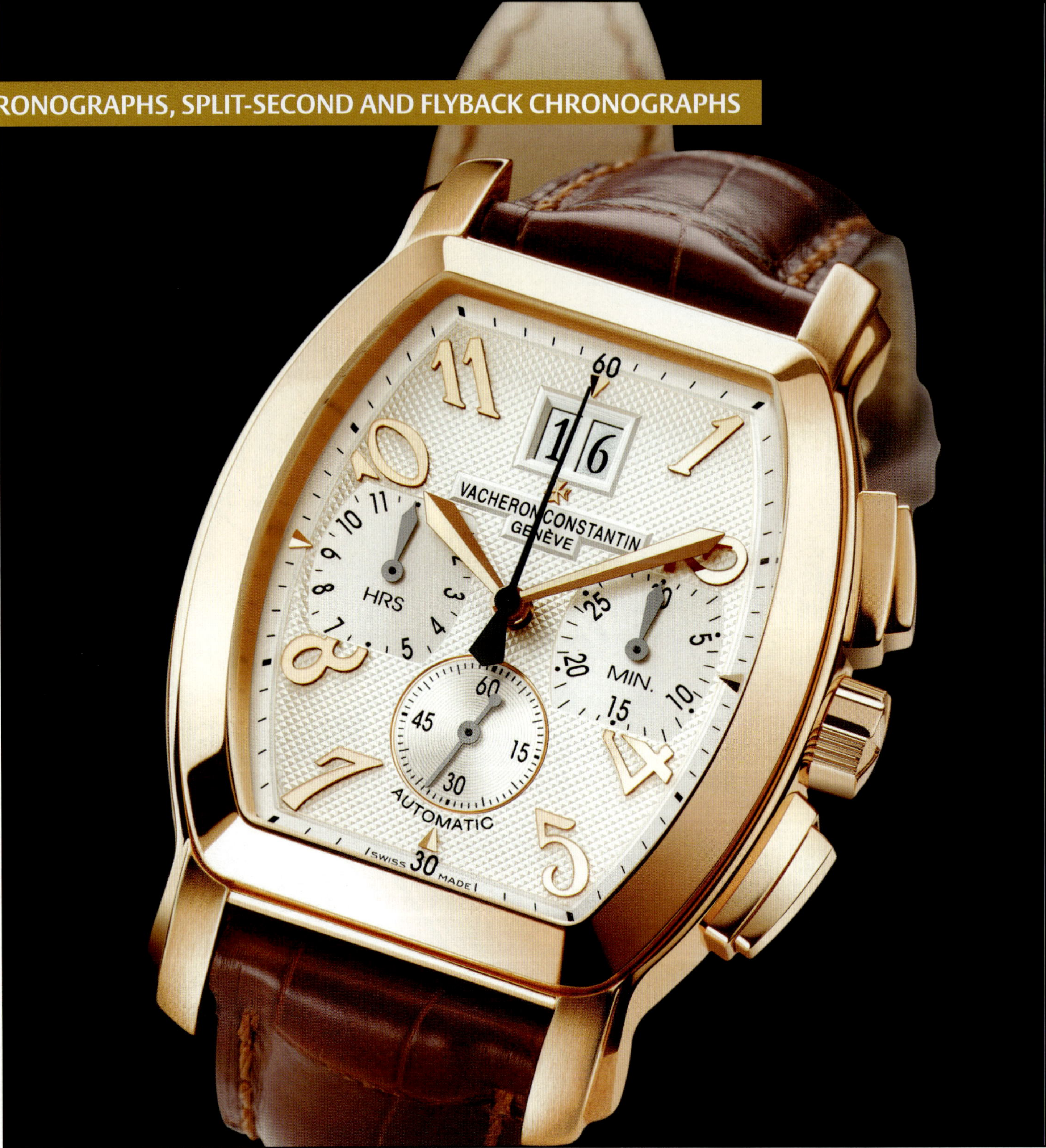

VACHERON CONSTANTIN

MALTE TONNEAU CHRONOGRAPH – REF. 49145

This 18K pink-gold Malte Tonneau Chronograph offers date indication via twin oversized apertures, in addition to the chronograph and time readouts. It is powered by the mechanical manual-winding Vacheron Constantin Caliber 1137 with 37 jewels and 40 hours of power reserve. The movement beats at 21,600 vibrations per hour. The chronograph offers a center seconds hand, 30-minute and 12-hour totalizers, and tracks to 1/6th of a second. This watch's hand-stitched alligator leather strap is secured with a pink-gold buckle.

VACHERON CONSTANTIN

MALTE TONNEAU CHRONOGRAPH – REF. 49180

The new Malte Tonneau Chronograph offers date indication via twin oversized apertures in addition to the chronograph and time readouts. It is powered by the mechanical self-winding Vacheron Constantin Caliber 1137 with 37 jewels and 40-hour power reserve. Housed in a 40x50mm white- or rose-gold case, the movement beats at 21,600 vibrations per hour. The chronograph offers a center second hand, 30-minute and 12-hour totalizers, and tracks to 1/6th of a second. This watch is water resistant to a depth of 30 meters (100 feet) and comes on a hand-stitched alligator leather strap with a gold buckle.

VACHERON CONSTANTIN

OVERSEAS CHRONOGRAPH – REF. 49150

Vacheron Constantin presents the self-winding Overseas Chronograph in a pink-gold version. The sporty, stylish 42mm case displays a Maltese cross-inspired bezel, luminescent hour markers, screw-down pushpieces, water resistance to a depth of 15atm (approximately 150 meters), and the Overseas' emblematic two-masted sailing ship motif engraved on the solid caseback. The case has a strong and instantly recognizable design and its large anthracite dial clearly sets off all the useful functions offered by the Vacheron Constantin 1137 movement, which beats at a rate of 21,600 vph. This model features two counters (30 minutes at 3:00, 12 hours at 9:00) and the date at 12:00. As with all the models in the line, the pink-gold Overseas Chronograph is equipped with an antimagnetic shield that protects the movement and complex gear trains from disturbances caused by local magnetic fields. The new Overseas Chronograph comes on either a pink-gold bracelet or a choice of two straps: hand-sewn alligator leather or dark brown vulcarbonized rubber.

VACHERON CONSTANTIN

OVERSEAS CHRONOGRAPH – REF. 49150/B01J

This 18K gold Overseas Chronograph houses the mechanical automatic-winding Vacheron Constantin Caliber 1137 with column-wheel chronograph. The movement beats at 21,600 vibrations per hour, is equipped with 37 jewels and offers 40 hours of power reserve. It is protected against magnetic fields by an inner iron case. Water resistant to 15atm, the watch offers hours, minutes, small seconds, large date and chronograph with three counters. In addition to a screw-down crown with case protector, the watch features a three-fold gasket and screw-down pushers. Its caseback is embossed with the Overseas sailboat and the hands and markers are luminescent.

ZENITH

CHRONOMASTER OPEN EL PRIMERO GRANDE DATE – MOON & SUNPHASE

The iconic ChronoMaster Open Grande Date enhanced with a new Moon & Sun Phase, an automatic column-wheel chronograph with large date and moon- and sunphase displays. Powered by the 4047 El Primero caliber made of 350 components, 32 jewels and beating at 36,000 vibrations per hour, this watch has a sapphire moonphase disc with a gold moon symbol and the patented three-disc mechanism. The 45mm case is made of 18K rose gold and reveals a silver Grain d'Orge guilloché dial. It is mounted on a black crocodile leather strap lined with silky Alzavel calfskin.

ZENITH

CHRONOMASTER T

Housing the El Primero 410 automatic chronograph movement, this ChronoMaster T is a COSC-certified chronometer. The movement consists of 357 components and 31 jewels, beats at 36,000 vibrations per hour and retains up to 50 hours of power reserve. The chronograph measures to 1/10th of second. With bi-directional winding, the central rotor is on ball bearings and the oscillating weight features a grained pattern. In addition to the seconds and chronograph function with 30-minute and 12-hour counter, the watch offers day, date and month readout, moonphase at 6:00 and tachymetric scale.

Coming up on the era of the "global village," watchmakers have developed quite a large palette of watches that display two, three, four or even twenty-four time zones. Over the last few years, we have witnessed an explosion in new models that play around with the design, display method, ease of use and other technical and aesthetic considerations. Modern brands offer a wide choice of timepieces combining multiple time zones with other functions much appreciated by travelers (alarm, 24-hour display, day/night indicator, linking the date to local time, etc.)—not to mention the numerous marriages between other useful complications such as the chronograph or perpetual calendar.

***Rolex**, Oyster Perpetual GMT-Master II*
***Jaeger-LeCoultre**, Reverso Squadra World Chronograph*
***Maurice Lacroix**, Pontos Décentrique GMT*
***JeanRichard**, GMT 2TimeZones*

***Girard-Perregaux**, ww.tc Financial*
***Concord**, C1 Worldtimer*
***Panerai**, Luminor 1950 Tourbillon GMT*

MULTIPLE TIME ZONES AND GMTs

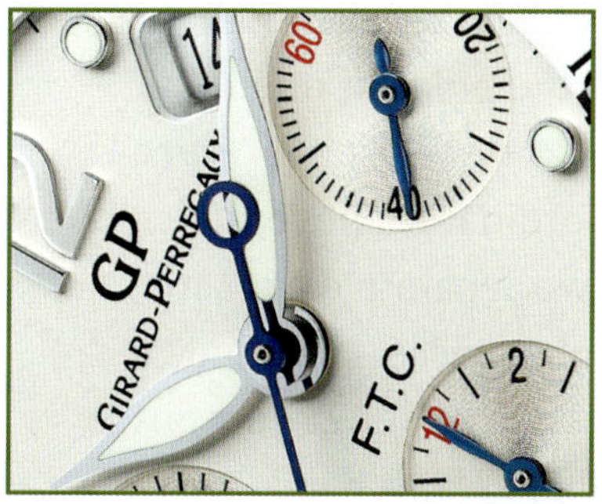

THIS PAGE
TOP LEFT
***Pierre Kunz**, Second Time Zone*

TOP RIGHT
***de GRISOGONO**, Fuso Quadrato*

CENTER
***Patek Philippe**, Calatrava Travel Time (ladies' version Ref. 4934)*

FACING PAGE
***Jaquet Droz**, Les Longitudes*

AROUND THE WORLD IN 24 HOURS

Until the end of the 19th century, each region had its own local time based, more or less, on its longitude. With an upsurge in long-distance travel, and especially the institution of the railroad, people began to feel the need for a unified time system. At the International Meridian Conference in 1884, it was decided to divide the planet into 24 time zones, taking Greenwich (at zero longitude) as the point of reference. The first dual-time-zone watches were equipped with fairly coordinated movements, displaying the time on two separate dials. Later, watchmakers perfected the device, using only a single movement, with a disengagement mechanism for the additional hour hand. Today, watchmakers rival each other to develop the most original systems for watches with two, three, four and even more time-zone indications.

THE HANDS OF TIME

The simplest system for simultaneously displaying two time zones is to add an extra hour hand in the center of the dial, taking care that it is

distinguished from the main hour hand by shape or color. This is the solution chosen by Panerai for its Luminor 1950 Tourbillon GMT, which also links a day/night indicator to the second hour hand, helping the wearer avoid calling people at inopportune times or waking them up in the middle of the night. To resolve the am/pm dilemma, other brands prefer to include a 24-hour display for the second time zone. The classic watch with a 24-hour display is the Rolex Perpetual GMT-Master, released in 1955.

The double-hour-hand system is open to a range of technical and aesthetic variations. Pierre Kunz gave its Second Time Zone model a central retrograde hand for the second time zone. On de GRISOGONO's Fuso Quadrato, the additional hand is camouflaged under a dial composed of 12 titanium "shutters" that the wearer can open at any time by sliding a bolt at 9:00.

The second time-zone hand occasionally leaves the center of the dial, occupying an off-center position in a small auxiliary display. This is the case with Piaget's new Polo FortyFive Chronograph, which positions a 24-hour display at 9:00. Regulator dials inspired Les Longitudes by Jaquet Droz. It features a subdial with Roman numerals at 3:00 for the 12-hour home time, a subdial with Arabic numerals at 9:00 for the 24-hour second time zone, and a central minute hand.

In most analog systems, the supplementary hour hand is always visible, even when the wearer does

THIS PAGE
LEFT
Jaquet Droz, *Les Douze Villes*

BELOW
Parmigiani Fleurier, *Kalpa Hemisphere*

FACING PAGE
LEFT
Jaeger-LeCoultre, *Reverso Grande GMT*

RIGHT
Piaget, *Altiplano Double Jeu*

not need it. Patek Philippe has found an ingenious and elegant way of getting around this on its Calatrava Travel Time—when the dual-time-zone system is not in use, both hour hands move in perfect synchronization, one atop the other. Montblanc's new Grand Chronographe Régulateur also features this capability, but in a subdial at 12:00.

DOUBLE HOUR/MINUTE DISPLAYS

Although the minute usually remains the same from one time zone to the next, certain brands choose to display both hours and minutes for each time zone, using two hands for each zone. This is the case with Oris and its Worldtimer caliber, whose date changes automatically, either forward or backward, when the wearer adjusts the time past midnight; on the Oris BC4 Flight Timer, a second crown placed vertically at 2:00 also permits the wearer to set the interior bezel to a third time zone. Blancpain's Léman Réveil GMT joins the two most useful complications for travelers in a single watch: the subdial at 3:00 shows home time; the alarm and the date functions on the central display are set to local (traveling) time—a detail that would have saved Phileas Fogg from thinking he had lost his bet (that he could traverse the world in 80 days) by just a few minutes, when he had actually gained a day by heading east! More daring in its design, the Pontos Décentrique GMT by Maurice Lacroix displays its two time zones on two completely off-

center subdials. de GRISOGONO strikes another blow for originality with its Meccanico dG, a completely mechanical system that joins an analog display for the first time zone with a digital display for the second (see "Retrograde Mechanisms and Jumping Hours" chapter).

Another possibility is the display of two time zones on two full dials via designs out of the ordinary—far out. Jaeger-LeCoultre uses its famous reversible case to magnificent effect on the Reverso Grande GMT, with two dials back to back. The

dial on the back also includes a "differential GMT" indicator, i.e. the number of hours between the displayed time zone and that of Greenwich Mean Time, or the time in another reference city. With its Altiplano Double Jeu, Piaget reinvents "secret" watches by offering two dials on two stacked cases, linked by a hinge and both equipped with ultra-flat mechanical movements. IceLink has chosen to indicate five time zones simultaneously on its 6TimeZone Mechanical, with the help of five small dials (plus one for seconds) and just one mechanical movement.

On the models presented up until now, the second time zone is usually adjustable in increments of one hour—leaving the minutes untouched. But there are countries in which the gap between local time and universal coordinated time (UTC), i.e. Greenwich Mean Time, is in finer increments, such as half an hour or even a quarter hour. This is the case in Iran (UTC +3h30), India (UTC +5h30) and Nepal (UTC +5h45). The Kalpa Hemisphere from Parmigiani Fleurier takes this quirk into account; its two time zones are equipped with a system that lets the wearer set the hour and the minute independently.

SYSTEMS WITH DISCS AND WINDOWS

Multiple time zones can also be displayed through discs and windows instead of hands—or in addition to them. Watchmakers usually use them in order to present additional indications such as the names or abbreviations of certain cities that represent specific time zones. The GMT 2TimeZones from JeanRichard actually has two windows, one for the hour of the second time zone, the other for the names of the 24 cities of reference. The Concord C1 Worldtimer stands out for its original Dubois-Dépraz mechanism, with a large opening in the shape of a circular arc that reveals two discs, one for the cities and one for the times. Pressing on the pushbutton allows the wearer to select the desired city; the corresponding time is then instantly displayed. On the Colosso from Hysek, the display of the second time zone is presented in an unusual manner: a system of Archimedes' screws raises or lowers two

THIS PAGE
LEFT
Hysek, *Colosso*

RIGHT
A. Lange & Söhne, *Lange 1 Time Zone*

FACING PAGE
LEFT
Jaeger-LeCoultre, *Reverso Squadra World Chronograph*

CENTER
Antoine Preziuso, *Transworld*

RIGHT
Jean-Mairet & Gillman, *GMT Sport*

arrows that point to all 24 hours. The top of the dial features a three-dimensional globe making a complete revolution every 24 hours, which can be set to local time or GMT.

Combining windows and hands, certain watchmakers are designing systems that indicate only one time zone at a time, but provide the opportunity to switch to another time zone at any moment. The model Les Douze Villes from Jaquet Droz joins a disc that bears the names of twelve cities with a jumping hour. Pressing on the pushbutton shows the desired city and its corresponding time; the large central hand indicates the minutes.

SYSTEMS WITH ROTATING BEZELS

Instead of a window, certain watches feature a rotating bezel that allows the wearer to select the name of one of the 24 reference cities. The A. Lange & Söhne Lange 1 Time Zone has two auxiliary dials equipped with hour/minute hands and day/night indicators. The permanent "home time" is usually displayed on the larger dials. Setting the second time zone (for local time) is done via a pushbutton that allows the wearer to turn the bezel bearing the names of 24 cities. The wearer can upend this system by choosing to place the local time on the main stage and synching it with the patented large date. The Swiss brand Vogard has patented a system called "timezoner®," which allows the wearer to set the second time zone with the bezel. All it takes is a pull on the security lever placed along the case and selecting the desired city while turning the bezel—the supplementary hour hand will show that city's local time on a 24-hour scale.

UNIVERSAL TIME WATCHES

In 1936, the Genevan watchmaker Louis Cottier invented an ingenious system that allowed the wearer to read the time on the whole planet in one glance at any given moment. The principle had been developed and perfected in the famous "universal time" watches from Patek Philippe such as the recent Réf. 5131. The center of the dial has hands showing the local time. It is encircled by two mobile discs, one on a 24-hour scale and the

other displaying the names of 24 reference cities. The local time is the one reflected in the city name at 12:00. To change the main time zone, one simply presses on the sole pushbutton at 10:00; the mechanism then simultaneously corrects the city disc, the 24-hour disc and the hour hand. Girard-Perregaux also offers a universal watch in its ww.tc collection (an abbreviation for "World Wide Time Control"). Designed for financial hotshots and nervous market dabblers, the ww.tc Financial also shows the times when the world's four major stock exchanges are open. On the Reverso Squadra World Chronograph, Jaeger-LeCoultre returns to its Reverso double-dialed case. The dial on the front displays the local time, complete with a day/night indicator and a large date, as well as chronograph counters. When the user rotates the case, a universal time appears in a round dial. All displays are powered by a single mechanical automatic movement.

The universal-time mechanism is not always relegated to the edges of the dial. Jean-Mairet & Gillman's Sport model displays it on a round subdial at 9:00 with a window for the date at 3:00. Audemars Piguet's Jules Audemars Metropolis joins it to a perpetual calendar. The two rotating discs for the universal time occupy a subdial at 6:00, and the three other auxiliary dials have calendar displays. On Antoine Preziuso's Transworld, the brand reinterprets the universal-time function in a very attractive way. The center of the dial is decorated with a mobile map of the globe, seen from the South Pole, which rotates every 24 hours; the (immobile) outside part of the dial has a 24-hour scale with day/night zones. This is quite an original and poetic way of reading the time, but it requires a certain familiarity with geography and the complexity of time zones!

AUDEMARS PIGUET

ROYAL OAK DUAL TIME – REF. 26120ST.OO.1220ST.01

Crafted in stainless steel, this Royal Oak Dual Time houses the self-winding caliber 2329/2846 and features a second time zone displaying hours and minutes with AM/PM indication, power reserve and date. The dial is engine-turned with Grande Tapisserie pattern and offers riveted gold indexes with facets. Also available with black or navy dial.

de GRISOGONO

MECCANICO dG

de GRISOGONO ushers in a new era with its creation of the very first mechanical digital display. A masterpiece with a movement comprising 651 elements, the Meccanico dG features two time zones: an analog display of hours and minutes in the upper part and a mechanical digital display of the second time zone in the lower part—a de GRISOGONO patent. Fawaz Gruosi has achieved what others do not dare dream: propelling haute horology into a new dimension. The exclusive hand-wound dG 042, de GRISOGONO caliber with a 35-hour power reserve is housed in a curved rectangular case of titanium and rubber. Water resistant to 30 meters, the case is fitted with a crown cover and correctors made of vulcanized rubber, a transparent black dial with green dauphine hands, and on a black natural rubber strap with titanium. Limited edition of 177 pieces.

GUY ELLIA

JUMBO HEURE UNIVERSELLE

One of the latest creations by designer Guy Ellia is the Jumbo Heure Universelle with a movement created by Frédéric Piguet. Caliber PGE 1150 features a 72-hour power reserve, a blue sapphire disc, and Côtes de Genève-finished bridges with rhodium plating. The day/night indicator, the grand date and 24 time-zone indications define its singular functions. The Jumbo Heure Universelle bears an exceptional Ø 50mm size that is rarely seen in the world of luxury watches. Mounted on an alligator strap with a folding buckle, this model is presented in black gold and is also available in pink gold and white gold.

IWC

BIG PILOT'S EDITION ANTOINE DE SAINT EXUPERY – REF. IW500422 / IW500421 / IW500420

The Big Pilot's Watch Edition Antoine de Saint Exupéry completes the limited Pilot's Watch collection, which IWC has dedicated four times to the man who brought passion to his work both as poet and pilot. In a break with the past, this edition is not dedicated to any particular work but to the author's entire literary oeuvre. With its characteristic tobacco-brown dial, "A" (for Antoine) at 9:00, and riveted calfskin strap, this immensely popular watch is recognizable at a glance to connoisseurs and collectors as an exclusive "Saint-Ex." It is also the largest pilot's watch from IWC and requires a case measuring Ø 46mm to house the IWC-manufactured 51111 caliber with automatic Pellaton winding and 7-day power reserve. The caseback is engraved with Saint-Exupéry as a military pilot. The 1,149 pieces in stainless steel, 500 in rose gold, 250 in white gold, and one unique piece in platinum—which will be sold to the highest bidder—total 1,900 for the year of the author's birth. The watch is accompanied by Saint-Exupéry's biography titled "L'archange et l'écrivain" by Nathalie Des Vallière's and produced in a special edition for IWC Schaffhausen.

PANERAI

LUMINOR 1950 3 DAYS GMT AUTOMATIC – REF. PAM00329

The P.9001 caliber, from the latest family of Officine Panerai's in-house movements, comes equipped with a GMT function with a 12-hour indicator, a seconds reset device (historically designed for watch synchronization) and a power-reserve indicator. This 227-component movement animates the Luminor 1950 3 Days GMT Automatic. To house these new movements, a specially made version of the Luminor 1950 case has been designed; it respects the proportions of the original but holds a slightly less convex sapphire crystal, which protrudes only from the bezel. The 44mm stainless steel case is water resistant to 30 bar and its sapphire crystal caseback reveals the power reserve, which can be read from a rotating disc on the movement.

PARMIGIANI FLEURIER

KALPA HEMISPHERES

This watch houses the manual-winding PF337 movement with a 50-hour power reserve and beats at 28,800 vibrations per hour. The 38-jeweled movement features Côtes de Genève decoration and hand-chamfered bridges. The watch's functions include hours, minutes, small seconds at 6:00, day/night indicator linked to local time at 6:00, second time-zone hour and minute display at 12:00, second time-zone day/night indicator at 1:00, large calendar window. It is crafted in 18K rose gold or steel. The watch is water resistant to 30 meters and features sapphire crystals with antireflection treatment.

RICHARD MILLE

RM 022 TOURBILLON 'AERODYNE DUAL TIME'

New for 2010, the RM 022 Tourbillon 'Aerodyne Dual Time' is a visual and mechanical evolution of the first Richard Mille timepiece. Within its newly sculpted case design is the manual-winding RM 021 caliber, built on a base plate of honeycombed orthorhombic titanium and carbon nanofiber. It provides hours, minutes, indicators for power reserve (approximately 70 hours), torque indicator and function indicator for Winding, Neutral, and Hand-setting operations. The finely finished pushbutton, located at 9:00, advances the second time zone in one-hour increments, utilizing a numbered, rotating sapphire disc visible at 3:00.

ULYSSE NARDIN

EXECUTIVE DUAL TIME – REF. 243-00-3/42

The 43mm Executive Dual Time features a second time zone with patented quickset on the main dial, permanent home time displayed in a window at 9:00, and big date in a double window. Caliber UN-24 is visible through the exhibition caseback. Shown in stainless steel and accented with a ceramic bezel and pushers, this watch is also available in 18K rose gold and on a leather strap.

ULYSSE NARDIN

EXECUTIVE DUAL TIME – REF. 246-00/42

The 43mm Executive Dual Time features a second time zone with patented quickset on the main dial, permanent home time displayed in a window at 9:00, and big date in a double window. Caliber UN-24 is visible through the exhibition caseback. Shown in 18K rose gold and accented with a ceramic bezel and pushers, this watch is also available in stainless steel and on a rubber strap with a ceramic clasp.

ULYSSE NARDIN

GMT ± PERPETUAL – REF. 322-66

This GMT ± Perpetual houses within its 42mm, 18K red-gold case the Caliber UN-32 with perpetual calendar, which is adjustable backwards and forwards from a single crown. The watch offers a second time zone on the main dial with patented quickset, and permanent home time is indicated by a third hand. This watch is part of a 500-piece limited edition and is also available with a silver dial.

ULYSSE NARDIN

LADY DUAL TIME – REF. 243-22B/30-02

Powered by Caliber UN-24, this 37mm Lady Dual Time in stainless steel features a unique time zone with quick setting and permanent home time, big date display, and small seconds at 6:00. The Lady Dual Time is also available in 18K rose gold, with or without a diamond bezel, and on a bracelet.

ULYSSE NARDIN

QUADRATO DUAL TIME – REF. 243-92/632

The Quadrato Dual Time measures 42x42mm and features a second time zone with patented quickset on the main dial, permanent home time displayed in a window at 9:00, and big date in a double window. Caliber UN-24 is visible through the exhibition caseback. Shown in stainless steel, this watch is also available in 18K rose gold, with various dial combinations, with or without a diamond bezel, and on a bracelet with ceramic center links.

ULYSSE NARDIN

QUADRATO PERPETUAL – REF. 326-90/92

This Quadrato Perpetual's 42x42mm, 18K rose-gold case houses the Caliber UN-32 with perpetual calendar, which is adjustable backwards and forwards from a single crown. The watch offers a second time zone on the main dial with patented quickset, and permanent home time is indicated by a third hand. Quadrato Perpetual is also available in 18K white gold, with or without a diamond bezel, with various dial combinations, and on a bracelet.

ULYSSE NARDIN

SONATA CATHEDRAL DUAL TIME – REF. 676-88/212

Presented in a 42mm, 18K rose-gold case, the Sonata is powered by Caliber UN-67. The watch is equipped with a chiming 24-hour alarm with countdown indicator and also features a dual time system with instant time-zone adjustor. Sonata is also available in 18K white gold and on a bracelet.

VACHERON CONSTANTIN
MALTE DUAL TIME REGULATOR – REF. 42005

This Malte Dual Time Regulator is presented in an 18K pink-gold half-hunter case with back lid, and houses the COSC-certified chronometer Vacheron Constantin Caliber 1206 RDT. The manually wound movement offers hours, minutes, date calendar at 6:00 and second time-zone indicator at 9:00 via a 24-hour subdial.

VACHERON CONSTANTIN

MALTE DUAL TIME – REF. 47400

This self-winding Malte Dual Time houses the Caliber 1222 and is available in 18K white or rose gold. It offers hours, minutes, date, power reserve, and second time-zone indication with day/night readout. The movement beats at 28,800 vibrations per hour and the watch is water resistant to 3atm.

VACHERON CONSTANTIN

OVERSEAS DUAL TIME – REF. 47450/B01A

Encased in 316L surgical-grade steel on a steel bracelet, this Overseas Dual Time watch is powered by the mechanical automatic-winding Vacheron Constantin Caliber 1122 with 40 hours of power reserve. The 34-jeweled movement beats at 28,800 vibrations per hour, and is protected against magnetic fields by a soft inner iron case. The watch offers hours, minutes, seconds, date, and dual-time readout with day/night indication. Eight screws fasten the bezel and the sapphire crystal is antireflective. Water resistant to 15atm, Overseas Dual Time features a silvered dial with applied, luminescent gold trapezoid markers and luminescent hands.

VACHERON CONSTANTIN
OVERSEAS DUAL TIME – REF. 47751

The Overseas Dual Time features the date, a second time zone, and a power reserve. Its 18K pink- or white-gold Ø 42mm case with clear-cut, harmonious lines gives this timepiece a very strong character. The white-gold bezel shimmers with 88 brilliant-cut diamonds and the matte-white varnished dial, with its luminescent, pink-gold leaf-shaped hands, provides perfect legibility for reading the various indications. This watch also has a solid caseback stamped with the Overseas medallion, a two-masted sailboat. Thanks to its screw-down crown, water resistance is guaranteed to a depth of 15atm, or approximately 500 feet. Each Overseas model features an antimagnetic shield that was researched and developed by Vacheron Constantin. Diamonds sparkle at their brightest when they come together with luminous materials, one of the reasons why the brand paired the Overseas Dual Time with a white vulcarbonized rubber strap in addition to the white alligator leather that features a triple-folding clasp.

ZENITH

CLASS TRAVELLER OPEN EL PRIMERO MULTICITY

This is the first automatic integrated column-wheel chronograph with a three-disc large date, world timer and power-reserve indicators. Equipped with the El Primero 4037 caliber with 351 components and 43 jewels, this 46mm Ti2 black titanium Class Traveller Open Multicity is fitted on a gray integrated hand-made alligator-leather strap with red stitching and lined with silky Alzavel calfskin. With a silver Grain d'Orge guilloché dial, this timepiece simultaneously shows the time in 24 world cities at a glance.

ZENITH

DEFY OPEN GRANDE DATE MULTICITY

This stunning timekeeper houses the automatic El Primero 4037 SC chronograph movement with large date and world timer. It is one of the most complicated World Timer calibers—351 components, 43 jewels, and a unique three-disc large date mechanism—within a 46.5mm brushed rose-gold case equipped with a unidirectional rotating bezel and screw-in pushers and crown. Water resistant to 100 meters, this watch is mounted on a brown leather strap and also available on a rubber strap or rose-gold bracelet.

PERPETUAL CALENDARS

CORUM
SUN
DAY
MONTH
AUG
RETROGRADE ANNUAL

CEO of Vacheron Constantin

Juan-Carlos Torres

'A complication is not just a product, it is a broader notion.'

Having planned for a return to more traditional demand since 2007 and 2008, Vacheron Constantin has not suffered as much as others from the financial crisis. In just a few years, the brand demonstrated the range of its horological expertise by presenting a complete collection of grand complications, the entire line of which will be unveiled in 2010.

Is the return to the classics in difficult times a real trend? Was this new look back foreseeable?
Vacheron Constantin's presentations in 2007 and 2008 were already foreshadowing this return to the classics. A little closer inspection reveals that this swing of the pendulum is not surprising—horology has always gone through cycles, and classic timelessness is always in demand. That is why Vacheron Constantin has always kept timeless, subdued watches in its collections.

In this context, are complications still fashionable?
The demand may have changed, but it still exists for exceptional timepieces and, by extension, for complications.

What is your definition of complication?
I have always advocated for a very particular notion of complication. A complication is not just a product; it is a broader notion. The challenge for the brand is not producing a complication—even a major one—but developing and preserving over time a complete collection of exceptional timepieces, from the flattest watch to the most complicated. The ability to maintain

FACING PAGE
Juan-Carlos Torres

THIS PAGE
TOP LEFT
Vacheron Constantin's headquarters

TOP RIGHT
The Self-Winding Quai de l'Île Date in palladium

CENTER
The Self-Winding Quai de l'Île Date in pink gold

LEFT
Quai de l'Île Day-Date and Power Reserve in pink gold

THIS PAGE
The Self-Winding Quai de l'Île
Date in pink gold

FACING PAGE
LEFT
Vacheron Constantin's
Caliber 1003

RIGHT
Vacheron Constantin has a long
and storied history

a timeless range of demonstrations of horological savoir-faire is a real test of the brand. In short, the most complicated thing is providing our clientele with what it wants in each segment.

The idea of diversity is important...

Let's just say that the true demonstration of our watchmaking expertise lies in the totality of our production.

Have you achieved this goal at Vacheron Constantin?

Can you ever finish a job like that? I don't think so, even after more than 250 straight years of activity—there are always innovations to incorporate, envelopes to push. That is why Vacheron Constantin works tirelessly to construct its collection of complications. Buildings are built brick by brick.

Manufacturing the watch is one thing, service after the sale is another. At Vacheron Constantin, this aspect seems essential.

Yes, it's one thing to produce a complicated watch; it's quite another to commit to repairing it year after year, decade after decade. I'm not sure that everyone understands that the second demand is no less complex than the first. At Vacheron Constantin, we attach enormous significance to this idea of after-sale service. In that arena as well, the idea of timelessness is of the utmost importance.

You mention lifetime after-sale service. What do you mean by that?

Vacheron Constantin makes it a priority to be able to repair any of our watches over its lifetime. So we do have a lifetime after-sale service guarantee for all of our models. That involves significant resources and an extremely high level of organization.

What will 2010 be like at Vacheron Constantin?

This year will be much like the brand itself—broadly embracing the vast range of complications, and demonstrating once more that haute horology is intimately entwined with the mastery of these artistic endeavors. From extra-flat movements to major complications to traditional savoir-faire, the year 2010 will be very rich for Vacheron Constantin.

President of Vacheron Constantin North America

Hugues de Pins

Hugues de Pins was named President of Vacheron Constantin in May 2009, replacing Julien Tornare, who was promoted to Director of International Sales for the Genevan brand. Benefiting from 15 years of experience in the luxury industry, de Pins did not take much time to understand the ins and outs of the North American market. His target market: in-the-know collectors. His credo: holding fast to true values. Despite the financial crisis and the accompanying upheaval, the young president, who was formerly posted in Dubai for five years for Vacheron Constantin, has faith in the future.

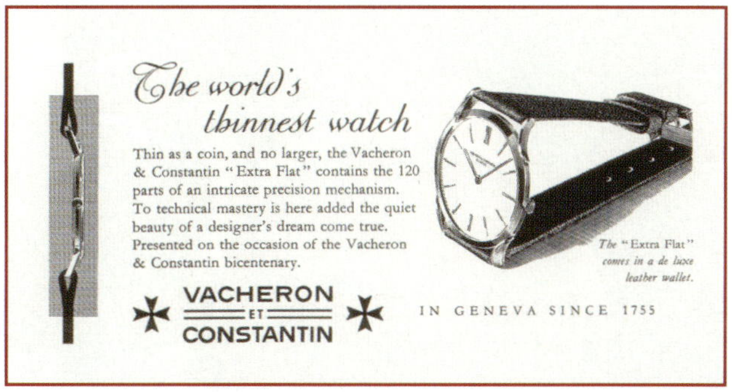

If you had to explain Vacheron Constantin to someone in a few words, what would you say?

I would tell them that Vacheron Constantin is a house with a unique, strong and recognized reputation. That reputation is due to the company's timelessness and longevity—255 years of history is not nothing.

How is Vacheron Constantin different from other haute horology brands?

I mentioned one of the most important reasons, our incredible history, but there are others. A brand's true character, like an individual's true character, is not based on a look, but on values.

What are Vacheron Constantin's values?

Firstly, a search for excellence: mechanical movements with superb finishings and decorations. We've based our whole philosophy on them. Then comes the Vacheron Constantin support for creativity and innovation: in that, our goal is to be always turned toward the future. The Quai de l'Ile and the Métiers d'Art collection, which are surprisingly daring, are perfect examples of this.

The "Métiers d'Art – Les Masques" collection pays tribute to art from different cultures...

And that is our third value: being open to the world. Of course, Vacheron Constantin is a Swiss brand, founded in Geneva, but we also have a

FACING PAGE
Hugues de Pins

THIS PAGE
TOP LEFT
Historical ultra-flat Vacheron Constantin timepiece from 1955

TOP RIGHT
1955 advertisement

ABOVE
The Vacheron Constantin Structura 10662

calling to spread horological art and culture throughout the world. That goes hand in hand with respect for and continuation of traditions. In haute horology, passing on expertise is fundamental. That is what allows the next generation to master an entire range of complications. Finally, sharing is important for us. It is a great joy to be able to share a passion with watch collectors and others who are fascinated by horology. We do a lot to promote these values and to share them: for example, we have dinners for collectors and the brand has started "The Hour Lounge," which provides an online meeting place for Vacheron Constantin fans.

What do you see as the most iconic model of the brand?

This may surprise you, but it's not the product that Vacheron Constantin promotes the most, nor is it the best known. For me, it is the Patrimony Traditionnelle Squelette Quantième Perpétuel. The platinum version is magnificent! It combines all the savoir-faire, all the qualities of an haute horology watch: the movement is produced entirely in-house, the art of skeletonization is at a whole new level, the perpetual calendar is brilliantly highlighted. It is a rare, valuable timepiece, timeless and elegant.

What is Vacheron Constantin's position on the North American market?

Vacheron Constantin has a history in the United States that stretches back to the middle of the nineteenth century—the beginning of the industrial age and the emergence of the first modern capitalists, bankers and industrialists. The American market is a market of collectors. Even though Vacheron Constantin is becoming more and more well known, it is largely known only to the cognoscenti of the watch world. With only 44 points of sale in North America, we are

FACING PAGE
TOP RIGHT
Archival photo of Vacheron Constantin boutique.

CENTER
Vacheron Constantin's Les Masques series.

THIS PAGE
RIGHT
The process of skeletonization.

CENTER
American 1921 model

BOTTOM
Vacheron Constantin Patrimony Traditionnelle
Quantième Perpétuel Squelette

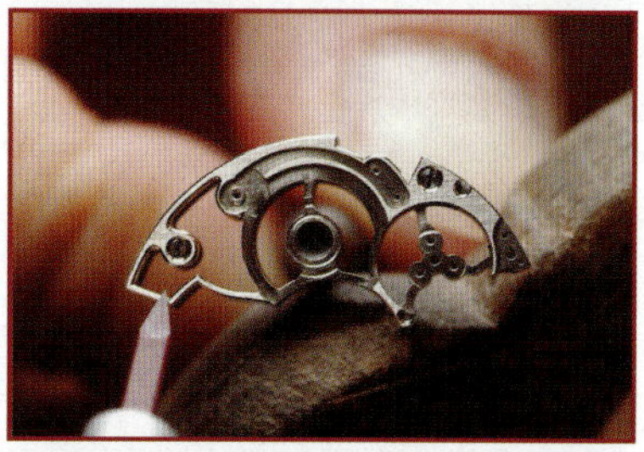

building a highly selective retail network. However, we are very well known among retailers.

How does the American market perceive Vacheron Constantin?

In the United States, our undisputed best seller is the American 1921. The Quai de l'Ile also sells well, as it does everywhere it is available—which is only 100 points of sale throughout the world, of which 17 are in the United States. Our American market is essentially a clientele of collectors, and their horological knowledge is unbelievable. Our American customers are also very loyal, and not as "trendy" as one might think. They are actually quite classic in their tastes.

Overall, how would you say the company has evolved over the past five years?

The 250th anniversary of Vacheron Constantin marked a real turning point for the brand; this event allowed us to refocus our attention on mastery of complications and multi-complications. Since then, we have invested a lot in the production process, both in Geneva and Vallée de Joux. We have a dual objective: we want to produce most of our movements in-house, and for all of them to earn the Geneva Seal. Of course, our clients view both goals extremely positively.

Our calendar system poses several challenges to watchmakers—especially the variable length of the months and the occasional occurrence of February 29. Perpetual calendar watches masterfully conquer this difficulty by continuously displaying the date, the day, the month and the year, all the while taking leap years into account. Long associated with a rather subdued, classical aesthetic, perpetual calendars are now undergoing a creative renaissance, with imaginative displays and many different technical optimizations. "Annual calendars" are also becoming quite popular—as the name suggests, they require just one correction per year.

***Piaget**, Emperador Coussin Perpetual Calendar*
***Pierre DeRoche**, GrandCliff Annual Calendar*
***de GRISOGONO**, Instrumento Novantatre*
***Girard-Perregaux**, 1966 Annual Calendar and Equation of Time*

***Hermès**, Dressage Annual Calendar*
***Corum**, Romvlvs Retrograde Annual Calendar*
***Patek Philippe**, Ref. 5135*

PERPETUAL CALENDARS

THIS PAGE
TOP LEFT
***H. Moser & Cie**, Moser Perpetual 1*

TOP RIGHT
***Breguet**, Classique*

FACING PAGE
LEFT
***Jaeger-LeCoultre**, Master Grande Tradition Tourbillon à Quantième Perpétuel*

RIGHT
***IWC**, Da Vinci Perpetual Calendar Digital Date-Month*

ETERNITY IN YOUR POCKET—MORE OR LESS

Calendar indications made a relatively early appearance on pocket watches. In the 17th century, astronomical watches were invented that displayed the hour, the date, the day and the month, as well as moonphase and the signs of the Zodiac. Watches with the date met with great success, but they were more often "simple" calendar watches, needing a manual correction at the end of each month with fewer than 31 days, or five times a year—as is the case with most current calendar wristwatches. Not until the end of the 18th century were "perpetual" calendars developed; these took the leap-year cycle into account and could handle months that were 28, 29, 30 or 31 days long, as well as the quadrennial return of February 29. This sophisticated function demands incredible feats of miniaturization—especially for wrist-worn watches—because the movement must possess a mechanical "memory" of 1,461 days (four years). Contrary to popular belief—a belief that watch brands refrain from correcting—perpetual calendars are not actually designed to function "from here to eternity," and each must be adjusted by one day on March 1, 2100. Because of a correction made to the Gregorian calendar, century-end years such as 1900, 2100 and 2200 are not leap years, though century-end years divisible by 400 are. Extremely rare "secular calendars" that take this quirk into account do exist.

ON DISPLAY

Perpetual calendars are known for their multiple displays—date, month, day, year and leap year—usually completed by the indication of the lunar cycle (see "Moonphase" chapter). These displays may use hands or discs with a system of windows. The classic models most often present three (or sometimes four) round subdials placed symmetrically around the center of the dial.

Jaeger-LeCoultre has reinterpreted this canonical aesthetic in its new Master Grande Tradition Tourbillon à Quantième Perpétuel with three auxiliary dials: month at 12:00, day at 3:00 and date at 9:00—the lower part of the dial shows off the large titanium tourbillon cage, surrounded by a Clous de Paris decoration. Playing with this geometry, Breguet offers a Classique men's watch with indications of the day, month, leap year and date aligned on the same vertical axis. For the Moser Perpetual 1, released in 2009, H. Moser & Cie offers an original, extremely purified vision of the perpetual calendar. The month is displayed via a small central hand pointing at one of the 12 hour-indexes—the numeral 5 for May, 10 for October, etc. Day and year indications have been deemed superfluous, and thus omitted. The date display employs an ingenious patented system called the "Flash Calendar," which allows the watch to go directly from the 28, 29, 30 or 31 to the first of the next month, without touching on the irrelevent dates in between. The calendar can be adjusted forwards or backwards at any moment, even around midnight—an activity that is strictly forbidden on most perpetual calendars for fear of damaging the movement. Also in 2009, IWC replaced the subdials with two double windows indicating the date and the month with two digits on the Da Vinci Perpetual Calendar Digital Date-Month.

THIS PAGE
TOP LEFT
***Jaquet Droz**, Perpetual Calendar*

TOP RIGHT
***Blancpain**, Perpetual Calendar with under-lug correctors*

CENTER
***Parmigiani Fleurier**, Toric Corrector Minute Repeater and Perpetual Calendar*

FACING PAGE
TOP
***Vacheron Constantin**, Malte Openface Retrograde Perpetual Calendar*

LEFT
***Patek Philippe**, Grande Complication Ref. 5104*

RIGHT
***Maîtres du Temps**, Chapter Two*

TECHNICAL WONDERS

In its Perpetual Calendar with under-lug correctors, Blancpain joins classic design with technical innovation. Instead of placing the correctors on the side of the case, the brand has developed an unprecedented system allowing it to incorporate the correctors in the four lugs that attach it to the strap, on the wrist side. A simple push corrects the date, day, month, leap-year cycle or moonphase. The Daniel Roth Instantaneous Perpetual Calendar is equipped with an unusual function: the instantaneous movement of the counters' hands at midnight each night. Its beautifully made automatic movement is partially visible through the skeleton dial. Patek Philippe's Ref. 5207 also boasts an instantaneous change of all the indications at midnight, but here it is applied—as an additional challenge—to a window display system. This multi-complication also possesses a minute repeater and a tourbillon.

RETROGRADE AND ROLLING SYSTEMS

Today, the perpetual calendar gives rise to all kinds of flights of fancy in terms of design and display. To vary the aesthetic of the dials, many watchmakers use "retrograde" systems (see also "Retrogrades and Jumping Hours" chapter). Such is the case with the Toric Corrector Minute Repeater and Perpetual Calendar from Parmigiani Fleurier, equipped with an in-house movement and a pusher that can instantly correct all the day/date functions and moonphase. Jaquet Droz, whose watches all boast an unusual aesthetic, offers a Perpetual Calendar with double retrograde display across the top of the dial—the day to the left, the date to the right. Piaget's Emperador Coussin Perpetual Calendar, with its extra-flat manufacture movement, also features a retrograde day and date display; the display of a second 24-hour time zone allows the wearer to travel the globe without undoing the calendar indications. 2009 was also marked by another "alternative" display, on the Chapter Two,

Roger Dubuis and Peter Speake-Marin) for the Maîtres du Temps brand. Other than the large date at 12:00, this model displays the months and the days all in letters (on two rollers placed at 12:00 and at 6:00) with two correctors incorporated into the caseback.

CLEAR AMBITION

Another popular trend is to apply different levels of transparency. Vacheron Constantin equipped its platinum Malte Openface Retrograde Perpetual Calendar with a double sapphire crystal that reveals a direct view into the heart of the mechanism. The retrograde date is displayed on

LEFT
Vacheron Constantin, *Patrimony Traditionnelle Skeleton Perpetual Calendar*

CENTER
Jaeger-LeCoultre, *Master Eight Days Perpetual Skeleton*

RIGHT
Omega, *De Ville Hour Vision Annual Calendar*

half of the dial. Small subdials use tiny white boards to indicate the day, month, and leap-year cycles painted in black on one of the sapphire crystals. The Genevan manufacture has also given the perpetual calendar on its Patrimony Traditionnelle Skeleton Perpetual Calendar a spectacular new design with an entirely open-worked and engraved movement. Patek Philippe has performed magic with its Grande Complication Ref. 5104, equipped with a transparent dial that reveals the mechanism in action. To meet this challenge, the manufacture invented an unusual display system: the names of the days and months, as well as the number in the leap-year cycle, are printed directly on the sapphire crystal; on these three circles are placed three small sapphire discs with a black rectangular area. As it turns, this dark "palette" sets off the white transfer by contrast. This platinum timepiece is also equipped with a minute repeater. The Master Eight Days Perpetual by Jaeger-LeCoultre, with an eight-day power reserve, has been released in a dazzling skeleton version, whose daringly curved bridges evoke latitude and longitude. Another player in the transparency game is the ingeniously constructed 220.Y Tourbillon 8-Day Perpetual Calendar from Daniel Roth. The timepiece swings upwards on a hinge at 12:00, revealing a second dial on the other side, with perpetual calendar and moonphase display.

TRIUMPH OF THE ANNUAL CALENDAR

Halfway between the simple calendar and the perpetual calendar lies the annual calendar, which recognizes months that last 30 or 31 days but must be corrected once a year at the end of February. The Dubois Dépraz manufacture was among the first to propose this mechanism, in a modular form. In 1996, Patek Philippe was equally original, presenting its patented Annual

LEFT
***Patek Philippe**, Grande Complication*

RIGHT
***Girard-Perregaux**, Cat's Eye Annual and Zodiac Calendar*

Calendar—an ingenious system hiding a high level of technical sophistication. The mechanism has been created since then with different cases and varied displays, in versions for men and women. In the last few years, several other brands have launched new perpetual calendar models with original looks, such as Instrumento Novantatre from de GRISOGONO, which features a large double window for the date, an arc-shaped opening for the number of the month and oversized numerals for 9 and 3. The Dressage Annual Calendar by Hermès, with an exclusive Vaucher Manufacture Fleurier movement, is distinguished by its retrograde display of the date with a hand sweeping across a 270° arc, as well as its two visible discs for the day and month—a principle that also guides the recent Dressage Perpetual Calendar. Pierre DeRoche, a brand founded by the brother of the directors of Dubois Dépraz, offers the GrandCliff Annual Calendar. This timepiece, equipped with an exclusive Dubois Dépraz caliber, adds to the annual calendar a chronograph with flyback function, 60-minute and 6-hour retrograde counters, and large date. To celebrate its 160th anniversary in 2008, Omega expanded its De Ville Hour Vision collection with a limited edition perpetual calendar. The watch beats to the rhythm of an automatic Omega caliber equipped with the brand's famous exclusive coaxial escapement. Corum recently added to one of its flagship collections a new model called Romvlvs Retrograde Annual Calendar. Girard-Perregaux went for two new calendar models in 2009 with its 1966 Annual Calendar and Equation of Time (see "Equation of Time" chapter), as well as a ladies' model, Cat's Eye Annual and Zodiac Calendar.

A. LANGE & SÖHNE

LANGEMATIK PERPETUAL

Powered by the self-winding Caliber L922.1 SAX-0-MAT, the Langematik Perpetual is the world's first self-winding wristwatch with an outsize date and a perpetual calendar featuring separate pushpieces for individual corrections of the calendar indications (date, day of the week, month, leap year, and moonphase displays), as well as a main pushpiece for advancing all displays. Caliber L922.1 SAX-O-MAT has a 46-hour power reserve, stop seconds with a patented zero-reset mechanism, plates and bridges made of untreated German silver, and a hand-engraved balance cock. The Langematik Perpetual's three-piece pink-gold case is fitted with antireflective sapphire crystals on the front and back, and a crown for winding the watch and setting the time. The solid silver and argenté dial is topped with luminous pink-gold hands. The watch's crocodile strap is secured via a solid gold buckle.

AUDEMARS PIGUET

JULES AUDEMARS PERPETUAL CALENDAR – REF. 26390OR.OO.D088CR.02

The ultra-thin profile of this watch is truly fascinating, and it is even more surprising when one considers that such a slim case houses the automatic-winding 2120/2802 movement that indicates the day, date, month, moonphase and leap-year cycle—all thanks to a mechanism barely 4mm thick! Also available with a brown dial.

AUDEMARS PIGUET

ROYAL OAK SKELETON PERPETUAL CALENDAR – REF. 25829PT.OO.0944PT.01

This Royal Oak model displays the date, the day of the week, the month, the four-year leap-year cycle and the moonphase. Its automatic-winding 2120/2802 movement possesses an engraved rotor in 21K gold. The case and the bracelet are in 950 platinum and the screws that hold the case together are in 18K gold. Water resistant to 20 meters, the Royal Oak Skeleton Perpetual Calendar boasts a transparent sapphire dial that reveals the delicate engraving on the movement. This model is also available in stainless steel or 18K pink gold.

BLANCPAIN

VILLERET LADY'S ULTRA-SLIM PERPETUAL CALENDAR

With unfailing precision, this slim case accommodates no fewer than 248 components that enable Calibre 5621 to give meticulous cadence to the hours and minutes, as well as the day of the week, date, month, leap years and moonphases. This caliber is housed within an 18K gold case with a diameter of 34mm. Water resistant to 30 meters, the case is fitted with a sapphire crystal, glareproof on both sides, and with a glareproof sapphire caseback.

BOVET

FLEURIER COMPLICATIONS: PERPETUAL CALENDAR, RETROGRADE WITH MOONPHASE

This 42mm BOVET perpetual calendar is a magnificent demonstration of how to display a full calendar and moonphases in letters, numbers and images. Retrograde indications, in which the hand flies back to the beginning of a scale after reaching a prescribed end, are popular because they challenge our view of time as a constant rotation of passing minutes, hours, days and months. It's simple enough, mechanically, to advance the date hand every 24 hours against a spring, which is released by the perpetual-calendar mechanism at the end of the month (28, 29, 30 or 31 days) so that it flicks back to the beginning. The difficulty that underlies all such retrograde mechanisms is that the hand flies back (through an arc of 225° in this watch) with such force that it bounces up again on the scale and catches on the second or date. BOVET gets around the bounce-back problem by slowing the return of the date hand with a train of wheels. The blue guilloché dial brings to the timepiece a subtle shining.

BREGUET

CLASSIQUE GRANDE COMPLICATION – REF. 5327BR/1E/9V6

This Classique Grande Complication wristwatch is crafted in 18K yellow, white or rose gold, and houses a thin, engraved automatic movement with perpetual calendar, precise moonphase, 46-hour power reserve, and 3Hz balance frequency. Its engine-turned dial is in silvered 18K gold with a chapter ring displaying Roman numerals, central months indication, and showing dates, days and leap years on three subdials, power-reserve indicator at 10:30, and moonphase at 1:30. It also features a secret signature. The engine-turned caseback is sapphire crystal and the case is water resistant to 30 meters.

CHOPARD

L.U.C LUNAR ONE WITH ORBITAL MOONPHASE – REF. 161894-9001

Measuring Ø 11.4mm and 20mm thick, the L.U.C Lunar One is powered by the mechanical self-winding L.U.C 96 QP movement. The 354-part movement is a COSC-certified chronometer and bears the Poinçon de Genève quality hallmark. It has a power reserve of approximately 65 hours and beats at 28,800 vibrations per hour. The L.U.C Lunar One features a perpetual calendar, date at 12:00, day of the week, leap year, 24-hour indication, power-reserve indicator, and moophase, which is presented in an extremely precise and original way. The moonphase rotates around the axis of the small seconds display, hence "orbital." This system's accuracy measures a mere 57.2-second difference per lunar cycle (or one day every 122 years). Water resistant to 30 meters, the watch is created in two limited editions: 250 pieces in pink gold and 250 pieces in 950 platinum.

GUY ELLIA

TIME SPACE QUANTIEME PERPETUEL

The Time Space, original ambassador of Guy Ellia, is transformed into a perpetual calendar for this version. A mechanical hand-winding Frédéric Piguet caliber harbored in a Ø 46.8mm black-gold case allows the owner to read the hour, minute, day, month, date and moonphases, while taking leap years into account. With a brushed bottom plate of 7.75mm, this watch symbolizes elegance, complexity and thinness. A specific automatic winder is integrated to the watch box. This model is also available in white gold and pink gold.

GUY ELLIA

TIME SPACE QUANTIEME PERPETUEL – FULL SET

The Time Space, original ambassador of Guy Ellia, is transformed into a perpetual calendar for this version. A mechanical hand-wound Frédéric Piguet caliber harbored in a Ø 46.8mm white-gold case allows the owner to read the hour, minute, day, month, date and moonphase, while taking leap years into account. With a brushed bottom plate of 7.75mm, this clear allusion to the Couteaux watches symbolizes elegance, complexity and thinness. A specific automatic winder is integrated into the watch box and this model is also available in pink gold.

IWC

DA VINCI PERPETUAL CALENDAR DIGITAL DATE-MONTH – REF. IW376101

In 1884, IWC secured the rights to the Pallweber system developed by Joseph Pallweber and started producing the first "digital" watches in IWC's history. Rather than an analog display with hands, digits were presented in separate windows; only the seconds were shown via a hand. Now, 125 years later, IWC presents the Da Vinci Perpetual Calendar Digital Date-Month with large-figure digital displays for the date and the month. The power required to switch both month and date discs at the end of the month is accumulated over the course of the entire month in a quick-action switch specially developed for this purpose. At the end of the month, the energy is released and displays are advanced, even the digital leap year if necessary. The chronograph can run continuously without having any noticeable effect on the watch's rate and, thanks to the flyback function, can be reset to zero without being stopped. The new IWC-manufactured 89800 caliber consists of 474 individual parts and builds up a power reserve of 68 hours. The movement is a massive watchmaking achievement.

IWC

DA VINCI PERPETUAL CALENDAR EDITION KURT KLAUS – REF. IW376205

IWC owes a great deal to Kurt Klaus, who spent more than fifty years with the company as a highly successful designer and inventor. His designs included an easy-to-use perpetual calendar that could be set using the crown and a moonphase display that required no correction buttons. The Da Vinci Perpetual Calendar Edition Kurt Klaus pays a fitting tribute and, for the first time, the special limited edition (originally available in stainless steel) is joined by a stimulating combination of a warm red-gold case and black dial. If the watch is not worn for some time, the displays—date, day, month, four-digit year and perpetual moonphase—can be advanced simultaneously, a day at a time, via the crown. Klaus's signature is located in the bottom right-hand corner of the dial, while the back features his engraved portrait.

IWC

PORTUGUESE PERPETUAL CALENDAR – REF. IW502218

This 18K white-gold Portuguese Perpetual Calendar watch is powered by the brand's 5000 caliber and offers ingenious displays. It houses the Pellaton winding mechanism with an entirely new moonphase display, a world-first patent. The Portuguese Perpetual Calendar offers a 7-day power reserve, all perpetual calendar readouts and moonphase.

JAEGER-LECOULTRE

MASTER EIGHT DAYS PERPETUAL – REF. 161242A

Classically designed, this Master Eight Days Perpetual houses the mechanical manually wound Caliber 876-440B that is crafted, assembled and decorated by hand. It beats at 28,800 vibrations per hour and consists of 262 parts and 37 jewels. It offers hours, minutes, date, month, day of week, four-digit year display, moonphase, power reserve, and a day/night indicator with red safety zone for changing of the perpetual calendar. The watch is crafted in 18K pink gold or platinum.

JAEGER-LECOULTRE
MASTER GRANDE REVEIL

The Ø 43mm Master Grande Reveil offers both an alarm function (with chime or vibration modes) and perpetual calendar. Available in stainless steel, pink gold or 950 platinum, it houses the mechanical automatic Caliber 909/1 with 363 parts and and 36 jewels, and offering a 24-hour indicator and moonphase indicator for each hemispheres. The 1000 Hours Control seal is engraved on the caseback of each platinum and pink-gold version.

PARMIGIANI FLEURIER

TORIC RETROGRADE PERPETUAL CALENDAR – REF. PF002614

This mechanical self-winding watch houses the PF333 caliber, created in house with a 22K gold oscillating weight and hand-beveled bridges. Beating at 28,800 vibrations per hour, the watch offers day, month, leap year, moonphase indicator and retrograde date. It is crafted in 18K rose gold with a slate-gray and rose-gold dial.

PATEK PHILIPPE

GONDOLO CALENDAR – REF. 5135P

Crafted in platinum and set with a single brilliant at 6:00, this Gondolo Calendar is powered by the automatic-winding Patek Philippe 324 S QA LU 24H caliber decorated with a Côtes de Genève pattern and beveled. The movement with its 21K gold rotor is visible through a sapphire caseback. The watch offers hours, minutes and seconds, annual calendar and 24-hour indication. The month readout is at 2:00, moonphase with 24-hour is at 6:00, day of week is at 10:00, and date is at 12:00. The solid gold dial with slate-gray sun-patterned finish features white-gold markers and diamonds. Hallmarked with the Geneva Seal, this tonneau-shaped watch is also available in pink gold, white gold or yellow gold with different dial colors.

PATEK PHILIPPE

GONDOLO CALENDAR – REF. 5135R

This Gondolo Calendar houses the mechanical automatic-winding Patek Philippe 324 S QA LU 24H manufacture caliber decorated with a Côtes de Genève pattern and featuring a 21K gold rotor. It offers hours, minutes, seconds, 24 hours and annual calendar (date, day, month, moonphase, and takes the days of a month into account over a whole year, except for February). It is crafted in an 18K pink-gold two-piece tonneau-shaped case with curved sapphire crystal, pink-gold crown and screw-on caseback, displaying the movement through a sapphire crystal. It is water resistant to 2.5atm.

PATEK PHILIPPE

PERPETUAL CALENDAR – REF. 5140

Housed in a three-part 18K white-gold 37.2mm case, this Perpetual Calendar beats to the mechanical automatic-winding Patek Philippe 240 Q caliber. The movement, with 22K off-centered micro-rotor, features the Geneva Seal and is decorated with a Côtes de Genève pattern. The perpetual calendar offers 24-hour indication, day, date, month, year, and moonphase, plus hour and minute. Water resistant to 2.5atm, the watch features a silvered solid gold dial with applied gold markers and hands.

PIAGET

EMPERADOR PERPETUAL CALENDAR – REF. G0A33018

Mechanically programmed to cope with the irregularities of our Gregorian calendar up until the year 2100, the perpetual calendar is one of the major complications of the watchmaking art, as well as one of the most widely used. Measuring 5.6mm thick, the Piaget 855P self-winding movement was designed, developed and produced entirely in-house. It displays the hours, minutes, small seconds at 4:00, month and leap years at 12:00, and retrograde day of the week and date displays at 9:00 and 3:00, respectively. In addition to the latter retrograde indications, this 855P movement stands out from most ordinary perpetual calendars with the addition of a double-hand dual time-zone display in a subdial at 8:00. The self-winding Piaget 855P movement beats at a cadence of 21,600 vibrations per hour and is endowed with an approximately 72-hour power reserve. Shown in white gold.

ULYSSE NARDIN

GMT ± PERPETUAL – REF. 320-60/32

This GMT ± Perpetual houses within its 42mm, 18K white-gold case the Caliber UN-32 with perpetual calendar, which is adjustable backwards and forwards from a single crown. The watch offers a second time zone on the main dial with patented quickset, and permanent home time is indicated by a third hand. This watch is part of a 60-piece limited edition and is also available on a bracelet.

ULYSSE NARDIN

GMT ± PERPETUAL – REF. 326-60/62

This GMT ± Perpetual houses within its 42mm, 18K rose-gold case the Caliber UN-32 with perpetual calendar, which is adjustable backwards and forwards from a single crown. The watch offers a second time zone on the main dial with patented quickset, and permanent home time is indicated by a third hand. This model is also available in 18K white gold, on a bracelet and with various dial combinations.

ULYSSE NARDIN

QUADRATO PERPETUAL – REF. 326-90/91

This Quadrato Perpetual's 42x42mm, 18K rose-gold case houses the Caliber UN-32 with perpetual calendar, which is adjustable backwards and forwards from a single crown. The watch offers a second time zone on the main dial with patented quickset, and permanent home time is indicated by a third hand. Quadrato Perpetual is also available in 18K white gold, with various dial combinations, with or without a diamond bezel, and on a bracelet.

ULYSSE NARDIN

MAXI DIVER PERPETUAL – REF. 333-90/3

This Maxi Diver Perpetual is powered by the Caliber UN-33 with perpetual calendar, which is adjustable backwards and forwards from a single crown. The 45mm titanium case is fitted with a turning bezel and black carbon-fiber structured dial. The watch is limited to 500 pieces and each comes with both a titanium/steel bracelet and a rubber/titanium strap.

VACHERON CONSTANTIN

PATRIMONY TRADITIONNELLE SKELETON PERPETUAL CALENDAR – REF. 43172

The Patrimony Traditionnelle Skeleton Perpetual Calendar houses the 1120 QP SQ self-winding caliber with 36 jewels, a 40-hour power reserve, and stamped with the prestigious Geneva Seal. The movement is distinguished by the Art Nouveau motif of its beautifully finished engraving; the elegant shapes of the Eiffel Tower inspired Vacheron Constantin's master engravers. The dial was designed to provide an excellent view of the skeleton movement and perfect legibility of the perpetual calendar indications. Vacheron Constantin designed a transparent sapphire dial enhanced by a silvered ring with the hour markers and minute track. The perpetual calendar indications sit on this transparent dial, consequently gaining in both size and legibility. This watch is available in 950 platinum or in 18K rose gold.

ZENITH

ACADEMY QUANTIEME PERPETUEL EL PRIMERO BLACK TIE

Crafted in platinum, this Academy Quantième Perpétuel El Primero Black Tie is powered by the proprietary El Primero 4003 automatic chronograph movement with perpetual calendar. The COSC-certified chronometer caliber consists of 321 components, including 31 jewels. With 50 hours of power reserve, the watch indicates date, moonphases, day, month and leap year, chronograph functions, and tachymeter readout. The case's 60 baguette-cut Top Wesselton diamonds (5.4 carats) encircle a solid gold dial with genuine Polynesian mother-of-pearl and 11 diamond indexes. It is released in an exclusive limited and numbered edition on a handmade lambskin "Black Tie" leather strap with satin trim.

ZENITH

ACADEMY QUANTIEME PERPETUEL EL PRIMERO CONCEPT

This limited edition 18K white-gold Academy Quantième Perpétuel El Primero Concept houses the automatic El Primero 4003 C (a COSC-certified chronometer with perpetual calendar that beats at 36,000 vph and carries 50 hours of power reserve), which is visible through the caseback. The movement with circular-grained mainplate is composed of 321 parts including a 22K gold oscillating weight with Côtes de Genève guilloché pattern. The perpetual calendar indicates date (in a ring around the 30-minute counter at 3:00), moonphase (inside the 12-hour counter at 6:00), day at 9:00 and month and leap year at 12:00. The sapphire dial is circled with a tachymetric scale.

ZENITH

ACADEMY QUANTIEME PERPETUEL EL PRIMERO

This Academy Quantième Perpetuel El Primero is a COSC-certified chronometer that houses the El Primero 4003 automatic chronograph movement with perpetual calendar. It consists of 321 components and beats at 36,000 vibrations per hour. With a 22K white-gold oscillating weight, the 31-jeweled movement offers 50 hours of power reserve and measures to 1/10th of a second. The 45mm platinum 950 PT case is water resistant to 30 meters.

ZENITH

ACADEMY TOURBILLON EL PRIMERO QUANTIEME PERPETUEL

This prestigious timekeeper offers two Grand Complications simultaneously—the tourbillon and the perpetual calendar—in addition to the legendary automatic column-wheel El Primero chronograph. The result is one of the most complicated El Primero—4033—ever manufactured: 492 components, 35 jewels, and the highest balance speed of 36,000 vibrations per hour. All calendar features are displayed with sword-shaped gold hands over the handmade guilloché dial. The tourbillon cage, positioned at 11:00, makes one turn per minute. Displaying a sapphire crystal caseback, this watch is available in white gold (shown), rose gold and also in platinum with diamonds. The Academy Tourbillon El Primero Quantième Perpétuel is an exclusive millesime and individually numbered edition.

RETROGRADE MECHANISMS AND JUMPING HOURS

opus
12
11
10
9
8
7
6
5
4
3
2
1
HW
60
45
30
15
00

President of A. Lange & Söhne in the Americas

Philippe Bonay

Philippe Bonay has long been familiar with the haute horology market, especially in North America. After having participated in the launch of Panerai in the United States, Bonay engaged in several activities before being offered the presidency of the US branch of the German brand A. Lange & Söhne. We spoke with this passionate, candid, straightforward manager in January 2010, just before he embarked on a new challenge: becoming president of Jaeger-LeCoultre in North America.

How does the public see A. Lange & Söhne?

Worldwide, A. Lange & Söhne products have earned an enormous amount of respect from true connoisseurs. Though that is true everywhere, it is particularly so in the United States, because the characteristic A. Lange & Söhne finishings and overall perfection match up exactly to the expectations of the American market.

In what way do they match up?

From our watchmakers to everyone who puts the finishing touches on an A. Lange & Söhne piece—we all have a true obsession with performance. Our products express that, naturally, through their innovation and originality. But that's not all: A. Lange & Söhne watches also stand out for their precision and reliability. These two assets are essential values for everyone who opens a manufacture in Glashütte, but it's not necessarily true for all brands in haute horology. Over the long term, however, it is the precision and the reliability of the products that makes the difference, and we in haute horology must never forget it.

Do you think that some brands have let the quality of their products slip?

I think that's obvious. In order to be able to offer reliable products, first you must have the industrial capability, which is of course crucial for ensuring quality, but you also must really want

FACING PAGE
Philippe Bonay

THIS PAGE
TOP LEFT
A. Lange & Söhne 1815 Moon phase

CENTER
Lange 1 Tourbillon

BOTTOM
A. Lange & Söhne Tourbograph Pour le Mérite

to provide that quality. Some have forgotten that a little. What's happening in haute horology today is a little like what happened with sports cars in the 1960s and '70s. Many companies weren't as interested in the reliability of their cars as they were in the cars' power and designs. Then Porsche came along with models that were not only innovative and well designed, but also reliable—and that brand rose to the top of the market. The watch industry is undergoing something very similar to that.

Is A. Lange & Söhne the Porsche of the watch world, reliability wise?

I don't know if I would compare us to Porsche, but what I do know is that a Lange watch does not come back to our service centers for a long time after it is sold. Their reliability is well known and that is A. Lange & Söhne's ace in the hole in the United States. Americans are very pragmatic consumers, and they hate things that don't work. What brings me the most pride is not just that our clients collect Langes, but also that they wear them every day.

A. Lange & Söhne won the "Golden Hand"—the most prestigious prize at the Grand Prix d'Horlogerie de Genève. What are your thoughts on this new accolade for the company?

The prize is primarily a recognition by watch connoisseurs for the work accomplished by the brand. The piece that earned this prize was the Lange Zeitwerk, an exceptional machine whose innovations and functions are truly inspiring. From all points of view, the Lange Zeitwerk is an objectively innovative watch that pushes the boundaries of haute horology. Progress always comes out of curiosity. At Lange, first we asked the question: "Can the principles behind mechanical watches and modern time indications be combined smoothly and convincingly?" Our answer was the first mechanical wristwatch equipped with a jumping digital display of eloquent clarity. This watch reinterprets time in an

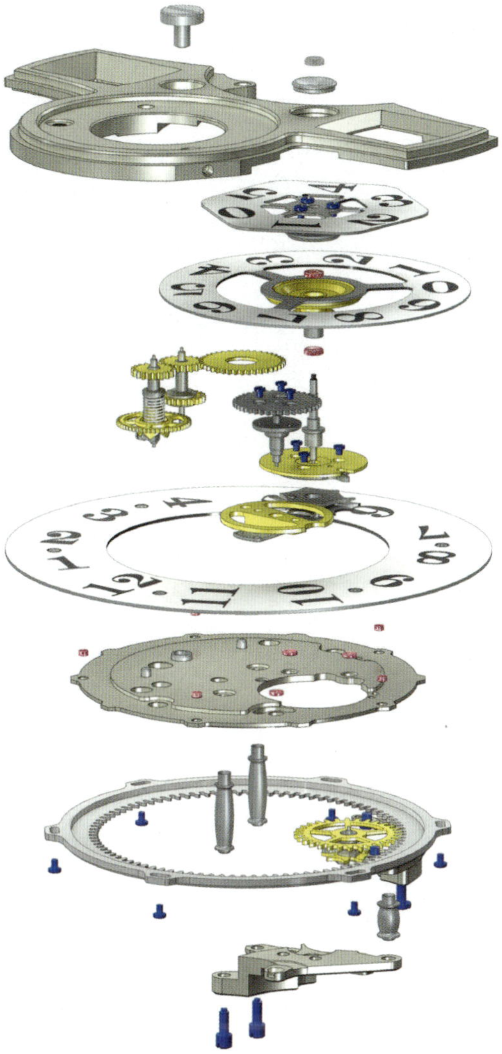

FACING PAGE
A. Lange & Söhne Zeitwerk

THIS PAGE
LEFT
An exploded view of the A. Lange & Söhne Zeitwerk disc mechanism

TOP RIGHT
A. Lange & Söhne Zeitwerk

CENTER
The disc display mechanism of the A. Lange & Söhne Zeitwerk

era of change. In so doing, it not only gives time a new face, but also shows a new path to horology. And it definitely gives its wearer a radically new way to interpret the passage of seconds, minutes and hours. It embodies the Lange signature to perfection.

Is that Lange signature known widely enough and understood deeply enough by watch lovers?
A brand—and with it the brand's unique character—is probably never known widely enough or understood deeply enough. But this brand speaks a truth that resonates in the market. We still have further to go with our public. Our new guiding principle is "watchmaking performance," and in those two words is expressed the entire DNA of A. Lange & Söhne. We still have to work on getting this image out there, and creating a little more heat around the brand. Lange is an exceptional brand that definitely deserves to be wider recognition. We have a lot of work ahead of us, especially in the United States. I am very confident that my successors will see this fabulous challenge to a successful conclusion.

Although a hand rotating endlessly around its axis seems to us to be the most "natural" way to represent the passing of time, for quite some time different display methods have required different methods of reading time whether by retrograde indication (whose hand sweeps over a circular arc before returning to the beginning) or jumping indications (which features a disc moving in a window). These alternative displays have become one of the favorite fields of exploration and experimentation of young watchmakers. Mechanical movements experiment with digital displays, using constructions as original as they are sophisticated, and exceptional timepieces are even using three-dimensional or linear indications.

***Pierre Kunz**, Seconde Virevoltante Rétrograde*
***De Bethune**, Digitale*
***Vacheron Constantin**, Patrimony Contemporary Bi-Retrograde Day Date*
***MB&F**, Horological Machine N° 2*
***Harry Winston**, Opus 7*

***Pierre DeRoche**, GrandCliff TNT Royal Retro*
***de GRISOGONO**, Meccanico dG*

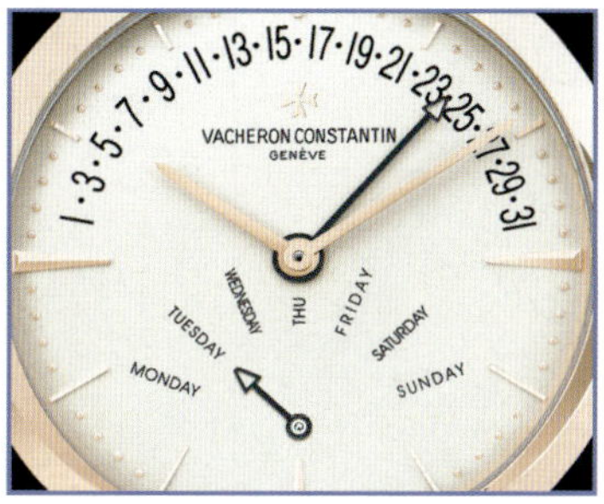

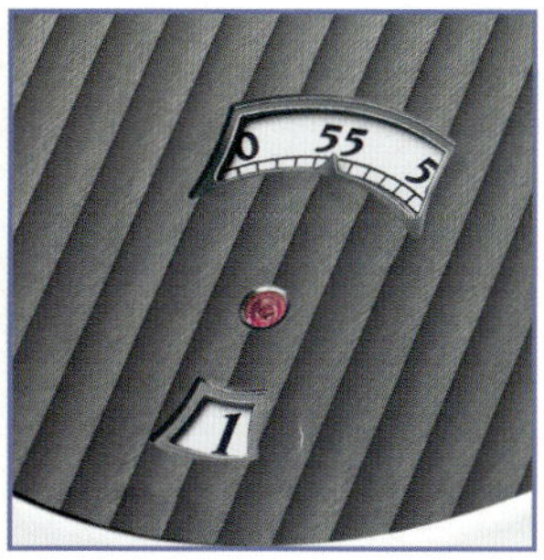

RETROGRADE MECHANISMS AND JUMPING HOURS

THIS PAGE
LEFT
Jean d'Eve, *Sectora II Automatic*

RIGHT
Pierre DeRoche, *GrandCliff Skyscrapers*

CENTER
Maurice Lacroix, *Double Retrograde II*

FACING PAGE
LEFT
Milus, *Tirion Triretrograde Seconds Skeleton in titanium*

RIGHT
Audemars Piguet, *Jules Audemars Jumping Hour Minute Repeater*

BELOW
Pierre Kunz, *Infinity Looping*

MOVING BEYOND CLOCKWISE

For many years, watchmakers have attempted to develop displays different than those involving hands turning...clockwise. This is why they invented the "retrograde" system, which employs a hand that sweeps an arc and then instantly returns to its point of departure to start over again. The retrograde display is quite fashionable right now; it allows for an original, even vivacious, design. One example is the Sectora II Automatic by Jean d'Eve, which displays hour and minute on a 120° arc (all on an asymmetric vertical dial), and another is the new GrandCliff Skyscrapers from Pierre DeRoche, with two vertical half-moon-shaped counters. Retrograde mechanisms can also be used for indications other than time. Maurice Lacroix's Double Retrograde II offers in addition to "traditional" hours, minutes and seconds a retrograde display for the date and the 24-hour clock. Vacheron Constantin's highly original Patrimony Contemporary Bi-Retrograde Day Date indicates the date on an arc from 9:00 to 3:00, echoed by a second "fan" from 7:00 to 5:00, for the day.

SPECTACULAR SPECTACLE

The dance of hands returning all the way to their first position often lends a spectacular visual aspect to retrograde timepieces, especially when the dials combine two, three or even four of this kind of indication or when the watchmakers have a little fun with complicating the "figures." On its Seconde Virevoltante Rétrograde, Pierre Kunz offers a truly acrobatic show with a seconds hand that dives down and swoops back up on a 417° orbit before returning to its initial position in five hundredths of a second and starting over! On its Infinity Looping, the Genevan watchmaker imagines a completely new way of telling time, which is not exactly retrograde, but stunning nonetheless.

Using a system with a satellite pinion that turns around a fixed rack, the hour and minute twirl around the dial, creating a rosette design. The Tirion TriRetrograde Seconds Skeleton in titanium by Milus presents a second retrograde in three 20-second sectors, placed at 2:00, 6:00 and 10:00. Each second-hand traverses its arc in turn and passes the baton to the next before springing back to its original position. Pierre DeRoche went even further in 2009, unveiling the GrandCliff TNT Royal Retro equipped with an exclusive Dubois Dépraz mechanism. The second is indicated by a succession of six retrograde displays, moved by a strip-spring system that is visible through the dial.

JUMPING HOUR

Another "dissident" time display is the jumping mechanism, a disc on which numerals are inscribed, and which "jumps" by a notch with each change of the hour or, in some cases, the minute. On Audemars Piguet's Jules Audemars Jumping Hour Minute Repeater, the hour appears in a beveled window at 12:00, while the minute hand

is anchored in the middle of the dial. The new Lange Zeitwerk from A. Lange & Söhne also joins digital and traditional displays, with jumping minutes at 3:00, a jumping hour on a double disc at 9:00 and two counter with hands for the small seconds and power reserve, respectively. De Bethune's Digitale presents a completely disc-based display, with an upper day/date/month window, a jumping-hour window below and a minute window between the two. On the Outland by RSW, the traditional hands are replaced by three concentric discs (for hours, minutes and seconds), moving in relation to a fixed point of reference.

SHOCK AND AWE

The jumping-hour display is very often paired with a retrograde minute. Gérald Genta has made a specialty out of this coupling, as on its Gefica Safari, which also has a retrograde date. The FG One by de GRISOGONO features two dials: one with retrograde minute on a 230° arc, instant jumping hour and a "dragging" second time zone, and the other with retrograde seconds complete with a day/night indication synchronized to the second time zone. The Horological Machine N° 2, from MB&F, combines a resolutely avant-garde look with a display on two dials that takes advantage of very sophisticated technical solutions, especially in its use of energy. The dial on the right shows jumping hours (with a visible disc) and retrograde concentric minutes (with a semi-circular arc and an arrow-tipped hand); the dial on the left shows a retrograde date and a moonphase on two hemispheres.

TIME FOR DIGITAL TIME

"Digital" mechanical displays are rapidly gaining favor among watchmakers, who see in them a fertile ground for all sorts of imaginative possibilities. Hautlence has designed a jumping-hour device

FACING PAGE
TOP LEFT
***Vincent Calabrese**, Baladin*

TOP RIGHT
***A. Lange & Söhne**, Lange Zeitwerk*

LEFT
***de GRISOGONO**, FG One*

THIS PAGE
TOP LEFT
***Harry Winston**, Opus 3*

TOP RIGHT
***RSW**, Outland*

LEFT
***Hautlence**, a model from the new HLQ collection*

and an innovative retrograde minute with a system of visible connecting rods that guarantees the transmission of energy. Vincent Calabrese offers in its Baladin a new way of telling time. The numeral of the jumping hour is displayed in a small round window; that window marks the minutes by spinning around the dial. For the Opus 3 from Harry Winston, Vianney Halter designed a completely digital display with jumping hours, minutes, seconds and date appearing in six separate "portholes." The ten independently rotating discs are powered by two mechanisms totaling 250 components. For Harry Winston's Opus 7, the young Swiss-German watchmaker Andreas Strehler designed an "alternative display" disc system. First, a push on the crown guard calls the hour on its disc against a marker at 10:00. A second push elicits the minutes, and a third push, the power reserve. The dual-time-zone watch Meccanico dG from de GRISOGONO joins an analog display for the first time zone with a digital display for the second, all powered by a completely mechanical movement with 651 components. The digital indication of the second time zone, which evokes old-fashioned

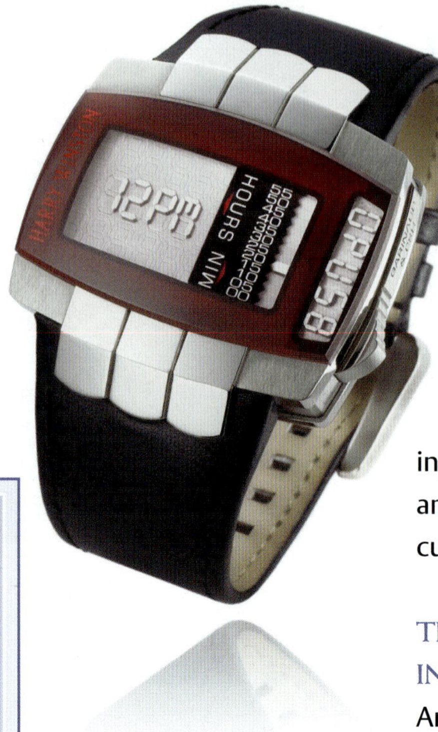

LEFT
***Jacob & Co**, Quenttin*

CENTER
***Harry Winston**, Opus 8*

RIGHT
***MCT**, Sequential One*

departure and arrival boards in airports, is composed of mobile micro-segments animated by a system of 23 gears. For Harry Winston's Opus 8, Frédéric Garinaud designed a spectacular digital display system of hours and minutes. When the wearer presses on the bolt on the right of the case, the "digits" showing the hour (on an AM/PM scale) rise up in relief from the dial, as the minutes are indicated on a vertical scale on the right. Another engrossing spectacle occurs on the Sequential One from MCT (Manufacture Contemporaine du Temps). The hours appear one by one in four display areas on the dial, with the help of an innovative system of triangular prisms similar to those seen on European rotating billboards. The minutes are shown on a 270º arc, but there is no retrograde action: at the change of each hour, the mobile minutes ring makes a quarter-turn to the left, uncovering the next hour (and concealing the other areas) and allowing the minute hand to continue its circular course uninterrupted.

THE FOURTH DIMENSION IN THREE DIMENSIONS

Another innovative approach is the use of three-dimensional displays. Daniel Roth has set the tone with its Ellipsocurvex Papillon, which features a pair of minute hands set in a straight line. When the first hand arrives at 60, it pivots 90° and disappears under the hidden part of the dial, while the other appears at 00 using the same pivoting mechanism. The imposing Quenttin watch, created by the American brand Jacob & Co., has no fewer than seven barrels all visible under the crystal assuring a power reserve of one month. The hour, the minute and the power reserve are all read off vertical discs that share an axis. The watch even has a tourbillon, visible through the case side. No less original, the Cabestan from Vianney Halter and Jean-François Ruchonnet of DMC Group is wound by a fixed crank. The hours, minutes, seconds and power reserve are shown on engraved rotating drums. But the star of three-dimensional displays is, without a doubt, the 201 by Urwerk a young brand famous for its futuristic timepieces and "satellite" displays, such as the UR-103T, whose

TOP CENTER
Urwerk, UR-103T

TOP RIGHT
Christophe Claret, DualTow

LEFT
Pierre Kunz, Vertigo

RIGHT
Urwerk, UR-CC1

four satellites make it look like a tarantula. On the UR-201, the hour can be read off the revolving extremities of a three-armed rotating star. Each of the four-sided extremities makes a quarter-turn every three hours in sequence to display the hour (1-4-7-10/2-5-8-11/3-6-9-12). Tiny telescopic rods extend in turn from the ends of the arms to follow the scale of minutes at the bottom of the dial, and then retract. A control board on the caseback, with racing-style gauges, allows the wearer to monitor the watch's performance.

LINEAR DISPLAYS

The latest trend, as evidenced by several noteworthy creations of 2009: linear displays, which break even more dramatically (from a visual standpoint, at least) with our traditional view of time as a closed circle. These straight-lined displays might evoke retrograde systems, such as on Pierre Kunz's Vertigo, with an hour hand that rises like mercury in a thermometer, only to plunge in a flash after hitting 12:00. But they also refer to other systems. On its DualTow, created to celebrate the manufacture's 20th anniversary (see "Chronographs" chapter), Christophe Claret presents a display of hours and minutes on notched rubber transmission belts inspired by vehicles with caterpillar tracks. The Opus 9 from Harry Winston, by designer Eric Giroud and watchmaker Jean-Marc Wiederrecht, proposes a linear display of hours and minutes via two small brass chains set with emerald-cut diamonds, with bright orange mandarin garnets as indexes. Urwerk set aside its satellite displays in 2009 when it presented the UR-CC1, inspired by speedometers from certain midcentury automobiles. The linear reading of the hours and minutes is done via two cylinders. Once it finishes its path, the minute cylinder is returned to its initial position in one-tenth of a second, and this retrograde movement sets off the advancement of the hour cylinder by one unit. The seconds are displayed via a disc in the upper half of the dial.

A. LANGE & SÖHNE

LANGE ZEITWERK

The Lange Zeitwerk is powered by the manual-winding Lange proprietary L043.1 caliber, which contains 388 components including 66 jewels. Decorated and assembled by hand, the movement beats at 18,000 semi-oscillations per hour and possesses a precision beat-adjustment system with lateral setscrew and whiplash spring. The case, which measures 41.9mm in diameter, is crafted in white gold, and the black dial is in solid silver. The dial sports jumping hour and jumping minute displays, a small seconds hand with stop seconds, and a 36-hour power-reserve indicator. The watch is also available in a yellow-gold case with a solid silver champagne-colored dial, in a pink-gold case with a solid silver argenté dial, and in a platinum case with a solid silver rhodiumized dial.

AUDEMARS PIGUET

JULES AUDEMARS SKELETON MANUAL WINDING REPEATER W/ JUMPING HOUR AND SMALL SECONDS – REF. 26356PT.OO.D028CR.01

Housed in a 950 platinum case fitted with a sapphire caseback and an opaline openworked dial with black printed numerals and a skeleton jumping hour disc, this Jules Audemars model marries two great horological specialties: the minute repeater and the jumping hour. This marvel of precision and harmony extends Audemars Piguet's savoir-faire in the realm of complicated watches. With its classically reinvented case and dial, the watch is a fresh addition to the Jules Audemars collection.

BOVET

FLEURIER JUMPING HOUR OPENWORK 42MM

BOVET's most unusual timepiece features a central jumping digital hour set in a rock crystal glass revealing the poetry of its original movement. The minutes are displayed on a blacked rotating ring with a white LumiNova triangle index. The 12 central hours are all on one blackened disk, offset so that its rim is leveled with the movement's rim. They jump instantaneously as the 60th minute reaches the dot at 12:00. A sapphire crystal caseback reveals the movement and its gold winding rotor, engraved in *fleurisanne* style. The jumping hour watches are also available in 18K red gold; with a 16-point Compass Rose painted in different colors on a mother-of-pearl or fired-enamel dial; or in a jewelry version upon which the Compass Rose is paved in diamonds and sapphires.

BOVET

FLEURIER JUMPING HOUR WITH MINIATURE PAINTING

BOVET's most unusual timepiece, the jumping hour model, is also one of the complicated timepieces that is most suitable for miniature painting. Thanks to this specific and original hour display, the dial still offers a generous space for creativity. BOVET has access to the most accomplished artists in miniature painting who create the spectacular effects of unique miniatures on mother-of-pearl. In this unique piece, the artist's talent brings to life a graceful orthodox icon representing "Vladimirskaya," Virgin and her child. Both holy figures are crowned and dressed with gold leaf.

LEVIEV

DOUBLE BARILLET

Shown here in 18K white gold, the LEVIEV Double Barillet wristwatch is manufactured by Muller & Laville, and is composed of 220 components. The dial features blued steel hands and is set with 41 diamonds with a 0.30 total carat weight; the watch's crown is set with 0.15 total carat. The self-powered movement has a twin barrel, 43 jewels, and a 120-hour power reserve, which is indicated at 5:00. The retrograde date is located at 1:30 and the watch is fitted on an alligator strap that fastens together with an 18K gold clasp and 18K gold cover. The LEVIEV Double Barillet watch is made in Switzerland and engraved with an individual serial number.

LEVIEV
DOUBLE BARILLET

Shown here in 18K rose gold, the LEVIEV Double Barillet wristwatch is manufactured by Muller & Laville, and is composed of 220 components. The dial features blued steel hands and is set with 41 diamonds with a 0.30 total carat weight; the watch's crown is set with 0.15 total carat. The self-powered movement has a twin barrel, 43 jewels, and a 120-hour power reserve, which is indicated at 5:00. The retrograde date is located at 1:30 and the watch is fitted on an alligator strap that fastens together with an 18K gold clasp and 18K gold cover. The LEVIEV Double Barillet watch is made in Switzerland and engraved with an individual serial number.

PIAGET

EMPERADOR COUSSIN REGULATOR – REF. G0A34025

The Piaget Emperador coussin regulator is available in 18K pink- or white-gold versions measuring 42.5mm in diameter and fitted with sapphire crystal casebacks. This finely satin-brushed midnight-blue dial is guilloché-worked at 12:00 for the retrograde seconds. At the heart of this Piaget Emperador coussin regulator model beats an ultra-thin, mechanical hand-wound movement measuring 3.92mm thick. Designed, developed and produced by the Manufacture de Haute Horlogerie Piaget, the 835P caliber is equipped with a large balance with screws and a large barrel providing a power reserve of approximately 65 hours. Like all movements by Piaget, this 835P caliber is graced with extremely meticulous finishes. The mainplate is circular grained, bridges are beveled, while the decorative elements such as the circular Côtes de Genève and blued screws are in line with the brand's aesthetic codes.

VACHERON CONSTANTIN

PATRIMONY BI-RETROGRADE – REF. 86020

Powered by the mechanical automatic-winding Vacheron Constantin Caliber 2460 R31 R7, this Patrimony Bi-Retrograde is hallmarked with the Geneva Seal. Beating at 28,800 vibrations per hour and offering 43 hours of power reserve, the 27-jeweled movement is equipped with a guilloché pink-gold rotor. Retrograde day is provided at 6:00 and retrograde date is shown at 12:00. The 18K pink-gold three-piece case is polished and water resistant to 3atm. The sapphire caseback reveals the exquisite movement.

With its slightly mysterious name, the equation of time remains one of the least known complications, appearing in a very small number of exclusive timepieces. It's true that the display of the difference between true solar time and mean solar time is not the most useful function for day-to-day living. However, the recent launch of several original models with equation of time and the appearance of the first wristwatches with a "running" equation of time could well signify the return to favor of this

***Audemars Piguet**, Jules Audemars*
Equation of Time
***Audemars Piguet**, Jules Audemars*
Clinton Foundation Equation of Time
***Blancpain,** Equation Marchante M.Y.S.*

***Arnold & Son**, True North Perpetual*
***Audemars Piguet**, Jules Audemars*
Equation of Time

EQUATIONS OF TIME

THIS PAGE
***Breguet**, Equation of Time*

FACING PAGE
TOP LEFT
***Girard-Perregaux**, 1945 Vintage Annual Calendar and Equation of Time*

RIGHT
***Girard-Perregaux**, 1966 Annual Calendar and Equation of Time*

BOTTOM LEFT
***Jaquet Droz**, Equation of Time*

CELESTIAL MECHANICS

There are actually two times: the true solar time and the mean solar time. The true solar time (the one we see on sundials) corresponds to the rhythm of nature. As it turns around the sun, the Earth follows an elliptical trajectory, and its axis is inclined with respect to the equator. As a result, the interval between two passages of the sun through the highest point in the sky (noon) does not have the same length over the course of a year. It lasts exactly 24 hours only four times a year: April 15, June 14, September 1 and December 24. On other days it is either longer or shorter, according to a path that is immutably expressed year after year. This difference, which goes from -16 minutes and 23 seconds, on November 4, to +14 minutes and 22 seconds, on February 11, is called the "equation of time." Mean solar time, that which we read from our watches (also called "civil time"), is just a pure convention, based on the average of all the days in the year.

THE ETERNAL RETURN

The greatest horologers rival each other in innovation, developing systems that reproduce the variations in equation of time an essential element of all ultra-complicated astronomical watches. The variable lengths of true solar days are repeated faithfully on the same dates every year, and it is possible to "program" them with the help of a cam that makes one rotation per year. The equation-of-time display can take several forms. Most watches with this complication have a small dial or sector that is swept over by a hand going from -16 to +14 minutes; the user must then mentally add or subtract this to the mean time to figure out the true time. This is the case with the Breguet Equation of Time, which has a perpetual calendar, and Daniel Roth's

Perpetual Calendar Equation of Time, which is equipped with an openworked dial that reveals the movement. There is also a sector indication to show the number of minutes between the mean solar time and the true solar time on the new 1966 Annual Calendar and Equation of Time from Girard-Perregaux, presented in the spring of 2009 and also equipped with an annual calendar that needs only one correction per year (see "Perpetual Calendar" chapter). On its crisp dial, the date is presented via a counter at 1:30, the equation of time is on an arc at 4:30, the month shows through a panoramic window at 7:00, and the small seconds tick at 9:00. The new in-house automatic movement powering this watch is equipped with a variable-inertia pendulum that assures the precision and stability of the settings. Girard-Perregaux, evidently a big fan of this complication, also offers it on a sophisticated version of its rectangular model 1945 Vintage, this time paired with a perpetual calendar. The sector indicator of the equation of time takes its place in the corner of the dial at 10:30, right next to the astronomical moonphase (see "Moonphase" chapter). On the Equation of Time from Jaquet Droz, the eponymous complication is truly the star, thanks

to its large hand that is decorated with a sun and runs along a 180° arc from 9:00 to 3:00. This unusual composition is completed by date and month subdials in the lower part of the dial.

RUNNING EQUATIONS

Simpler to use but more complex to create, watches with a running equation of time have two minute hands on the same axis, one indicating the mean time and other showing the true solar time. This complication requires no mental calculation, as the true time is always displayed directly on the dial. This system, long exclusive to pocket watches, first appeared on wristwatches in 2004—a true feat of miniaturization. The Jaeger-LeCoultre Gyrotourbillon 1, most noted for its spherical tourbillon (see "Tourbillons" chapter), presents a running equation with an additional minute hand tipped with a golden sun, all on an off-center hour/minute subdial. Blancpain's Equation of Time Marchante is also notable for its double equation-of-time display: in the center is the running equation with a supplementary sun-tipped minute hand, and at 2:00 lies a subdial with a retrograde hand to indicate the number of minutes' difference—all combined with an extra-flat perpetual calendar. Blancpain has also joined the running equation with a perpetual calendar in a model from the Villeret collection called Equation Marchante Pure, which does not have an additional sector display.

FACING PAGE
LEFT
Jaeger-LeCoultre, *Gyrotourbillon 1*

RIGHT
Blancpain, *Equation Marchante Pure*

THIS PAGE
LEFT
Audemars Piguet, *Jules Audemars Equation du Temps Squelette (Winner in Full Calendar watch category at the Grand Prix d'Horlogerie de Genève 2008)*

ABOVE
Arnold & Son, *True North Perpetual*

TAKING LONGITUDE INTO ACCOUNT

In 2005, Audemars Piguet took another big step by proposing the first equation-of-time system adjusted to the exact degree of longitude—not just the general time zone—in an adaptation that assures a much more precise reading. The highlighted dial allows the wearer to determine true noon (when the sun is at the highest point in the sky) for the indicated city. The Jules Audemars Equation du Temps Squelette is also the first wristwatch to display the times of sunrise and sunset according to three parameters: the date, longitude, and latitude. It is available in a precious skeletonized version, with a completely openworked and engraved automatic movement, which took the Grand Prix d'Horlogerie de Genève 2008 in the Full Calendar category. Arnold & Son, legacy of the famous British watchmaker John Arnold, drew inspiration from the work of its founder to create another equation-of-time watch that takes longitude into account via a dial with two movable rings. The True North Perpetual contains another unusual attribute: when the 24-hour solar hand shows exact solar noon, the wearer need only aim it in the direction of the sun for the exterior mobile dial to show true geographic north.

AUDEMARS PIGUET

JULES AUDEMARS EQUATION OF TIME – REF. 26003BC.OO.D002CR

This Jules Audemars Equation of Time watch is created in 18K white gold and houses the self-winding Caliber 2120/2808. Visible through the sapphire crystal caseback, the 41-jeweled movement depicts conventional time and real solar time and offers hours and minutes, sunrise and sunset times, equation of time, perpetual calendar and astronomical moon. The solar culmination time is calibrated to the reference city chosen by the owner. This model is also available in 18K yellow gold.

AUDEMARS PIGUET

JULES AUDEMARS EQUATION OF TIME SKELETON – REF. 26053PT.OO.D002CR.01

This Jules Audemars Equation of Time is created in platinum and houses the self-winding, hand-engraved, openworked caliber 2120/2808. The sapphire reveals the elaborate engraving and blued hands. Visible through the sapphire crystal caseback, the 41-jeweled movement depicts conventional time and real solar time and offers hours and minutes, sunrise and sunset times, equation of time, perpetual calendar and astronomical moon. The solar culmination time is calibrated to the reference city chosen by the owner.

AUDEMARS PIGUET

ROYAL OAK EQUATION OF TIME – REF. 26603OR.OO.D092CR.01

This Royal Oak Equation of Time is housed in an 18K pink-gold case and powered by the automatic-winding 2120/2808 movement, which beats at 19,800 vibrations per hour. Visible through the sapphire caseback, the movement indicates the moonphase, the times of sunrise and sunset, as well as the difference between mean solar time and true solar time. Boasting a perpetual calendar, this timepiece displays the day of the week, the date, the month and leap years. The solar zenith corresponds to the reference city chosen by the watch's wearer. This model is also available in stainless steel with a silvered dial.

BLANCPAIN

VILLERET EQUATION MARCHANTE PURE

The Equation Marchante Pure, based on the Le Brassus model that was the first wristwatch capable of displaying the separate solar and civil times by two minute-hands, was launched in 2005 as part of the Villeret collection characterized by its pure lines and formal beauty. This limited edition of 50 pieces is crafted in platinum and houses the 364-part caliber 3863A, equipped with 72 hours of power reserve.

In the opinion of many connoisseurs, the audible indication of time—whether it be "in passing" sonnerie mechanisms or "minute repeaters" that sound on demand—constitutes the most sophisticated horological complication. The complication requires extreme technical ability coupled with an authentic ear for music in order to guarantee both optimal operation and sound. Today, these artisanal skills are no longer the only crucial factors involved in making these models. Watchmakers are also exploring all the potential of high-tech metal alloys and reinventing striking systems to achieve the best possible acoustics. They are using the very latest software programs to master the sound components. The field of minute repeaters and sonneries and other striking mechanisms is thus in full bloom—even though these ultra-complicated timepieces continue to be the exclusive preserve of a handful of manufactures and exceptionally gifted artisans.

***Parmigiani**, Kalpa Minute Repeater*
***Kari Voutilainen**, Masterpiece N° 6*
***Ulysse Nardin**, Hourstriker Erotica*
***Audemars Piguet**, Jules Audemars Jumping Hours Minute Repeater*

***Jaeger-LeCoultre**, Master Minute Repeater Antoine LeCoultre*
***DeWitt**, Minute Repeater Rose Gold*

MINUTE REPEATERS AND SONNERIES

MORNING BELLS

Sound indications showed up very early in the history of the pocket watch. At the end of the 15th century, there were already records of watches with a "passing strike" that sounded the hours in passing, like church bells. The quarter-hour repeater, a function that sounded the hours and quarter-hours on demand—a very practical system for knowing the time at night—was invented two centuries later. At that point, these watches contained hammers striking small bells. It is English horologer Thomas Mudge who is widely credited with perfecting the minute repeater in 1750. At the end of the same century, the famous Abraham-Louis Breguet came up with the idea of replacing the bells with gongs: hardened steel strips coiled inside the case that allowed for a slimmer watch and a clearer sound.

TIME'S TINKLING TUNE

In the 20th century, miniaturized to accommodate the new wristwatch format, mechanisms with sound became one of the greatest demonstrations of horological know-how. It takes peerless skill to create this complex system of mechanical "memory," with "feeler-spindles" picking up information on the hour, quarter and minute "snails" in order to transmit it to the "gathering-pallets." It takes an extremely sensitive ear to adjust the chimes as one might tune a musical instrument, especially when it comes to the sonnerie known as "carillon" or "cathedral," which rings on three or four chimes. There are two types of sound indications: sonnerie in passing (grande or petite), and sonnerie on demand (the repeater). "Grande sonnerie" refers to the striking of each hour and quarter-hour on the quarter-hour, and "petite sonnerie" to the striking of only the hours or the quarter-hours. The minute repeater is generally equipped with two chimes, a low tone for the hours and a high one for the minutes, with the quarter-hours marked by two high-low tones.

FACING PAGE
LEFT
Jaeger-LeCoultre, *Master Grande Tradition à Répétition Minutes*

CENTER
Audemars Piguet, *Jules Audemars Tourbillon Minute Repeater Chronograph*

RIGHT
Jaeger-LeCoultre, *Master Minute Repeater Antoine LeCoultre*

THIS PAGE
Roger Dubuis, *Excalibur RD08*

STROKES OF BRILLIANCE

For several years, watchmakers have been reviving general interest in minute repeaters by beating new technical and aesthetic paths. In 2005, Jaeger-LeCoultre launched the Master Minute Repeater equipped with an innovative system of sound transmission: it is sent directly outside the watch by the sapphire crystal, to which are welded the heels of the gongs—themselves crafted from a secret, exclusive material. The result is a sound of unequalled power, richness and purity. The brand's Master Grande Tradition à Répétition Minutes, released in 2009, is based on the same principle of sound transmission through the crystal, but its gongs now feature a square section tapered towards the end in order to intensify the sound volume and increase its duration. The two hammers are visible through an opening in the dial at 4:00. The minute repeater is paired with a regulator-style display with central minutes and hours on an off-center subdial at 12:00. The watch also possesses an exceptional power reserve of 14 days. Other companies have begun to develop new striking systems, such as Audemars Piguet in its Jules Audemars Tourbillon Minute Repeater Chronograph, or new trigger systems, such as Roger Dubuis with its Excalibur RD08 movement that activates its minute repeater with a turn of

THIS PAGE
LEFT
Breguet, *Classique 5447 Minute Repeater and Perpetual Calendar*

CENTER
Blancpain, *Léman Aqua Lung Minute Repeater*

BELOW
Citizen, *Eco-Drive Minute Repeater Perpetual*

FACING PAGE
Cvstos, *Challenge RMT-S*

the rotating bezel. Not to mention the Classique 5447 Minute Repeater and Perpetual Calendar by Breguet, which boasts varied technical optimizations, some of them patented. Blancpain has tackled head-on one of the biggest traditional problems facing minute repeaters: a break in the water resistance seal at the location of the slide that triggers the chime. This is an Achilles' heel that can prove fatal in especially humid climates. With its Léman Aqua Lung Minute Repeater, the manufacture proposes a minute repeater that is water resistant to 100 meters. To achieve this, Blancpain has designed an ingenious device that links the exterior slide and the interior winding lever with a series of racks, gaskets and a transmission shaft. This movement is also the flattest minute repeater in the world, with the smallest diameter. The Challenge RMT-S watch, from the Genevan brand Cvstos, with an anti-shock tourbillon cage, also joins a minute repeater and water resistance to 100 meters—but with a much more futuristic aesthetic perspective. At the risk of offending any purists, we must also mention one more technical innovation: the unusual combination of a quartz movement with a minute repeater in Eco-Drive Minute Repeater Perpetual by the Japanese brand Citizen, whose Eco-Drive system draws all of its energy from natural or artificial light.

VISUAL HARMONY

In the classic minute repeater, nothing appears to signal the presence of this sophisticated complication—nothing, that is, except the small slide or pusher on the side of the case, as in the Bulgari Minute Repeater, whose movement is made by Parmigiani Fleurier, or in the new Portuguese

CVSTOS
MINUTE REPEATER ACTION INDICATOR
RMT-S
3x20 SECONDS
CHALLENGE

TOP LEFT
***Harry Winston**, Westminster Tourbillon*

TOP RIGHT
***de GRISOGONO**, Occhio Ripetizione Minuti*

BELOW
***Vacheron Constantin**, Maîtres Cabinotiers Skeleton Minute Repeater*

BOTTOM
***IWC**, Portuguese Minute Repeater*

Minute Repeater from IWC, with a large case and a manual-winding pocket-watch movement. But many watchmakers prefer to show the mechanism through openworked dials. This is the case with the Zenith Grande Class Traveller Répétition Minutes El Primero and Parmigiani Fleurier's Kalpa XL Minute Repeater, which bears a large circular opening. Harry Winston's Westminster Tourbillon joins a flying tourbillon to a minute repeater that reproduces the famous melody of Big Ben. The lack of a dial allows the wearer to admire the four hammers that strike the four cathedral chimes. Vacheron Constantin aims for the most possible transparency—and the least possible thickness—with its Maîtres Cabinotiers Skeleton Minute Repeater. The 3.3mm-thick movement is made of more than 330 components, most of them openworked, decorated and chased. Playing the iconoclast once again is de GRISOGONO with its Occhio Ripetizione Minuti. Based on the same principle as the reflex camera, the watch has an aperture as a dial: when the wearer activates the minute repeater, the 12 ceramic shutters open to reveal the movement for the duration of the cathedral sonnerie's chime.

TOP LEFT
Zenith, *Grande Class Traveller Répétition Minutes El Primero*

LEFT
Parmigiani Fleurier, *Kalpa XL Minute Repeater*

BELOW
Kari Voutilainen, *Masterpiece N° 7*

BOTTOM
Chopard, *L.U.C Strike One*

THEY'VE GOT RHYTHM

Other watchmakers offer variations on the frequency and the type of sonneries. On its L.U.C Strike One, Chopard presents a mechanism that strikes once at the passing of each hour (hence its name). An opening at 12:00 shows the small hammer at work. In the one-of-a-kind Masterpiece N° 7, Finnish watchmaker Kari Voutilainen offers, with a minute repeater that sounds not the hours/quarter-hours/minutes, but the hours/ten-minutes/minutes, a system that can allow for a more intuitive telling of time. Edox also opts for an hour/minute sound indication in its Classe Royale Five Minute Repeater, with a square case and a sonnerie mechanism visible through the openworked dial. The Japanese brand

Seiko pays tribute to the ancient "hour repeater" in a high-end model called Credor Spring Drive Sonnerie. The sound mechanism operates on three modes: the wearer can choose an hour-count sonnerie on the hour, a three-strike sonnerie every three hours (12:00, 3:00, 6:00 and 9:00), or silence. Using the exclusive Seiko Spring Drive technology, the watch's hands move "as regularly and as silently as time itself."

A DIVINE SOUND

The final word in sound mechanisms is the practice of joining the on-demand and in-passing sonneries in the same movement. Philippe Dufour, one of today's greatest artisan watchmakers, created in 1992 the first minute-repeater wristwatch with grande and petite sonneries. F.P. Journe, another first-rate inventor, followed up with the Sonnerie Souveraine. This wristwatch, which took almost six years to perfect, is distinguished by its extreme functionality. The watchmaker developed several systems to protect and ensure easy use of the watch, such as an activating device based on watertight pushers. Journe also put a lot of effort into limiting the amount of power needed for the sonnerie. This exceptional piece has been awarded ten different patents. Another characteristic of the Sonnerie Souveraine is that, in order to guarantee the most perfect sound possible, Journe opted to house it in a steel case—a first for the brand's collections. A superb example of a minute repeater (or of any complicated watch), the Grande Sonnerie from Daniel Roth joins a tourbillon, a minute repeater, a grande and petite sonnerie, a four-hammer Westminster chime and a double power-reserve display for the movement and the sonnerie, as well as a large moonphase and a hand display for the date. 2009 gave us two masterpieces that will go down in the history of the audible complication. The first, Jaeger-LeCoultre's Hybris Mechanica à Grande Sonnerie, joins the Hybris Mechanica 55 trilogy of ultra-complicated watches (see "Multi-Complications" chapter). Its movement of more than 1,300 components includes (in addition to a flying tourbillon, perpetual calendar and many jumping or retrograde displays) a grande and petite sonnerie as well as a minute repeater, all with a Westminster chime that lasts longer than usual. To improve the functioning and the sound quality of the sonnerie, the watchmakers designed new hammers with articulated heads, ensuring a more efficient use of energy. The

FACING PAGE
LEFT
***Edox**, Classe Royale*
Répétition 5 minutes

CENTER
***Philippe Dufour**, Grande Sonnerie*

RIGHT
***Ulysse Nardin**, Genghis Khan*

THIS PAGE
LEFT
***Seiko**, Credor Spring Drive Sonnerie*

CENTER
***F.P. Journe**, Sonnerie Souveraine*

RIGHT
***Jaeger-LeCoultre**, Hybris Mechanica*
à Grand Sonnerie

second groundbreaking new arrival of 2009 is from Gérald Genta. The brand uses an exclusive software program that measures the sound of its watches with respect to intensity, accuracy and cadence. The new Arena Metasonic, released last autumn, benefits from all these technological advances. Using a program that can analyze different kinds of materials, the brand has also perfected a new, patented alloy with which to create the watch's case middle. Called Magsonic, the material's secret composition guarantees the best possible diffusion of sound towards the exterior of the watch. The case construction is inspired by a snare drum and the titanium caseback and bezel are affixed to the exterior with pillars.

TIME FOR ANIMATION

In terms of the "spectacle," watches bearing automata undoubtedly hold the spotlight, despite their extreme rarity. Ulysse Nardin continues this tradition with several highly esteemed creations. One of them is the Genghis Khan, the first minute repeater with tourbillon, Jaquemarts and a Westminster chime. The 18-karat gold case houses four gongs that strike different notes (E-C-D-G). It marks the hour with a G, the minute with an E, and the quarter-hours on four gongs using three different sound sequences. The onyx dial is decorated with hand-engraved gold figurines that, when the wearer activates the sonnerie, are animated in perfect synchronization with the sound of the striking gongs. Inspired by a Caravaggio painting, Daniel Roth's Il Giocatore Veneziano joins a minute-repeater mechanism (with cathedral chime) with an automaton that tosses dice through seven different cycles with 72 combinations each—504 possible rolls of the dice in all. The automaton's movement functions independently of the minute repeater, so it can be activated either at the same time as the sonnerie or on demand.

AUDEMARS PIGUET

JULES AUDEMARS MANUAL WINDING MINUTE REPEATER WITH JUMPING HOUR AND SMALL SECONDS – REF. 26151OR.OO.D002CR.01

Housed in an 18K rose-gold case, this Jules Audemars model marries two great horological specialties: the minute repeater and the jumping hour. This marvel of precision and harmony extends Audemars Piguet's savoir faire in the realm of complicated watches. With its classically reinvented case and dial, the watch is a fresh addition to the Jules Audemars collection. It is also available in 950 platinum on a black crocodile strap.

AUDEMARS PIGUET

TRADITION MINUTE REPEATER PERPETUAL CALENDAR – REF. 26052BC.OO.D092CR.01

Part of the new Tradition collection, this exceptional timepiece is inspired by a Lépine pocket watch created in 1923 by Audemars Piguet. The 50x50mm case houses the manual-winding 2855 movement, whose minute-repeater movement chimes the hours, quarter-hours and minutes upon request. The piece's opaline dial offers perfect readability of the day, date, month, leap year and moonphase indications provided by the perpetual calendar module. This timepiece is available in a limited edition.

CHOPARD

L.U.C STRIKE ONE – REF. 161912-1001

The L.U.C Strike One houses the 33x5.7mm L.U.C 96 SH caliber, which offers an hour-strike function with on/off setting, 65 hours of power reserve (Twin Technology—two spring-barrels), and a small seconds indicator at 6:00. The chronometer-certified movement bears the Geneva Seal quality hallmark and its bridges are decorated with a straight-line Côtes de Genève pattern. L.U.C Strike One is produced in a limited edition of 100 timepieces in 18K white gold.

de GRISOGONO

OCCHIO RIPETIZIONE MINUTI

The exceptional Occhio Ripetizione Minuti boasts a mechanism very similar to the one found in a reflex camera. Comprising 12 titanium blades, the diaphragm opens to reveal the movement as the mechanism chimes. The watch's sapphire crystal caseback reveals the movement of the three hammers (to strike the hours, quarter hours, and minutes) on the gongs, as well as the movement's signature decorative finishing. Originally released in a more sedate version, this model is now available in a spectacular diamond-set version, which features 154 baguette-cut diamonds (18 carats in total) on the bezel, case flanks and lugs.

GUY ELLIA

REPETITION MINUTE ZEPHYR

The ambassador of Guy Ellia's complicated timekeeper, the Repetition Minute Zephyr with its complications and intricate manufacturing process, is considered a particularly exceptional piece. The Caliber GEC 88 was created by Swiss manufacture Christophe Claret and features a power-reserve indicator, minute-repeater function and five time zones with day/night indication. The movement beats at 18,000 vibrations per hour in a solid, convex, high-resonance sapphire crystal case of impressive proportions (53.6x43.7x14.8mm). Mounted on an alligator strap with a folding buckle, this model is also available in pink gold or titanium.

IWC

PORTUGUESE MINUTE REPEATER – REF. IW524204

The Portuguese Minute Repeater houses the caliber 95290 with 43 hours of power reserve, 54 rubies, and a stunning minute-repeater function with small seconds and stop device. It is offered in limited editions of platinum and two colors of gold.

JAEGER-LECOULTRE

MASTER MINUTE REPEATER ANTOINE LECOULTRE

Crafted in titanium, this timepiece possesses acoustical qualities that surpass all expectations and offer a new standard for repeaters. Its crystalline chime, which has exceptional purity of sound, is the fruit of a collaborative effort between a musical conductor and the watchmakers and technicians at Jaeger-LeCoultre. The materials used for transmitting the vibrations at greater speed are new: the gongs are made of steel and sapphire crystal acts as the sound transmitter. The manually wound Caliber 947 mechanism is endowed with 360 hours (15 days) of power reserve—indicated on the dial. Created in a limited edition of 200 pieces, the Master Minute Repeater Antoine LeCoultre houses 41 jewels and beats at 21,600 vibrations per hour.

ULYSSE NARDIN

CIRCUS – REF. 740-88

Circus's minute repeater is powered by Caliber UN-74 and chimes on two distinct gongs, activating the animated Jaquemarts upon an Aventurine dial. Crafted in 18K white gold, Circus is offered as a limited edition of 30 pieces.

ULYSSE NARDIN

EROTICA – REF. 6116-103/P0-P2

Fitted with Caliber UN-611 (visible through an exhibition caseback) with automatic chime activation and the 18K gold animated Jaquemart, the 42mm Erotica is shown in 18K rose-gold and is also available in platinum and on a bracelet.

ULYSSE NARDIN

HOURSTRIKER – SONNERIE EN PASSANT – REF. 6109-103/E2

This 42mm Hourstriker - Sonnerie en Passant is presented in platinum. Visible through an exhibition caseback, Caliber UN-610 operates the automatic chime activation and the animated Jaquemarts. The Hourstriker - Sonnerie en Passant is also available in rose gold, with various dial combinations and on a bracelet.

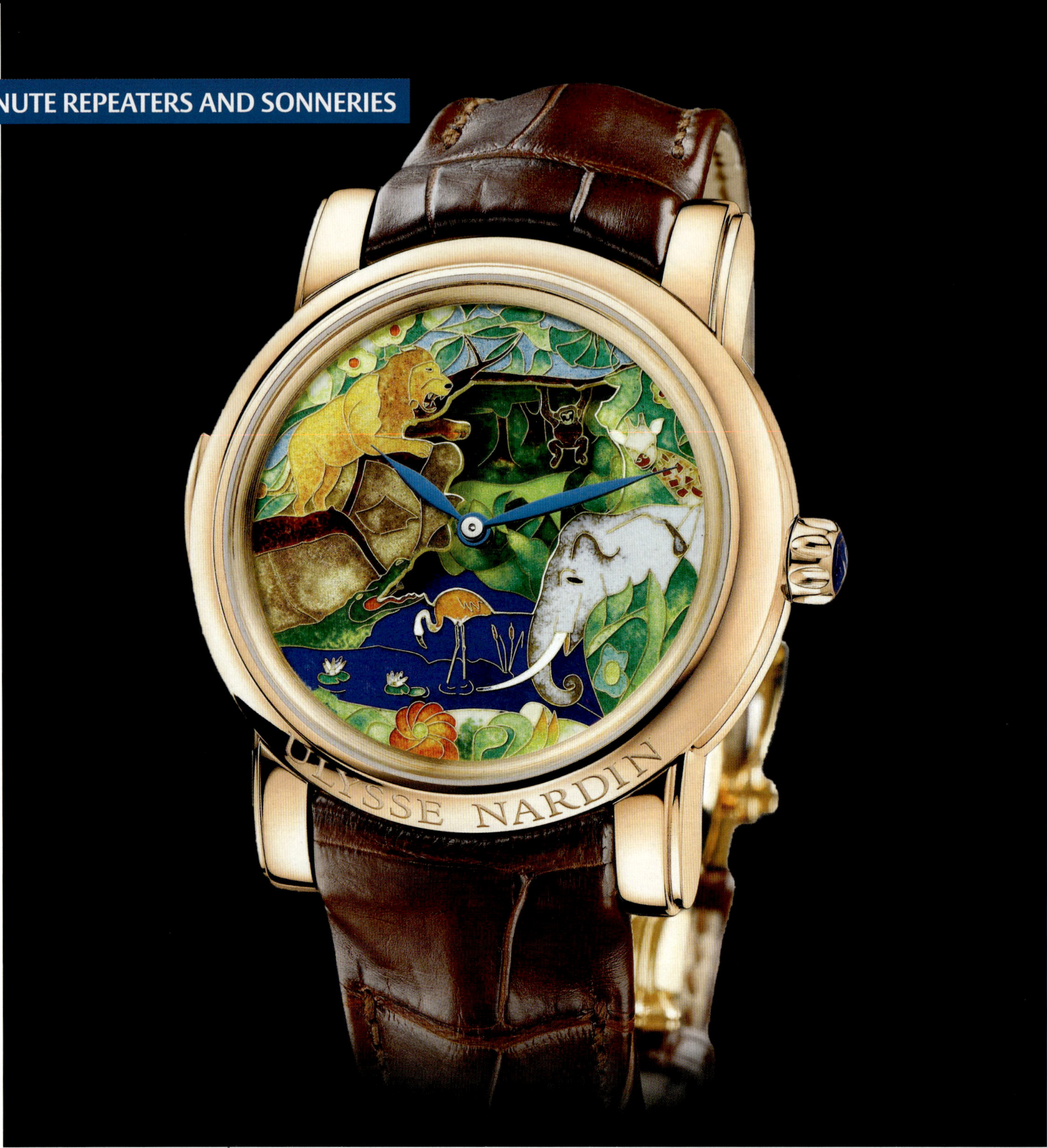

ULYSSE NARDIN

SAFARI – REF. 726-61

This minute repeater is equipped with two different chimes and two animated Jaquemarts on its cloisonné enamel dial. Safari is available in a 42mm, 18K rose-gold or platinum case with an exhibition caseback, through which Caliber UN-72 is visible. Each version is limited to 50 pieces.

VACHERON CONSTANTIN

PLATINUM SKELETON MINUTE REPEATER – REF. 30030/000P

Fully skeletonized, this Platinum Skeleton Minute Repeater is fitted with the manually wound, extra-flat Vacheron Constantin Caliber 1755 SQ. This exceptional 30-jeweled movement is 3.3mm thick and is decorated and chased entirely by hand. The repeater is operated via a slide on the left side of the case. The Platinum Skeleton Minute Repeater was created in a limited edition of just 15 numbered pieces.

ZANNETTI

REPEATER GLADIATORE – REF. REPRA184334

This 44mm Repeater Gladiatore is housed in a three-piece 18K pink-gold case that is engraved completely by hand. Its mechanical manual-winding five-minute repeater movement is Swiss Made and re-elaborated by Zannetti. The skeletonized dial features four round applied gold markers and pink-gold dart-style hands. Mounted on a hand-sewn Louisiana alligator leather strap with an 18K pink-gold ardillon buckle, this model is also water resistant to 20 meters. Limited edition.

ZENITH

ACADEMY OPEN REPETITION MINUTES CONCEPT

The Academy Open Répétition Minutes Concept houses the El Primero 4043 automatic chronograph movement with minute repeater. The 461-part movement with 45 jewels beats at 36,000 vibrations per hour and offers 50 hours of power reserve. The chronograph measures short time intervals to 1/10th of a second. With bidirectional automatic winding, the watch features a central rotor on ball bearings and a 22K gold oscillating weight. The transparent sapphire dial features two one-of-a-kind apertures on the chiming mechanism and the high-speed regulating organ. The 45mm double-gadrooned white-gold case is individually numbered at the back, where the transparent crystal reveals its mechanical beauty.

Born in the 1950s with the surge in popularity of water sports, diving watches have become recognized as the quintessential athletic watches—ready to face up to the most extreme conditions. For many brands, and many clients, they are the supreme symbol of reliability and robustness—even though they are only rarely used at the depths for which they were designed, and many of them never leave terra firma. Appealing to private or professional users, watchmakers continually improve the performance of diving watches, aesthetically as well as functionally. Mechanical depth gauges are also enjoying a dramatic revival of diving watches.

Favre-Leuba, *Bathy V2 Profondimètre*
Rolex, *Sea-Dweller Deepsea*
Jaeger-LeCoultre, *Master Compressor Diving Pro Geographic*
IWC, *Aquatimer "Cousteau Divers"*

Officine Panerai, *Luminor 1950 Submersible Depth Gauge*
CX Swiss Military Watch™, *20000 FEET*
Omega, *Seamaster Planet Ocean Liquidmetal® Limited Edition*

DIVING WATCHES

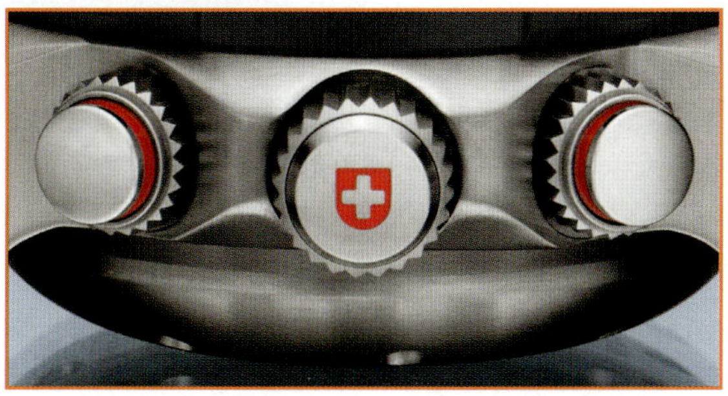

THIS PAGE
TOP RIGHT
***Rolex**, Submariner*

LEFT
***Blancpain**, Fifty Fathoms Automatique*

CENTER
***Rolex**, Sea-Dweller Deepsea*

FACING PAGE
***Breitling**, SuperOcean Heritage Chronograph*

THE WORLD IS YOUR OYSTER

The water resistance of watches has always been—along with lubrication—one of the principal concerns for watchmakers. Not everyone aspires to be the next Jacques Cousteau, but a good seal is welcome protection, even on dry land, against a movement's two worst enemies: humidity and dust. The first water-resistant case, Rolex's famous Oyster, was created in 1926. In 1953, the legendary brand created a watch for Captain Jacques Piccard to accompany his diving bell to 3,150 meters (10,335 feet) underwater; in 1960, the Deep Sea Special plunged 10,916 meters (35,813 feet) underwater to the Mariana Trench. Beside explorers and scientists, the first users of diving watches were often members of the armed forces. This was the case for the Officine Panerai models from the 1930s and '40s, which were made for the Italian Navy; the watches' dials bore luminescent indications and their famous crown system guaranteed water resistance to 200 meters.

In the 1950s, the first collections of diving watches appeared in retailers' shops. Rolex set the tone in 1953 with its famous Submariner, water resistant to 100 meters (now to 300 meters). The same year, Blancpain would release its Fifty Fathoms, created in collaboration with two "combat swimmers," officers in the French Army. This watch, initially resistant to 300 feet (50 fathoms—hence the name), was distinguished by its black dial, bezel and strap. Blancpain revisited the timepiece, creating a collection that includes a version with a flying tourbillon, flyback chronograph and water-resistant pushers functional at a depth of 300 meters. The completely white Fifty Fathoms Automatique has since joined the lineup. In 1957, Breitling launched the SuperOcean, a diving watch with a monohull case and armored glass guaranteeing water resistance to 200

meters; in 2007, the brand celebrated the watch's half-century by releasing the SuperOcean Heritage, also available in a chronograph version.

Rolex reaffirmed its sovereignty over the ocean's depths recently by launching the Sea-Dweller Deepsea, water resistant to 3,900 meters! To resist such intense pressure, this extraordinary instrument benefits from a patented new case design called Ringlock, with a steel ring placed in the case middle between the crystal and the caseback. The double system for changing the bracelet's length allows the utmost comfort in all its variations. The COSC-certified chronometer is equipped with the Rolex Parachrom hairspring, which is resistant to shocks and magnetic fields.

WRIST INSTRUMENTS

To earn the title "diving watch," a timepiece must not only possess a water resistance well above average (minimum 100 meters), usually provided by a screw-in crown and caseback; it also must offer all the functions indispensable to amateur or professional divers, such as a turning

bezel that controls the time of immersion—if possible, using a unidirectional system, to avoid any accidental change in the programmed time; the dial usually has large numerals and prominent hands, all coated in luminescent materials; and the strap—in rubber or metal—is often equipped with a mechanism for changing its length to fit over diving suits. The highest-performance models are equipped with a valve that releases helium; this very volatile gas, used to facilitate respiration in pressurized chambers, easily enters watchcases, but it must be evacuated upon ascent to avoid excessive pressure.

Playing on these diverse attributes, brands today propose a wide choice of diving watches—from chic sports models primarily destined for poolside cocktail parties, to professional instruments ready for descent into the deep sea. The HydroConquest line by Longines combines a water resistance to 300 meters with reinforced protection from its crown. The British-Swiss brand Graham has updated its Chronofighter, initially created for bombardiers in World War II who wore gloves and could therefore more easily handle a pusher and a crown placed on the left of the case. This diving chronograph, named Chronofighter Oversize Diver and water resistant to 300 meters, also boasts a helium valve. The titanium Oris Regulateur Der Meistertaucher, water resistant to 1,000 meters, uses a regulator dial to highlight the most important indication for a diver—the minute function, placed at the center.

FACING PAGE
TOP LEFT
Graham, *Chronofighter Oversize Diver*

TOP RIGHT
Richard Mille, *RM 025*

CENTER
Oris, *Regulateur Der Meistertaucher*

THIS PAGE
TOP
Omega, *Seamaster Ploprof 1200*

LEFT
Breitling, *Avenger Seawolf Chrono*

CENTER
Blancpain, *500 Fathoms*

Watchmakers often equip their diving watches with chronograph functions, but it bears remembering that many of these instruments, even the ones that are completely water resistant, cannot activate those functions while underwater, or water will seep in through the pushers. Breitling achieved a major advance in this field with its Avenger Seawolf Chrono, the only chronograph to be functional to 1,000 meters. To accomplish this, the brand developed a patented device that uses magnetic pushers with commands activated through the metal of the case, with no direct contact between the pusher and the movement.

NEW WATER VOYAGES

In 2009, Blancpain presented the "big sister" of Fifty Fathoms, the new 500 Fathoms, water resistant to 914 meters with a titanium case, helium decompression valve and large phosphorescent Arabic numerals; the watch also possesses a transparent sapphire caseback, a rare achievement for a timepiece that is water resistant to such depths. Omega reinterpreted its 1970 Seamaster 600, also called PloProf (for *plongeurs professionnels*—professional divers), in a modernized version that is water resistant to 1,200 meters and whose movement is equipped with a co-axial escapement. A security pusher allows the wearer to turn the bezel in either direction and to set it in the chosen position, which prevents any accidental manipulation during the dive. In autumn 2009, the brand also presented a new Seamaster Planet Ocean Liquidmetal® Limited Edition, whose bezel joins black ceramic and Liquidmetal®—two ultra-hard materials that are ultra-resistant to scratches and corrosion. Richard Mille enters the deep with its first diving watch, the RM 025, with tourbillon and chronograph—housed (a first for the brand) in a round case that is water resistant to 300 meters. On its Diverscope JR1000, JeanRichard offers an internal rotating bezel activated with two

THIS PAGE
TOP LEFT
***CX Swiss Military Watch™**, 20000 FEET*

TOP CENTER
***JeanRichard**, Diverscope JR1000*

BELOW
***TAG Heuer**, Aquaracer 500M Calibre 5*

FACING PAGE
TOP LEFT
***Vulcain**, Cricket Diver X-Treme*

TOP CENTER
***Jaeger-LeCoultre**, Master Compressor Diving Pro Geographic Navy SEALs*

RIGHT
***IWC**, Aquatimer Deep Two*

crowns: the steel case is coated in injection vulcanized rubber, which provides a high resistance against collisions, scratches, abrasions and UV rays. TAG Heuer is also plunging into the deep with its new Aquaracer 500M Calibre 5; the case is equipped with six studs to facilitate handling with diving gloves, and the readable, elegant dial is lined with vertical stripes. CX Swiss Military Watch™ entered the record books with its 2009 release of 20000 FEET—this mechanical timepiece, functional at more than 6,000 meters underwater, underwent a full battery of tests proving that it was impervious to extreme pressure, dynamite and bullets! Among diving watches, we are also seeing more and more models equipped with an alarm function, which audibly alerts the diver at the end of the dive time, such as Vulcain's automatic Cricket Diver X-Treme.

FORCES BELOW

For several years, we have been seeing the triumphant return of a function that is not quite horological, but quite useful for divers: the bathymeter, or depth gauge. This is the perfect alternative—or the perfect complement—to the electronic watch computers that have been flooding the market. Jaeger-LeCoultre's Master Compressor Diving Pro Geographic Navy SEALs, water resistant to 300 meters, stands out for its mechanical depth gauge placed on the left side of the case and equipped with a membrane that expands or contracts depending on the water pressure. The membrane's movements act on the large blue arrow hand via a clever transmission system partially visible on the dial. The depths measured range from 0 to 80 meters. Jaeger-LeCoultre also paid tribute to its partnership with the US Navy SEALs by creating two other limited edition diving watches: the Master Compressor Diving Chronograph GMT Navy SEALs, with a chronograph and second time zone, and the Master Compressor Diving Alarm Navy SEALs, with an alarm function.

Favre-Leuba—one of the oldest Swiss watchmakers now enjoying a renaissance—also distinguished itself in the field of diving watches by presenting the Bathy V2 Pro, water resistant to 300 meters. This worthy descendant of the famous 1966 Bathy model possesses a mechanical depth gauge based on a copper beryllium membrane. Four large openings visible on the side of the case allow water into the double caseback and the membrane contracts under the pressure. A complex mechanism then transforms this contraction of just a few tenths of a millimeter into an extremely precise needle movement on the dial: less than 0.18 deviation. This model, with depth sensor to 45 meters, will be supplemented in the future with versions equipped with a depth gauge suited for up to 150 to 300 meters.

IWC's new Aquatimer collection, launched in 2009, is spearheaded by the Aquatimer Deep Two model, equipped with a mechanical depth gauge with two different-colored hands, one indicating the current depth (up to 60 meters), the other indicating the maximum depth achieved by the diver. With these two references, the diver can plan for the stages of decompression and pause at the necessary depths to finish the dive safely. The collection also includes three chronographs, as well as an Aquatimer Automatic, water resistant to 2,000 meters.

Officine Panerai has opted for the electronic option. Its Luminor 1950 Submersible Depth Gauge joins an automatic caliber to a membrane system that activates a large yellow central hand on the dial. To guarantee maximum security, the brand had the Swiss Department of Measurement (l'Office fédéral de métrologie Suisse (METAS)) individually test and certify the calibration of each depth gauge. The crown-protecting lever system assures water resistance to 120 meters.

AUDEMARS PIGUET

ROYAL OAK OFFSHORE DIVER – REF. 15703ST.OO.A002CA.01

For its new diver's watch, Audemars Piguet has opted for a pared-down approach. The Royal Oak Offshore Diver is equipped with the stellar Manufacture Audemars Piguet automatic 3120 caliber. The case components—particularly the gaskets, the thickness of the back and that of the crystals—have been adapted to guarantee water resistance to depths of 300 meters.

BLANCPAIN

500 FATHOMS GMT

More than half a century after creating the first modern diver's wristwatch, the famous Fifty Fathoms, the manufacture in Le Brassus unveiled its new 500 Fathoms GMT. Its brushed titanium case houses an exclusive mechanical movement: Calibre 5215. Featuring a delicately engraved oscillating weight shaped like a boat propeller, this self-winding caliber incorporates a unique system of micrometrical balance-regulating screws: the rate is controlled by means of inertia-blocks placed around the "felly" or rim of the balance. A quarter-turn of two diametrically opposite screws results in a gain or loss of thirty seconds per day. This heightens the level of precision considerably and negates any risk of the movement's operation being disrupted by jolting or jarring. To ensure optimal operating autonomy and constant energy, the new Calibre 5215 is equipped with three series-coupled barrels guaranteeing a 5-day power reserve.

BREITLING

SUPEROCEAN HERITAGE 46MM – REF. A1732024/B868

The mechanical automatic-winding Breitling caliber 17 (ETA2824-2base) beats at 28,800 vph and is a COSC-certified chronometer. This polished stainless steel case bears curved, antireflective sapphire crystals on both sides, a clockwise-turning bezel with knurled rim and aluminum ring with five-minute markers. The black dial features a brushed sunray pattern, luminescent dots and rhodium-plated Sports hands, and date at 6:00. Shown on a rubber Ocean Racer strap with fold-over clasp mechanism with comfort-enhancing extension that is adjustable in seconds, this watch is available on bracelets or straps, in a Ø 38mm size, and is water resistant to 20atm.

IWC

AQUATIMER AUTOMATIC 2000 – REF. IW356802

The Aquatimer Automatic 2000, with its tested pressure resistance to 200 bar, still holds the horological record for water resistance. Its automatic 30110 caliber contains 40 jewels, beats at 28,800 vibrations per hour and offers 21 hours of power reserve. The stainless steel watch features a rhodium-plated black dial and a black external mechanical rotating bezel with the familiar luminous yellow 15-minute segment of the previous Aquatimer. Yellow is also used for the minute hand, which indicates the dive time, to ensure a clear distinction. A second variant has a white dial with orange or white numerals on a white or dark blue background on the rotating bezel and an orange hour hand. Shown here on a black rubber strap, the Aquatimer Automatic 2000 is also available on a stainless steel bracelet.

IWC

AQUATIMER DEEP TWO – REF. IW354701

The Aquatimer Deep Two boasts a 46mm case that is pressure resistant to 12 bar. The watch shows not only the actual dive depth, but also the maximum depth reached during a particular dive, doubling as a complete second safety system alongside the dive computer. The Aquatimer Deep Two features a semi-circular indicator on the dial, which records depths down to 50 meters. Its pressure-measurement system is contained in a second large crown on the left side of the case. The water pressure acts directly on a membrane inside this crown and forces a pin into the interior of the case, triggering a system that results in the depth indicator (blue) moving over the white measuring field as the depth of water increases or decreases. The maximum depth indicator (red) always remains at the greatest depth reached. It can be released by a button underneath the depth-gauge sensor crown on the left side of the case.

JAEGER-LECOULTRE

MASTER COMPRESSOR DIVING PRO GEOGRAPHIC

The Master Compressor Diving Pro Geographic, easily recognized by its 46.3mm diameter and its characteristic appearance due to the presence of the depth gauge, houses a new *Geographic* sports movement. The user must simply position the city symbolizing a given time zone in the aperture at 6:00 and the corresponding time is automatically shown on a 24-hour subdial at 9:00. This indication highlights the "rack" required to transmit the depth indication, read off by a pointer on the logarithmic scale of the depth gauge shown on an outer dial ring. The date appears in an aperture at 3:00 and the luminescent movement-operating indicator is located in the lower part of the dial. Equipped with the automatic Jaeger-LeCoultre Caliber 979 and water resistant to 300 meters, the Diving Pro Geographic model is available in satin-brushed grade-5 titanium.

PANERAI

LUMINOR SUBMERSIBLE – REF. PAM00024

Inspired by the model designed for the Egyptian Navy in 1956, the Luminor Submersible inherits the historic version's striking personality through its characteristic rotating bezel (which enables the duration of a dive to be read quickly) and its reliability under extreme conditions. The addition of an automatic mechanical movement enhances the great functionality of its predecessor, a testimony to Panerai's constant dedication to technical development and quality standards. This 44mm model is water resistant to 30 bar.

PANERAI

LUMINOR 1950 SUBMERSIBLE DEPTH GAUGE FOR THE PANGAEA EXPEDITION

REF. PAM00307

Recognized for creating the first professional diver's watches in history and supplying them—along with wrist depth gauges—to the Royal Italian Navy in the first half of the 20th century, Officine Panerai reaffirmed its tradition in the field of professional precision instruments with the combination of these two indispensable measuring devices in a single instrument: the Luminor 1950 Submersible Depth Gauge. Unlike historic wrist depth gauges, which were functional to 30 meters, this innovative device can measure depths to 120 meters and record the greatest depth encountered in the course of a dive. This is achieved by an independent, sophisticated electronic device fitted within the 47mm titanium case. In a numbered limited edition, the back is engraved in celebration of the famous explorer Mike Horn's Pangaea Expedition.

ROLEX

OYSTER PERPETUAL DATE SEA-DWELLER 4000 – REF. 16600

This Oyster Perpetual Date Sea-Dweller 4000 houses an automatic-winding Rolex 3185 caliber, which is COSC certified. Its polished and brushed Ø 40mm stainless steel case is fitted with a thick (3mm) sapphire crystal that resists high pressures, a counterclockwise-turning ring with graduated scale for the calculation of dive times, and a pressure-compensating valve for helium release. The piece is water resistant to 122atm and available on a brushed steel Oysterlock bracelet with fold-over clasp with Fliplock safety stop that comes with an additional link, an extension plate of the clasp, and a screwdriver to extend the bracelet to fit over a diver's suit.

ZENITH

DEFY XTREME SEA OPEN

Cased in 46.5mm of black titanium with graduated unidirectional rotating bezel in black titanium, fitted with carbon-fiber inserts, the Defy Xtreme Sea Open is powered by the El Primero 4021 SX automatic chronograph movement with harmonic plate. The caliber consists of 248 parts and 39 jewels. The balance, chronograph and pallet bridges are built of shock-absorbing Zenithium Z+. It has a 30-minute counter at 3:00, small seconds at 9:00, power-reserve indicator from the hour axis, and central seconds blue varnished hand. Water resistant to 1,000 meters, the high-tech case features a helium valve at 10:00 and black titanium screw-in pushbuttons with carbon-fiber guilloché patterns and protective crown device. The carbon-fiber dial is a multi-layered construction with shock-resistant Hesalite glass. Composite lateral inserts reinforce the black titanium bracelet with blue-tinted central links.

BRAND DIRECTORY

A. LANGE & SÖHNE
Altenberger Strasse 15
01768 Glashütte
Germany
Tel: 49 35053 440
USA: 310 205 5555

ARTYA
Route de Thonon 146
1222 Vesenaz
Switzerland
Tel: 41 22 752 49 40

AUDEMARS PIGUET
1348 Le Brassus,
Switzerland
Tel: 41 21 845 14 00
USA: 212 688 6644

BELL & ROS
350 Rue Saint Honoré
75001 Paris, France
Tel: 33 1 42 86 61 27
USA: 203 604 6840

BLANCPAIN
Le Rocher 12
1348 Le Brassus
Switzerland
Tel: 41 21 796 36 36
USA: 201 271 1400

BOVET FLEURIER SA
9 Rue Ami-Lévrier
1211 Geneva 1
Switzerland
Tel: 41 22 731 46 38
USA: 305 502 9001

BREGUET
1344 L'Abbaye
Switzerland
Tel: 41 21 841 90 90
USA: 866 458 7488

BREITLING
CP 1132
2540 Grenchen, Switzerland
Tel: 41 32 654 54 54
USA: 203 762 1180

CHANEL
25 Place du Marché St. Honoré,
75001 Paris, France
Tel: 33 1 55 35 50 00
USA: 212 688 5055

CHOPARD
Rue de Veyrot 8
1217 Meyrin-Geneva 2
Switzerland
Tel: 41 22 719 31 91
USA: 212 821 0300

CONCORD
MGI Luxury Group SA
Rue de Nidau 35
2501 Bienne, Switzerland
Tel: 41 32 329 34 00
USA: 800 547 4073

DE BETHUNE
6 Granges-Jaccard
1454 La Chaux L'Auberson
Switzerland
Tel: 41 24 454 22 81
USA: 212 729 7152

de GRISOGONO
176 bis Route de St. Julien
1228 Plan-les-Ouates
Switzerland
Tel: 41 22 817 81 00
USA: 212 439 4240

F.P. JOURNE
Rue de l'Arquebuse 17
1204 Geneva, Switzerland
Tel: 41 22 322 09 09
USA: 305 572 9802

FRÉDÉRIQUE CONSTANT SA
Chemin du Champ des Filles 32
1228 Plan-les-Ouates, Geneva
Switzerland
Tel: 41 22 860 04 40
USA: 877 619 2824

GREUBEL FORSEY
Eplatures-Grise 16
CP 670, 2301 La Chaux-de-Fonds
Switzerland
Tel: 41 32 751 71 76
USA: 310 205 5555

GUY ELLIA
21 Rue de la Paix
75002 Paris, France
Tel: 33 1 53 30 25 25
USA: 212 888 0505

HUBLOT
Chemin de la Vuarpilliére 33
CP 2464
1260 Nyon 2, Switzerland
Tel: 41 22 990 90 00
USA: 800 536 0636

IWC
Baumgartenstrasse 15
8201 Schaffhausen
Switzerland
Tel: 41 52 635 62 37
USA: 212 891 2460

JACOB & CO
Richelien 39
1290 Versoix, Switzerland
Tel: 41 22 775 33 33
USA: 212 888 2330

JAEGER-LECOULTRE
Rue de la Golisse 8
1347 Le Sentier Switzerland
Tel: 41 21 845 02 02
USA: 212 308 2525

LEVIEV
31 Old Bond Street
London W1S4QH
United Kingdom
Tel: 44 20 7493 3333
USA: 212 763 5333

MONTBLANC MONTRE
Hellgrundweg 100
22525 Hamburg, Germany
Tel: 49 40 84 001 0
USA: 908 508 2334

PANERAI
Via Ludovico di Breme 44/45
20156 Milan, Italy
Tel: 39 02 363138
USA: 212 888 8788

PARMIGIANI FLEURIER
Rue du Temple 11
2114 Fleurier, Switzerland
Tel: 41 32 862 66 30
USA: 949 489 2885

PATEK PHILIPPE
Chemin du Pont du Centenaire
141, 1228 Plan-les-Ouates
Switzerland
Tel: 41 22 884 20 20
USA: 212 218 1272

PIAGET
37 Chemin du Champ-des-Filles
1228 Plan-les-Ouates
Switzerland
Tel: 41 22 884 48 44
USA: 212 355 6444

RICHARD MILLE
11 rue du Jura
2345 Les Breuleux Jura
Switzerland
Tel: 41 32 959 43 53
USA: 310 205 5555

ROLEX
Rue François Dussaud 3-7
1211 Geneva 24
Switzerland
Tel: 41 22 302 22 00
USA: 212 758 7700

STÜHRLING ORIGINAL
449 20th Street
Brooklyn NY 11215 USA
Tel: 718 437 8723

TAG HEUER
Louis-Joseph Chevrolet 6A
2300 La Chaux-de-Fonds
Switzerland
Tel: 41 32 919 80 00
USA: 973 467 1890

ULYSSE NARDIN
3 Rue du Jardin
2400 Le Locle
Switzerland
Tel: 41 32 930 74 00
USA: 561 988 8600

VACHERON CONSTANTIN
Rue des Moulins 1
1204 Geneva,
Switzerland
Tel: 41 22 930 20 02
USA: 212 713 0707

ZANNETTI
Via Monte d'Oro 19
00186 Rome, Italy
Tel: 39 06 68 192 566

ZENITH
2400 Le Locle
Switzerland
Tel: 41 32 930 62 62
USA: 973 467 1890